Violet Margaret Princess Cannon was born and bred in Bradford, West Yorkshire, and raised in the traditional Romany way. At thirty-one, and in contrast to the media's portrayal of Gypsies and their culture, Violet has an education, a job and a divorce to her name. She has spent the last eight years working with Gypsies and Travellers, fighting to gain the community recognition as an ethnic minority in its own right. Violet is the founding member of the Northern Network of Travelling People and the Chairperson of the Romany Women's Union.

Gypsy Princess

*The true story of a
Romany childhood*

VIOLET CANNON

headline

First published in 2011
by HEADLINE PUBLISHING GROUP

4

Cataloguing in Publication Data is available from the British Library

ISBN 978 0 7553 6283 7

Typeset in Adobe Garamond by Palimpsest Book Production Limited, Falkirk, Stirlingshire

Printed and bound in Great Britain by CPI Group (UK), Croydon, CR0 4YY

Headline's policy is to use papers that are natural, renewable and recyclable products and made from wood grown in responsible forests. The logging and manufacturing processes are expected to conform to the environmental regulations of the country of origin.

HEADLINE PUBLISHING GROUP
An Hachette UK Company
338 Euston Road
London NW1 3BH

www.headline.co.uk
www.hachette.co.uk

For my precious Mam and Dad, who taught me how to believe in me and what true love really is. My brother and sister, and their spouses, who I owe so much to. My nieces and nephews – from the oldest, Margaret Violet, to the youngest, Charlotte Ann, and the six* in the middle who make me laugh, cry and smile. I wouldn't be without any of you. My friends, who got me through my hard times and shared my good times – Ellie, Linda, Deryllyn, Paula, Sonny, Small Pa, Frank and Mark.

And last but certainly not least, God, who helped me through the times when I thought I could not physically go on.

All of these people have changed and moulded me, given me the inner strength to tell my story and supported me with their love. Thank you all, I love you x

*I will be in so much trouble if I don't name them all, so here goes: Maria Cizzier, Thomas James, Violet Teresa, Bernadette Dawn, Maria Suzanna and Ely Thomas Henry.

Contents

Acknowledgements

I'd like to thank my agent, Diane Banks, co-author, Shannon Kyle, and all at Headline. Thanks for believing I had a story worth telling.

Cast List

Violet
Violet Snr: Mam
Tom: Dad
Tom: brother
Maria: sister
Grandad Tom: Dad's father
Granny Winnie: Dad's mother
Grandad Jimmy: Mam's father
Granny Suzanna: Mam's mother
Winnie, Margaret and Mary: aunties
Joanne, Sarah and Martina: cousins
Lina, Sabrina and Chanelle: friends
Philip and Josh: Tesco colleagues
Tomboy, John, Henry, Moses, George: love interests

Chapter One

Twenty-first Century Gypsy Girl

My name is Violet Cannon. I live in a trailer and I'm a Romany Gypsy, as were my parents, grandparents and all my family as far back as anyone knows.

Whenever a fellow Romany Gypsy asks who I am, I don't just give my Christian name. I reply: 'I'm a Cannon: my mam, Violet, was a Hall, whose mam was a Stuart; my dad was a Smith Cannon, whose mother was a Varey . . .' and usually within a few moments I'll get a nod of recognition. Because Gypsies always know someone who knows someone.

Growing up as a Romany, living on the edge of society, I've travelled from one end of the country to another, making my home on patches of wasteland, on disused industrial estates, in idyllic English countryside and even on the edge of a cliff. We might be there for a few days or weeks or months – or however long we want before setting off for other adventures. It's our freedom that sets us apart.

No one even knows exactly how many Gypsies there are, although we do know at least four million exist in Europe, because we choose to live under the radar, in our secret closed world. Only now, after TV shows like *Big Fat Gypsy Wedding*, has our ethnicity been placed under the spotlight like never before in our history. From being ignored, and sometimes resented, being a Gypsy is suddenly big news. Big fat news, in fact.

For me and my family, the programme is 'must-watch' telly. But it's also like witnessing a car crash. It's both hilarious and terrible in equal measures. Once I found myself sitting in a ballgown, waiting to go out to a big do, having to finish watching *BFGW* first while the taxi waited outside. I just couldn't miss it. The over-the-top bridezillas desperate to outdo each other, the outrageous wedding clothes, the family squabbles, the secrecy surrounding venues . . . Some of it is familiar but most of it is a massively heightened version of Romany life. And much of it we just don't recognise at all.

Once my dad's cousin John appeared on the programme, the last in the current series. He agreed to do it just for a laugh. The way his wife, my aunt Violet Taylor, was portrayed was actually very funny. She was filmed rushing for miles to bring him a stew while he parked up his wagon and horses on the way to Appleby Fair, after he'd ordered her to come and deliver it.

'Come on, woman,' he snapped at her down his mobile phone, as the cameras showed my poor aunt jumping in her car, driving and getting lost on the way.

Although we all laughed, we knew John would be in big

trouble afterwards. My aunt is no one's fool and I knew she'd have been absolutely seething inside. But the cameras were only interested in portraying the stereotypes; they wanted to show poor Gypsy women who are made to cook and clean by their husbands, waiting on them hand and foot.

What my auntie is, though, is loyal to her husband, and she didn't want to show up John on camera, however cheeky he was. So she agreed to do as he said, although he was obviously having a laugh, seeing how far he could push it. After they filmed her rushing over with his freshly made stew, they didn't show what happened later. She'd told him she would serve the pot of stew over his head, not on his plate.

It's believed there are around twelve million Gypsies living worldwide, but nobody actually knows where Gypsies come from. One school of thought is we descended from Joseph's tribes, as the story in the Bible says one disappeared from Egypt. Some say the term 'Gypsy' is derived from the word 'Egyptian' or even from a Greek village called 'Gyppe'. The other idea is we descended from an army. As a people we are quite a closed, tight-knit group, and we are natural-born fighters and loyal to the core, so that theory is one that makes sense to me.

It also explains the use of the word 'Gorja', which is the term we use for non-Gypsy people. In Sanskrit, the language our Romany words come from, it literally means 'civilian'. The word 'rom' or 'roma' means 'people'. Having our own language also sets us apart. Although it is dying out these days, most Romanies in this country use a mixture of Romanese (a word spelled in many different ways) and English. Romanese lacks many adjoining words such as 'to' and 'from'. There are hundreds of dialects of Romanese but we also see it as very bad manners to talk in our language in front of someone who doesn't understand us.

Some Gorja don't realise how Gypsy culture has seeped in to the mainstream already. Words such as 'bungalow', 'lollipop' and 'chav' all originate from Gypsy talk. The word chavvy, used to describe a child, was once a common term for us, and men would greet kids with the phrase, 'All right, chavvy!' We stopped using it though when Gorja people picked it up. The same happened with our word 'cushti', which was used by the character Del Boy in *Only Fools and Horses*. Again, the menfolk stopped using it as it became associated with the programme and wheeler-dealer types.

And it's not just language. We used to wear sovereign rings as kids; our mams and grannies were covered in gold as it's a sign of doing well for yourself in our culture. My grannies loved those large gold clown necklaces too, but then other Gorja people started wearing them, so we stopped.

Romany Gypsies are one of the largest ethnic minority groups in Europe, so it's incredible that many governments still don't record us in their census. Although British Gypsies won their fight to be recognised as a group (yes, we had to campaign, despite some families going back 500 years in this country), this year I wasn't even sent a copy of a census, even though I've paid my taxes to the government like everyone else since I started work.

Some Gypsies see all this recent publicity as a good thing. After all, if the public starts to understand us, the government can't oppress us so easily, can it? And oppressed we have been, throughout history. The first recorded persecution took place in the Middle Ages. Gypsies enjoyed freedom in Spain until the Christian *Reconquista* (re-conquest) in the thirteenth century, but since then my people have been killed, forced to flee their homes and even been made slaves in Hungary and Romania, right up until 1855. As recently as the 1970s, in Switzerland and Scotland, Gypsy children were taken away and adopted. A deeply moving book, *Never to Return*, was written by a man called Sandy Reid, who'd been snatched from his Traveller's camp as a boy and made to start a whole new life away from his family. I cried all the way through when I read it.

A line from the film *Rabbit-Proof Fence*, the story of an Aboriginal girl, spoke volumes to me. It said: 'We'll breed the black out of them.' You see, that was the idea – to have Gypsy kids adopted, to stop them from even existing . . .

Chapter Two

Hedgehogs, Vardos and
Falling in Love

Mam was born on 19 December 1955, the youngest girl out of nine. Her siblings were Anne, Townson, Margaret, Billy, Joe, Wally and Danny. She also had another brother Jimmy who died as a baby from meningitis. Her parents, Jimmy and Suzannah Hall, lived a very basic existence, travelling constantly and making a meagre living, though the family never went hungry. Her parents slept in a wagon every night with their youngest child Danny and the girls, while the other boys would sleep in the 'accommodation', which was basically a cart with a tent sheet pulled over the top. Sometimes they'd even sleep underneath the cart.

Whenever I or my brother, Tom, or sister, Maria, complained about anything, Mam would reminisce loudly about her own childhood, telling us we didn't know what a hard life was. 'Don't you moan,' she'd laugh if we shivered on a cold morning. 'I used to have to smash the ice off the top of the water dish before I could wash my face.'

Having lived off the land, Mam used to tell us how they collected what they could find to eat and would regularly enjoy roast hedgehog for dinner. They'd kill it in a trap, wrap it in clay and then cook it on the fire. When it was hot enough they removed the clay and all the spikes just fell off easily. Then they'd pick it apart and eat it straight off the bone. Apparently it tastes like a cross between chicken and pork. It sounds cruel but no different to eating a chicken or pig when you think about it.

I never met my Grandad Jimmy, but Mam paints such a clear picture of him, it feels like I did. He used to say to Mam: 'There's many a good heart under an old raggy coat.'

Mam always says her family was not as well off as Dad's, and they lived hand-to-mouth, surviving off Jimmy's wheelings and dealings. He'd buy and sell absolutely anything from scrap metal to jewellery. He'd sit in pubs and whatever anyone was selling he'd buy himself and sell on for a higher price. He became such a well-known Romany wheeler-dealer that he even had a song written about him, called 'Jimmy Hall'.

He also had a heart of gold, helping the poorest people he came across and showing genuine love and warmth towards them. Mam explained how any homeless person he met was always welcomed home and given some toast and sent off with a milk bottle full of hot milky tea. Jimmy told Mam you never knew if you'd be in that situation yourself and so must always help.

While Grandad Jimmy is a memory of mine made up from a mixture of faded photographs and old anecdotes, his wife, my Granny Suzanna, is very much part of who I am today.

Like my mam I've inherited her outspoken nature and temper, but I have always loved her dearly despite her being such a cantankerous force of nature. These days I see her personality shining through not only myself but my sister Maria's little girl, Maria-Suzannah, now aged seven, who has her beautiful red hair and temperament too.

Granny Suzanna was a big woman in every sense of the word. Standing in her socks at six feet tall, she was the definition of that much-used phrase 'big boned'. With her broad shoulders and big hands she wasn't someone to be messed with.

She also happened to be the cousin of my paternal grandfather Thomas Smith Cannon, making my own parents related by blood. My grandfather Thomas was a bit of a rogue himself by all accounts and always found himself in fights. One day he found himself in a tight spot with five or six Irish Travellers. My Granny Suzanna overheard the furore from her trailer and came rushing out to see what the fuss was about. Ordering her cousin to stand back to back with her, she rolled up her sleeves, held her knuckles aloft and screamed: 'Come on then! Let's be 'aving yous!' Returning punch for punch, between them they managed to see the gang off and Granny Suzanna probably saved my grandad from the hiding of his life. Thomas nicknamed her 'Big Geoff' from that day on. Granny Suzanna had three older sisters and as there were no other boys in her family she was treated as one by her father. She learned to tend horses and grew up to be a rather masculine girl.

Grandad Tom hated Bradford, so I bet he never imagined

that four generations of Tom Cannons would end up living in the area: my dad, my brother, and his son, also named Thomas Cannon (TJ). It's normal for Romany people to give their children exactly the same names as their parents or grandparents. In our eyes it keeps our family bloodline going, and gives us a sense of belonging. Of course it can get confusing, but that's why we often have nicknames.

In the 1960s my grandad traded his much-loved wooden wagon and horse for a modern, shiny, chrome trailer, which was all the rage in those days. Nowadays a hand-painted old wagon is called a 'vardo' and is much sought after, the equivalent of a classic car. But they are impractical in many ways, and expensive to buy and maintain.

Nevertheless, Grandad Tom came to regret his decision: he loathed pulling his new motorised trailer so much that when he parked it on Low Moor camp in Bradford, he ended up staying on the site for ten years with his wife Winnie, rather than admitting he'd made a mistake and swapping it back.

My grandad, who is eighty-four today, was a tall, big hulk of a man. He reminds me of the brother in the film *The Quiet Man* with Maureen O'Hara, proud, stubborn and a terrible joker. He'd tease us relentlessly. 'You open your mouth every time you drink from that cup,' he'd say, as I sipped from his cups of hot tea. Or: 'Do you want a sweet?' said with a twinkle in his eye as I popped it in my mouth. 'Tastes all right, don't it? . . . Considering it's straight from a skip.'

The trouble was poor Grandad carried on his little wisecracks until I was a teenager, when I definitely didn't find them funny any more.

He was always a dapper dresser, and was never without his waistcoat, cravat, hat and braces, although since Granny Winnie died the braces didn't always match. He loved to hear me sing as a child and every time we went to visit, about three times a week, he had me singing 'Cockles and Mussels' and 'Tomorrow' from *Annie*, as I had curly ginger hair. Unlike a lot of Gypsy men he never smoked. His biggest vice was toffees and every Christmas and birthday we'd buy him some.

We loved hearing stories of how back in the sixties Grandad Tom was one of the best horsemen around. He'd breed and tend his horses with such love and care that they'd be worth a fortune and he soon became fairly wealthy from them. All these years later the pride in his and my dad's faces is obvious as they retell the stories.

He specialised in horses with feathered feet known as Gypsy Cobbs, which are the strong breed used for pulling wagons. Every year, like most Romanies, he'd attend Appleby Fair in Cumbria, where horses are traded. It's a very important date in the Gypsy calendar. Most horses sold for around £100 but his would fetch anything up to £350.

Grandad Tom was very proud and had an inexhaustible work ethic, inherited by our father and myself. Once he was snowed in during winter and couldn't get his horses out of the fields to the fairs. So to feed his family he took on a job delivering coal for a Gorja man, something most Romany men would always refuse to do. My dad was just nine years old at the time, but even today, decades later, he remembers the name of this man, Ronnie Dove.

Luckily we lived near the sites of our grandparents on both sides. Every day after school Mam or Dad took us for a visit. They were keen we were close to both sides of our families and knew everything about our backgrounds. With no recorded history, Gypsies rely on passing down the stories of our family history orally to keep the Romany spirit alive.

Mam and Dad had known each other, through friends and family, for years before they got married at aged eighteen and nineteen respectively. Of course the fact that Mam's mam (Granny Suzanna) and Dad's dad (Grandad Tom) were first cousins meant they moved in the same circles. It's a bit of a Gypsy cliche, and we're not all inbred or anything, but that's how it went in our family. In any case, when Mam and Dad decided to get married, they dashed off and got hitched without telling anyone. Probably because my dad's family wouldn't have approved of my mother's, being so much better off, but who knows? They're still not telling.

The story goes that my Granny Winnie, my dad's mother, had just seen her sister Josie faint after she'd been told that her daughter Coralina had just eloped with a man named Alan. Originally Mam and Dad were going to marry with them in a double wedding, but in all the chaos they ended up marrying separately.

Just as my Granny Winnie knelt her tiny frame down to

console Josie, telling her not to worry – 'everything will be fine; it's lovely your daughter has married young; you've gained a son and not lost a daughter' etc. etc. – her daughter, my Aunt Mary, rushed over to break the news that *her* son Tom had in fact also married my mam Violet that day too.

In a fit of shock, it was Winnie's turn to keel over while Josie tried to revive her, repeating her own phrases: 'Don't worry, everything will be fine . . . You've gained a daughter not lost a son,' etc. etc. . . .

Violet and Tom – Mam and Dad – first got together at Appleby Fair in 1972, then married at Bradford registry office in 1974. They were pictured proudly wearing matching brown suits: Mam's was made from suede with a velvet overcoat, while Dad wore a brown wool three-piece suit. It was the seventies though so I can forgive them for looking so terrible!

Terrified of what her family would think of her sudden wedding, it was left to Dad to break the news to Mam's family. So he made his way down to Poplar Farm in Bradford, where Mam's brothers and parents lived in trailers. He says he'll never forget how he had to walk past Uncle Towie and Uncle Billy's trailers knowing they would knock seven bells out of him if they knew that he'd married their sister without telling anyone.

'I've married your daughter,' he said breathlessly when he reached Granny Suzanna's trailer, wanting to make his announcement as brief as possible.

Granny Suzanna looked confused. 'No son, you've got it wrong,' she said. 'My Violet's been at work all day.'

So Dad pulled out his marriage licence as proof but Granny Suzanna just looked at him blankly. She was unable to believe her daughter would do such a thing. Plus she couldn't read. Strangely my mam's best friend Mabel ended up getting the blame for getting them together, as Granny Suzanna refused to believe any of it was her precious daughter's fault. For years she wouldn't speak to her and poor Mabel's name was mud.

After working for years and always saving half of whatever cash he earned, Dad had £500 in his pocket by the time he was a teenage married man. So he went to Tingley, Leeds, and bought an Eccles Emerald, a fancy and popular Gypsy trailer, for £300, and then splashed out another £200 on pans, quilts, bedding and all the other bits and bobs they needed to set up home.

Afterwards, with no food, my mam sent for her big sister Anne to help. 'I don't know what he wants or likes,' she said, shrugging. 'Can you take him to the supermarket and ask?'

Ever the older, wiser sister, Anne did just that and bought Mam's first load of shopping as a newlywed. As the youngest daughter of nine, Mam hadn't been trained up as much by Granny Suzanna as the eldest, Anne, had. My mam was the babby girl of the family, and in most Gypsy families they are usually spoiled rotten.

Just after my parents married, Granny Suzanna and Grandad Jimmy drove around the area looking for them to see if Mam was OK. Eventually they tracked them down and gave them a talking to. Granny Suzanna, a forthright woman if ever there was one, was most incensed that her daughter could have run off like that.

'What did you think yous were doing?' she said.

'I'm sorry, Mam,' said my mother. 'We just had to get on with it.'

It was a regular thing for Gypsy couples to run off and elope in those days, and both of them knew my dad was from a good Romany family, the Cannons – the horse-selling folk. So they let bygones be bygones and welcomed him after a few stern words.

For a while afterwards Mam and Dad lived with Mam's sister, Auntie Margaret, around Keighley, before settling in a campsite with her brother, Uncle Billy and his wife Auntie Winnie in Bolton Woods, north Bradford. They had six children: Jimmy, Violet, Billy, Sarah, Joanne and Mabel-Marie.

Mam was, and still is, a loving, understanding and compassionate woman. Like my Granny Suzanna she can be as stubborn and feisty as they come, but as a mother we were lucky to have her. Dad is the total opposite, a complete softie as far as us kids were concerned. Unlike other Gypsy men he didn't spend all his time at work and in the pub either. Well, he worked like a trojan, but when we kids came along, home time was 'our' time. I've countless fond memories of my dad taking time to talk to us and teach us things. For my dad, his family was his life.

My dad's family, especially his proud father, found it harder to accept the new bride in to their family. This wasn't helped when

Grandad Tom turned up at Mam's trailer to meet her properly for the first time now that she was his daughter-in-law, only to find her dancing madly around to her favourite Motown tune on a blaring cassette machine. Not a good first impression.

Mam and Dad had told no one they were courting, and Grandad Tom had only met Mam through family gatherings, so they didn't know her very well. But they soon warmed to her kind, compassionate nature.

Not only was Mam and Dad's love for each other plain to see, but also their strong work ethic was something they very much shared. Right from the start they went to work, shunning treats and holidays. Their mantra was: 'We want to get on,' and that meant earning enough to buy their family a good trailer and one day buy a plot of land of their own.

Although Mam never wanted to change anything about the man she married, one thing she quickly realised was that she had to do something about his dress sense. He was quite old-fashioned when they'd met, all three-piece suits and a 1950s-style side parting. Mam loved 1970s clothes and fabrics of all kinds and often had them made specially. After just a few short months Dad had swapped his suits for bell bottoms, his hair was down past his collar and he'd even donned a colourful flowery shirt. He may have arrived a bit late, but thanks to my trend-setting mother, Dad's wardrobe finally caught up with the era.

Chapter Three

Making Babies

Right from the moment she had the ring on her finger Mam started buying baby clothes and putting them away. That's just what most newlywed Gypsy wives did. No one knows how big the average Gypsy family is as there aren't enough records, but it's more than the average 2.4 kids, that's for sure. Many families back then seemed to have a good four kids each.

After months of trying, Mam had drawers full of bibs, wool booties and knitted Babygros but nothing happening inside. She was devastated. In those days, you never visited a doctor or had any tests. You just waited and hoped for the best.

Gypsy people have very fatalistic attitudes of 'what will be will be'. Anecdotally, I've heard that the average lifespan for Travellers is only fifty (again there is not enough written evidence as few Gypsies are academic) and many of us die from strokes or cancer. But we grew up not worrying about day-to-day risks like many Gorjas do. We didn't wear seat belts while driving in cars or go to the doctors unless we absolutely had to. The bury-your-head-in-the-sand approach doesn't necessarily make you live longer but it definitely stops you worrying so much!

However, after two long, empty years of waiting Mam was suffering. Her sister-in-law, my Auntie Winnie, already had three children, Jimmy, Violet and Billy, and was expecting again. Desperate to share her joy, Mam came up with an idea.

'Winnie, can you let me have your next bairn?' she begged. 'Please. I will do anything to be a mam and you've already got three kids yourself.'

My auntie was shocked at my mam's distress. Usually so steadfast and strong, Mam was turning in to a shadow of herself, and as the months grew in to years with still no bump her heart was starting to break in two. Feeling a gnawing sense of guilt about her own fertility, Auntie Winnie badly wanted to help.

'I'd do anything, anything for a child,' Mam sobbed. 'It's not fair. We've tried so hard but it isn't gonna happen for me. I'm never gonna have one of my own, am I?'

After months of trying to soothe her sister-in-law, rehearsing well-worn platitudes about waiting and 'when it's right, it's right', and letting the fates decide, even Auntie Winnie was running out of hope too. It was heartbreaking.

After holding Mam tight as she sobbed yet again, my auntie sat deep in thought. She knew Violet and Tom would make fabulous parents, and she also knew they already had three mouths to feed . . . The babby would also be brought up on a site nearby, so she could see her all the time. Thinking about it, the idea made perfect sense.

'OK,' she whispered, eventually. 'I will let you have the next one.' Somehow she also managed to persuade her husband Billy it was a good idea. She'd give birth and hand the baby over to Mam to bring up as her own.

My mam began sobbing again, this time with utter gratitude. 'You know I will be the best mam I can possibly be,' she cried.

But when Winnie's baby, a girl named Joanne arrived, my auntie's maternal instincts erupted with their full force. However much she loved her childless sister-in-law she just couldn't bear to hand her newborn baby over. In floods of tears she had the difficult conversation with Mam to say it wasn't going to happen.

Suddenly Mam's unhappiness felt even more acute. Her arms ached to hold a baby but she knew it wasn't to be. She ran back to her trailer and in front of my bewildered dad, she pulled open the drawers, flinging all the baby clothes she'd carefully collected around the trailer in to a pile. Then she gathered them all up in to bin bags and rushed back to her sister-in-law's trailer.

Once there, she took a deep breath and calmly told her: 'Have all these clothes, they are no good to me now, I'll never be a mam.' She returned to my dad and agreed they'd have to accept a childless marriage. This was a hard thing to do as the family ethic is so strong in our people.

Everyone we knew had children, except for my Aunt Mary and her husband Uncle Jimmy. We nicknamed Mary 'Auntie Sweetshop' as she would ply us kids with pop and sweets whenever we went near her. She adored us and saw it as her role to spoil us rotten. It was sad she never had any kids of her own, this being very unusual. Mam of course also felt this pressure, but mainly from herself. She didn't want to let my dad down and desperately wanted kids as she couldn't imagine life without motherhood – to be fair, most Gypsy women couldn't.

Meanwhile my cousin Joanne grew up knowing the story of how my lovely mam almost came to adopt her and she swears she wishes she had done so! Her father Billy is a good man but very strict and she didn't always find growing up that easy. Uncle Billy decided to bring his whole family up as strict Romanies, and most Romany fathers are strict enough already. He purposefully picked the most isolated roadsides to park on, so no one could pull up alongside, and he was against letting his girls mix even with other Travellers let alone any Gorjas at all. In his own way he was desperate to preserve the culture of our people, which he'd seen change so much within a generation. Carts and horses had been replaced by trailers, fewer roadsides were available for us to park on and more and more Romanies were mixing with Gorja people. Joanne found it a stifling, isolating childhood in many ways, although as a child she luckily had us all to play with. Funnily enough, Joanne was born with a big gap between her front teeth, just like Dad, and Mam would later joke she could've easily passed for their own.

As the Gypsies say: 'What is meant to be, is meant to be,' and as soon as Mam accepted her situation, things did change. By the end of 1976 Mam's dream came true: she discovered she was expecting. Overwhelmed with hormones and joy, she collapsed in to Dad's arms in tears when she found out. They were finally going to be a proper family at last, just when they'd given up.

My brother, Thomas Peter Cannon, was born on 1 July 1977 at Bradford Royal Infirmary. For centuries Gypsies have been born in vardos, with many communities shunning local hospitals, but over the years fewer Gypsies minded Gorja hospitals as they were seen as safe places to have a child. Mam had to have a C-section as her labour went on for so long. Doctors warned her she would need C-sections for any subsequent babies too. Of course this straight away put paid to her dreams of having four or five children, the norm for a Gypsy woman in those days.

The same day my brother was born, a horse owned by Grandad Tom gave birth to a foal he named Peggy. Tom Cannon Senior happily gave the baby horse away to Tom as a gift, as he believed sharing the same birthday was a sign that he should have her. This horse was seen as an investment too, for when she gave birth her foals would be sold for money to give to my brother Tom. Peggy died when she was thirty-one, which is a ripe old age for a horse, and over the years she must have provided Tom with thousands of pounds of income. I suppose it was our version of a bank investment. Almost no older-generation Gypsies use bank accounts – most money is kept under mattresses – but they always encouraged other ways to invest, be it buying a piece of jewellery or an animal.

Of course Mam was absolutely thrilled with her baby boy and threw herself in to her new role as Mammy with a capital M. But some things are also sent to try us, as Tom proved himself to be a very difficult toddler, and soon Mam found herself struggling to get all her domestic jobs done.

She had the trailer to keep spotless; the dinner, usually a bacon stew or a casserole, to get going; a clingy toddler to look after; and generally she had to keep the home in good running order. My dad was far from a despot, but Mam liked to keep things good for him. He wanted for nothing and always had a steaming dish of something delicious waiting for him when he got home from working on the scrap yard. Of course she didn't have all the mod cons back then either. No vacuum cleaner or washing machine, so the chores took much longer. It was a bit like being a 1950s housewife even though it was the late seventies. With Tom whining and never wanting to be left alone, Mam struggled.

'That child plays you like a fiddle,' tutted my Auntie Margaret, as Tom clung to Mam's leg while she washed the pots. ''E needs teaching he can't have you on a piece of string.'

Mam raised an eyebrow. 'Well, he is difficult, yes,' she sighed.

As Margaret had already raised several boys by then, she was happy to offer advice.

'Take his harness and tie it to the tow bar and leave 'im,' she said. 'That'll teach 'im 'e can't be on your hip all day long.'

Reluctantly Mam agreed, despite Tom's wailing and

protesting. She managed to whizz through her jobs that day, and eventually Tom calmed down.

Mam tried again for another baby when Tom learned to walk and this time she didn't have to wait long at all. Within a matter of months I was on the way. Six months expecting me (we never use the term 'pregnant' as it's too close to the 'act' beforehand; in our eyes that's inappropriate language), her father Jimmy died. As with all Gypsy rites of passage, the funeral was massive. Relations, however distant, came from all over to pay their respects. Even if you barely knew the person who'd died you still came to make sure the grieving relations didn't want for anything.

Romany families stay with the body of the deceased until they're buried, night and day, in their trailer, which is filled with fresh flowers and incense to mask the scent of the corpse. It's a time for families to reminisce, comfort each other and try and come to terms with what has happened.

Mam, a true daddy's girl, was beside herself. She chose to stay by her father's body nonstop for a week, despite being six months' expecting and exhausted. But just as she thought things couldn't get any worse, Tom toddled over one morning, and managed to pull on a tablecloth, on top of which stood a hot cup of tea.

'Tom!' Mam screamed, leaping to scoop him up.

His wails sent the men running to help and Mam was given a lift to the hospital. There, they said they needed to keep Tom in to treat his superficial burns.

Poor Mam, already griefstricken, was torn in two. To leave her dad's body alone felt like a terrible betrayal and yet her son needed her as well.

In the end she chose to patch Tom up and then take him every morning and evening to the hospital to get his dressings changed, meanwhile staying by Jimmy's side. By the time he was buried, ten days later, Mam was nearly in hospital herself with complete exhaustion. The day after the funeral she immediately packed all her brightly coloured clothes away to display her grief. Close relations follow this tradition and it's a way of letting others know you're still mourning.

When I arrived by C-section, also at Bradford Royal Infirmary, on 14 August 1979, Mam couldn't have been more thrilled. Naming me Violet-Margaret, she finally had a much-wanted girl, although people have never used my full double-barrelled name as Mam intended.

People called me the spit out of my mother's mouth, as we looked so alike. Not only were our long faces and features the same, we share a mane of frizzy red hair and big blue eyes. She also used to be very petite like me before she had kids. All the pictures of Mam before she had us showed such a stylish woman. She loved her flares and her leather waistcoats, whereas afterwards she wore nothing but long black skirts and jumpers.

'I just had you to worry about then,' she used to say. 'Not myself any more.' And that was her philosophy: children come first.

As is customary for Gypsies, I was showered with gifts when I was born. But instead of getting an animal as an investment, like Tom, I was given jewellery.

Granny Winnie gave me a tiger teeth coral bracelet and American dollar earrings and bought me a gold bracelet with charms added to it every year. Later I got a pound charm, which was a pound note encased in a little glass and gold container, and when I was a little older, I was given a penknife with a blade that actually flipped out.

Jewellery is important to men, women and children alike in our culture. It shows you've got a bit of wealth and traditionally Gypsy women have always worn gold necklaces, bracelets and of course hoop earrings to show how well they were doing. We grew up as children wearing half-sovereign and beefy full-sovereign rings, the girls as well as boys. My grannies would proudly wear gold necklaces too, like the clown figurine pendants with limbs that moved. This was long before they became seen as 'chavvy'. Once Gorjas started wearing them, we stopped. One of my all-time favourite presents was a replica of Princess Diana's engagement ring – a midnight-blue sapphire with diamonds round it – that I got for my twentieth birthday. It was amazing.

One reason Mam couldn't wait to have a girl was so she could dress me in pretty clothes. As soon as I was born I was placed in the most carefully chosen outfits to be cooed at and admired by adoring family members.

Mam was crazy about one dress, which she ordered specially

from America after having saved up for three months, then waiting a further two months for delivery. After carefully dressing me in the yellow garment she proudly showed me off to everyone who passed her trailer. New mams were always extremely proud of the latest addition to their broods, and now she had a girl, Mam was determined to show me off. But despite her painstaking choice of outfits, she didn't always get the response she wanted.

'That dress makes that child look ill,' Aunt Winnie said, with her usual forthright honesty.

Mam was gutted. But she couldn't deny Winnie was right. As a toddler I had very fine blonde hair before it went red so I almost looked bald, and my skin broke out in to a rash at the slightest thing. Eventually Mam realised that all the pretty, delicate lace dresses and tiny knickers she'd carefully clothe me in every day were actually irritating the hell out of my very sensitive skin, and she promptly ditched the lot. Buying a whole load of new functional cotton Babygros she became resigned to having a plainer but happier-looking baby girl.

It wasn't just bad skin I'd inherited, much to my mother's dismay. It was also a small gullet, which meant I gagged and brought up food very easily. As a growing toddler I almost lived on mashed potato and custard. Try as she might to get fruit and vegetables down me, Mam ended up chewing up a lot of food and then re-feeding it to me herself like a mammy bird, except she used a spoon.

When my Auntie Winnie found out what she was doing she was disgusted.

'Violet,' she said, 'why on earth can't you just buy a food processor?'

Mam just laughed. 'And where do you think I am going to fit a food processor in to this place?' It was true. The trailer didn't have space for many extras. Such was our way of life, everything was stripped down to the basics, although of course there was always room for the Crown Derby china collection.

But my mam's troubles didn't end with my clingy elder brother and my own allergies and eating problems. In fact my very first memory of my childhood is peering in to a glass incubator at a tiny, beautiful, baby doll and being told by my weeping mother that it was my sister Maria. I was three years old and didn't understand, but Maria had been born with a hole in her heart and wasn't expected to survive. I just remember wondering if this pretty doll was actually real and being upset for my mam, who couldn't stop crying.

Next my dad brought Tom to hospital to see his new baby sister. Mam could never bear to cut Tom's gorgeous blonde hair and had proudly grown it down below his shoulders. But Dad had other ideas, so with Mam tied up in hospital with Maria, he took the opportunity to make his son a 'boy' again and got the whole lot lopped off. Already distraught about her newborn baby, the sight of her Tom's shorn hair made Mam cry even harder. He looked like a little lamb.

After a few weeks, Maria rallied and the hole in her heart

closed up – Mam swears by the power of prayer. My sister was let home and suddenly we were a family of five. Although nobody could have been happier to have a baby sister, her appearance in my life only served to make me feel bad about myself. Not only did I have the less-than-coveted position as a middle child, but even at a very young age I started to wonder about my place in the world.

My second memory of early childhood happened a month later. Following the drama of Maria's birth, Tom and I were treated to a theatre show in Bradford Alhambra, starring Russ Abbott off the telly. We were beside ourselves with excitement; we absolutely loved him.

I was dressed up in my best frock with my hair curled to perfection and I wore a real mink coat, while Tom was dressed in a smart little suit. We looked like two immaculately turned-out mini adults, so when children were picked out to go on stage to take part in the show Tom and I were both chosen.

I am not sure they would have done that if they'd known we were Gypsy kids but we certainly looked very cute in our beautiful clothes. Once we were in front of the blinding lights Tom got stage-fright when Russ Abbott asked him what he wanted for a treat, so I piped up and told him Tom wanted some books and a pen. We took part in a silly game and then Russ Abbott asked me if I had a boyfriend. I nodded and when he asked who it was I pointed to Tom, giggling. I don't think I've ever embarrassed anyone as much as my brother that evening. Afterwards we were let off stage with our books and pens and Tom started rowing with me.

'I wanted a car not felt pens!' he shouted. 'You should have said a car!' I just shrugged – it wasn't my fault he was shy.

For just a few weeks after Maria was born we lived in a rented house in Low Moor, but like most Romanies, Mam and Dad hated four walls and we soon moved in to a trailer back on the site in Bolton Woods again.

Chapter Four

The World Was Our Trailer

Yes, there wasn't much room, but our trailer made for the cosiest home you could wish for. At twenty foot long it wasn't very big, especially for a growing family, but we were used to lack of space. It was mainly white and rectangular in shape, with rounded corners and four stripes of chrome running across them, six inches deep, two in the middle and one along the bottom. It was kept spotlessly clean. When the sun shone directly on to it, your eyes would ache with the dazzle. Walking towards the mirror-like sections meant you could clearly spot anyone behind you. Outside were two big silver milk churns used for carrying water, which were also polished to perfection.

We Romanies love the light so windows are very important. Our trailer had three windows running down the front side, three foot by two foot each, through which you could see the cushions on the couch. The windows were made from pattern-edged etched glass. A formica step, matching the outside of the trailer, led up to the door. Once inside, the seating areas around the edge of the living space turned in to beds at night, while on the other side was the stove and kitchen area. The beds were covered with Welsh tartan blankets, made from angora wool. These were always hand-washed and hung up on the line to dry and I was never allowed to sleep directly underneath them, I always had to have a sheet separating me from the precious blanket. Even as a young child, I thought some of the décor was garish. We had burgundy and pink satin throws and cushions with gold frilled edges . . . yuck! They were fashionable at the time, so my Aunt Winnie also made them to sell on.

Lace is another massive feature of any Gypsy trailer. It's everywhere: thick, heavy, high-quality French 'macramé' lace. Every available tabletop and surface had a runner. Some pieces of lace had 'inner' sections that you could remove so you could colour-coordinate if you moved trailer without having to buy a new lot.

As you walked through the door, you were facing the white formica kitchen, scrubbed to perfection, with two cupboards towards the back and one at the side. Above that were lockers with etched glass front panels, showing off the dinner service, and next to them were the food cupboards. We had Minton Haddon Hall bone china, with delicate, pretty cups and saucers. We ate off the plates every day but used really big breakfast cups for morning coffee.

The kitchen was separated from the living area by a tiny strip of formica. On the sideboards sat lace doilies and blue cut-glass baskets filled with random bits, and a fruit bowl and vase to match. There was a mirrored cupboard and a wardrobe with a full-length mirror, as well as a fireplace with an open fire. Across every available surface there were more mirrors and glass, all sparkling from Mam's elbow grease.

I have no idea how she managed to keep it all so clean with three kids running in and out. I don't remember her ever telling us off for touching the mirrors or causing finger marks. On every shelf, china was laid out and on the sideboard sat decorative red and blue 'hawking baskets', filled with fruit. A few years later Tom and I would manage to shatter one after a play fight grew a bit too boisterous.

Directly above that was an airing cupboard filled with sheets and below a horseshoe-shaped seating area with a leather couch (if it wasn't leather it was covered in plastic) that pulled out in to a double bed.

Next to the seating area some formica doors pulled along to make a bedroom area. On the near side was a chest of drawers and another sideboard where Mam's Old Imari Crown Derby patterned dishes were displayed, then on the far side was another big long bunk, six foot long, which pulled out in to another double bed. This was where we children slept. Across the white formica ceiling sat cut crystal lights with gold edging. Although gold is extremely popular with most Gypsies my mam didn't like it much as a rule. She preferred pink.

This site in Bolton Woods was to be our main home for years, although we did swap trailers a few times and move about from time to time as all Gypsies do. We would stay in one place and then one day Dad would move the jacks and off we'd go, travelling wherever and whenever the mood took us. Sometimes we would stay on our own, but usually we would meet up with one of our many family members. This was just how Mam and Dad grew up and this is what they wanted for us. When we learned to talk we used a mixture of English and Romanese at home, but mainly Romanese. I would give examples but we don't like telling people our language. It's one of the ways we can identify each other as true Gypsies.

The site in Bolton Woods was on top of a steep bank in a hilly part of Bradford. Over the years we stayed in many areas of the city including Low Moor, Tong Street, Canal Road and Bolton Road. To the side of us was a disused pub and on the other side a printing press works. The site was essentially a piece of waste ground that no one was using, so no one bothered us. Along the edge sat giant Yorkshire boulders that we soon learned to climb over. Later on as kids we'd hold little shows on there using it as a stage. Underfoot was grass everywhere, all around the camp.

By the age of three my hair had grown to a sufficient length for Mam to 'do' something with it. Like all Gypsy mams she wanted her little girl to have the archetypal curls bouncing over her head as she played outside. As a result she'd spend half an hour every single morning teasing my frizzy mop in to a head of adorable shiny ringlets. Wet-combing every section with great patience, she'd twizzle it around her finger until the curl took and then ping it free. Neighbours would marvel at my lovely shiny, bouncing locks but accuse Mam of putting rags in it every night, something that was seen as cheating.

'No I have not,' Mam would boast. 'And no hair products neither.' She even started 'doing my hair' every day on the trailer steps, so everyone could see she never used rags. In my mother's eyes my hair was a force to be reckoned with, but one she'd win over.

During this time she had a lovely little saying she repeated to us every morning: 'You're better than no one and no one is better than you. But if they think you are, then you must know you're better than them . . .'

Mam was our role model. I wanted to be like her. Soft and loving, she also had real strength, and everyone liked her – I never met anyone who didn't. She taught us all the important things in life, like the fact that wealth and status means nothing but what's inside people's hearts is everything.

Mam also had fun dressing me in 'Granny Grunts', a traditional Victorian-looking embroidered smock with little bells on it, which had became popular with Gypsies. They cost a small fortune as they were handmade and you could only buy them from America. I was one of the first on my site to be dressed in them. My Auntie Maureen, one of Mam's cousins, who made curtains, couldn't wait to start making them too, so Mam lent her one of the dresses to use as a template and then sell on.

Clothes were a big part of our culture. Right from a young age, dressed as little walking, breathing dolls, we always took notice of our appearance. The mothers would all try and outdo each other's daughter's outfits, often hand-sewing them. One of my favourite outfits when I was very young was a red leather suit similar to Michael Jackson's that Mam had made for us herself. I also loved my leather miniskirt and my waistcoat emblazoned with silver and gold leaves. I thought I looked like the bees' knees. While girls usually stuck to fancy dresses, little boys often wore suits. Tom looked every inch the cheeky wee chappie in his three-piece suits.

My dad was a typical Gypsy man, but with a heart of gold. Tall, with dark brown hair and lightly tanned skinned, he had bright eyes that crinkled when he smiled. As a child he was my hero. I was always happy to see him pulling up in his van from a day at work, his cheeks always shiny, smiling widely and showing the gap in his front teeth that was big enough to fit a pound coin through. He always wore suit trousers and a shirt and smart jumper, wherever he was going, be it the scrap yard or horses' stable. He never wore jeans and the first time he bought trainers we all fell about laughing. They didn't look right. Not on my dad.

Animals are another huge part of any Gypsy community. We love them like our families, although they're never allowed in our trailers. They are seen as dirty, however much they get petted. When I was three years old I managed to get my first pet of my own, a Jack Russell I named Tiny. My friend Jolene, who was the same age, told me her dad was breeding them and, even though he hadn't checked with my parents first, he said I was allowed to choose one when the new litter was born.

As soon I saw Tiny I picked her out. I'd fallen in love with her because I thought she looked like me, all squashed face and white fur with orange blobs on it, the same colour as my hair. Still without breathing a word to my parents I then waited until she was six weeks old, and brought her home by myself.

As I marched in to our trailer, holding her out in the palm of my hand, my dad shook his head, guessing what I was about to say. 'Take it back, my Violet,' he said, gently. 'Yous too young for a dog.'

Tears filling my eyes, he led me back to Jolene's trailer, where Jolene's dad claimed he thought my parents had known all about it. Of course after several more tears and a stubborn refusal on my part to let go of little Tiny, I arrived back home with him, triumphant and proud to be a mammy to a pet dog.

Tiny went everywhere with me, she was devoted to me. With her by my side I was told I could roam around anywhere as long as I stayed within the site walls.

She soon had pups and I kept her daughter Missy, short for Mischief. I named her that after I caught her with the head of my much-loved 'Peaches and Cream' Barbie in her mouth. I started screaming when I found various skinny Barbie limbs strewn around outside our trailer, not to mention her peach puff dress and cape torn in to rags.

As she grew in to a toddler, my sister Maria's hair sat

beautifully straight as if ironed, even first thing in the morning. She'd leap out of bed and run outside, not needing a minute's attention with Mam. A wee and fragile thing, she quickly had everyone wrapped around her little finger with her sunny smile and her big eyes. She was always full of energy, running around, playing and dancing. She was great fun, but also hard work. We spoiled her really, after all she was 'the Babby'. As I watched her blossom, I started to feel less attractive. From the very beginning I just thought Maria was the most beautiful child in the world, and as I watched how everyone else around me fell in love with her, I began to feel I couldn't compare.

Maybe it's because we often have the same names as our close relations or maybe we simply like to bestow terms of endearment on our loved ones, but in our community everyone has their own nickname. Sometimes though people are just damn unlucky with the nicknames they get lumbered with. And the chances are you will get called something silly as many nicknames come from babyhood. Mine is 'Princess', something Tom coined for me. For some unknown reason my Aunt Margaret was called 'Pud Pud'. Maria was always 'the Babby'.

Once I came home to find one of my mam's friends around. She was introduced to me as 'Aunt Mamma Cow'. I swallowed down the giggle that was threatening to erupt from me. How on earth could I call this grown woman that name in a respectful way? Later Mam explained that her name was actually Vera, but when she was born her mam thought she looked like a baby cow so the name stuck. When her sister arrived she was duly named 'Mouse'. Incidentally, all other women are always referred to as 'aunt' and men as 'uncle', regardless of their real relationship to you.

Anyway, Mamma Cow was a frequent fixture at Mam's kitchen table for a while, but I always put off using her proper name, just sticking to Auntie.

One of the stereotypes about Gypsies is that people associate us with being dirty or untidy but for true Romanies the absolute opposite is the case. Mam cleaned like a demon every day and us kids grew up spotless and immaculate. We were always dressed in the best clothes, our hair done as if going to a party, even if we were running wild in the fields. True, not everyone on the sites we lived on looked like this, but for our mam high standards were important, and she was always conscious about the impression we made on other people. The smell of bleach even today makes me smile and brings back happy childhood memories of being warm and safe in our shiny trailer. Mam doused and cleaned and scrubbed everything in it. Especially teacups. To give someone a cup of tea with stains in it would be absolutely shameful.

If I got a pound for every time I've been called 'scum' or 'dirty', I'd have a trailer fit to house a millionaire by now. For someone as clean and as hard-working as I am, it's amazing how many times I've been called 'filthy' and 'lazy' too. As a child I could never understand where this came from because cleaning up after ourselves was absolutely ingrained in to our consciousness.

One Easter, we'd set up site on a piece of wasteland in

Thornbury. My dad's sister Aunt Mary and her boys came with us and she boiled up some eggs for us to paint with bright colours before rolling them down the hill.

Laughing and shouting, we started off doing it as carefully as possible, as the rules say the winner is the one with the shell still intact. Then we could give them a good old throw and smash them to pieces on the grass.

A few days later, just as we moved on, the black binbags came out and the adults and kids went round picking up every last piece of rubbish, wrapper, egg shell, whatever it was, checking almost every blade of grass as we went.

On my patch, I collected what I saw and then handed the bag to Mam.

'Finished, Mam,' I said, moving off to play.

'Er, no you haven't, my Violet,' she said, pulling me back. 'What about *that*?'

I followed her finger and spotted a Marathon wrapper (the old name for a Snickers chocolate bar). I hated peanuts and never ate them.

'But that's not mine, Mam, you know I never eat them kind of sweets, don't you?'

'It doesn't matter, my Violet, go and pick it up.'

'I ain't picking it up, it's not mine!'

Her eyes caught mine and flashed the signal for me not to press the argument further. 'It doesn't matter, Violet, whether it belongs to you or not. It's rubbish and we pick up every single tiny piece at all times. Now go and do it.'

So I did and always have done since.

Some people blame Irish Travellers for leaving rubbish-strewn fields wherever they go, and some people don't. Personally I've always got on with Irish Travellers; my sister-in-law is half-Irish and in Bradford we were happy to mix. Granted there are lots of wannabe Travellers, people who jump on to the bandwagon, so to speak, and want to pretend to be proper Gypsies. At the end of the day there is good and bad in everyone. But as far as I could see, my people were always incredibly careful to leave their places spotless and just as they found them.

What makes the cleanliness even more remarkable, of course, is the lack of water on the sites. There were rarely any standing pipes or taps, so we had to rely on the goodwill of neighbours and local folk to give us water. Often, if a Gypsy person is admitted to hospital, doctors will discover they are dehydrated, as we never get much to drink.

As kids we'd stagger around with churns and billy cans, being careful not to spill and waste a precious drop. Once my auntie needed water to make up her babby's bottles. 'Will you go across to the garage,' she said, 'and ask them to fill a can up for us?' So off I went, can swinging in my hand, ready to ask the Gorja garage man to spare a bit of water. Barely able to reach the counter, with a smile on my face, I stood on tiptoe to ask the man: 'Please mister, my auntie needs water to feed a bairn, will you fill it for us?'

The man looked at me, peering down his nose like I was a

piece of something unpleasant on his shoe. His stare made me shuffle my feet uncomfortably. It was not a feeling I was used to. 'Go away, Gypsy scum,' he snapped. 'And no, you can't have any water. Let the Gypsy baby die.'

So I returned, empty-handed, and my auntie sent a couple of the men instead. I don't know what they said, but they came back with brimming cans. It was one of my first experiences of seeing how unwelcoming the outside world could be towards us.

Washing was a similar scenario. When I was very young we'd use rainwater we'd collected to wash ourselves in the mornings. I'd roll my sleeves up and dip my hands in tentatively, seeing how cold it was first. Then I'd cup both palms, fill them with water, screw up my face, and quickly rub the water in. As long as we had clean faces and no sleep left in our eyes, Mam was happy.

We'd also have a strip wash every day. I don't remember anyone smelling, ever. When you think about it, people today almost wash themselves too much. There were no fancy shower gels either – just good plain soap and a scrubbing brush.

Mam and my aunties always took all the girls on a big jaunt to the laundrette once a week or so. They'd absolutely stuff the car with clothes or drag enormous bags filled to the brim with sheets, towels and clothes of every description for a big wash. After helping our mams sort the washing in to white and colours, we'd fight over whose turn it was to fill up the giant machine with soap and then sit mesmerised as it whirled and spun in to action. Washing, like cleaning and cooking, was very much women's work and not something the men ever had to worry about.

In later years we still didn't have showers or baths so finding somewhere off-site for a wash was the only way if we had no access to water. We'd go in to sports centres, swimming pools and public loos. Wherever we went though we were never welcome. If a leisure centre charged 50p one day it'd go up to a £1 the next and so on until we couldn't afford it. As a small child I was protected from much of this by Mam. She'd simply make a joke about forgetting to bring enough money.

Going to the toilet is also less-than-straightforward when you live in a trailer. In the same way as we don't have animals in our houses, believing them to be dirty, we also grew up without any toilets. As children we were taught to control our bowels and bladders from a very young age. You only went to the toilet when you really needed it and doing a number two meant going off-site.

When we were out and about we'd use pubs, leisure and shopping centres and all sorts to go to the loo. At night-time, we used dishes to pee in. Even using that word I can't stand, to be honest! All bodily functions are something you do in private and are seen as 'dirty'. It's not something you joke about or tell people.

If you were caught short after being out all day, you'd quietly tell your mam or dad and they'd ask what you needed to do. If you needed a number one you would be sent outside and for anything else they'd have to take you off-site, maybe to the supermarket or to Granny Suzanna, who was at that time living on a permanent council site.

One evening, around 6 p.m., I got caught short.

'I really need to go, Mam!' I cried, jiggling around.

'OK. What do you need, my Violet?' she asked.

'A number one!' I replied.

'Well, go out to the grass round the back of the container,' she replied, 'but be quick and discreet.' The container was a shed where we kept our bikes.

I shot off and did what I needed to do but as I ran back, I felt something furry with a wiry tail shoot over my bare feet.

'Arghhhh!' I screamed, jumping as if the grass had morphed in to hot coals. 'It's a long tail! It's a long tail!' That's the name we have for rats.

Shrieking as if the devil himself were after me, I ran as fast as I could and bolted up the trailer stairs. But my lovely brother Tom had overheard my cries. Banging on the door, I became hysterical, realising it was locked.

'Open it, open it!' I screamed.

'Nooo way,' shouted back Tom. 'I don't want no long tail in here with us!'

I couldn't believe he'd locked me out, and it took Mam leading him by the elbow to move him away from the door. It may have been the first but it certainly wasn't the last time my naughty big brother caused me trouble.

Chapter Five

Smelling of Roses

Education for Gypsies was non-existent for generations. Due to this there is little documentary evidence about our history. Few books have been written about our culture, and the lack of written records means that most of our knowledge of the past is learned through word of mouth and not recorded like in other cultures. Only in the most recent generation has education become widespread, and arguably a necessity. I was one of the lucky ones in that my mam had learned to read and write. Mam only went to school for a very short while, but she did enough to reach a basic level of literacy. She bought cheap paperback Mills & Boon books and devoured them, managing to improve her skills on her own.

From a young age I would sit with my mam while she taught me to read using *Topsy and Tim* books she'd borrowed from the library. She also encouraged us to read comics and any other books she could lay her hands on. Well I say 'us' but it was more like just me. Tom couldn't have been less interested. But Mam believed it was important for us to get an education and took it seriously. She could see how rapidly the world was changing and she instinctively understood that people need to reach a decent level of literacy and numeracy if they want to get ahead. She followed her instincts and agreed to send us to school, even though she wasn't thrilled about us mixing with Gorja people there.

In some ways we didn't need encouraging. Our Gypsy site on Bolton Road was right next to a paper mill. Regularly we went right up to it, exploring and investigating the place in our little gang. Sometimes the mill owner would spot us larking around and playing with offcuts he'd left outside. We would walk away with armfuls of card and paper bundles, all to be taken back to the trailer and cut up in to pieces, driving Mam mad with all the bits. There we would play teachers and use them as pretend registers.

In 1982, I joined Wapping Nursery and Primary School in Bradford. Tom started school in the infants and I went to the nursery. We'd recently pulled the trailer up on to an old piece of ground next to a pub and had been left alone there, so we were able to attend regularly.

On the first day, Mam dressed me in my usual look: a pretty dress, a head of ringlets and some gold dollar earrings. Tom wore some smart trousers and a little waistcoat, scowling and complaining as he walked.

Mam held our hands more tightly as we approached the gate. 'Now you be good as gold,' she said, kissing our heads. 'And try and listen to what the teacher's saying.'

We said goodbye and turned to the playground, full of Gorja kids of every description, milling around, holding the hands of their mams. This was the first time for both of us that we'd hung out with Gorja children, and from the off it was obvious we were different, although initially I was too young to pick up on this or allow it to upset me. All I knew was they lived in houses and spoke English, whereas we also spoke Romanese, moved around a lot and our family were our best friends.

The main thing I noticed in the classroom was not so much that I was the only Gypsy girl in my class, but that I was one of the very few white girls. Bradford has so many ethnic minorities and I was around kids from many different cultures, from Indian and African to Arab.

On my first day of 'big school' aged three, the first thing I didn't hesitate to do was to let the teacher know that Mam had already taught me all the basics of the alphabet and numbers and words. 'The cat sat on the mat' was no problem for this Gypsy girl.

Despite my first hesitant steps in to the world of Gorja education, at that age life for me continued to revolve around my family and community. We would come home from school ravenous, and the smell of our mam's cooking would greet us like an old friend as we approached the trailer, welcoming us back in to our society again.

Growing up, there was only one type of food we ate: good,

proper stuff, often straight from the ground. A meal wasn't considered a meal unless it contained meat and the lack of space meant we had little refrigeration and almost no frozen food. Mam went shopping in the local supermarket, and prepared most of the meals from scratch. My favourite dish was bacon ribs, potatoes and cabbage. Some Gypsies would drive literally hundreds of miles to find a good butcher who did proper bacon ribs. It's like a staple food for us, and people believed a decent cut was worth the extra effort. I also loved Gypsy toast (eggy bread) for breakfast and Yorkshire puddings made in cast iron pans. Ooooh, and you can't beat the taste of toast or jacket potatoes cooked on a proper fire.

Every morning we'd have toast for breakfast and Dad would make us kids a milky coffee, splitting one cup between the three of us. Dinners were roast beef, fry-ups or stew. Mam was always making stews, getting out the biggest pot we had and filling it to the brim with chopped veggies to bubble all day long in time for the end of the working day. Very occasionally we had fishfingers or butterscotch- or chocolate-flavoured Angel Delight but convenience foods were in short supply. We ate with our plates balanced on our knees, on the couch. Even now I don't like eating at tables and prefer sitting on the floor.

Electricity came from a crank generator that Dad would turn on after dark. Being a softie though he couldn't resist us kids' demands to watch children's ITV, and he put it on early for us so we could have our fill of *Supergran*, *Rainbow*, *Grotbags*, *Round the Twist* and *Sooty and Sweep*. We'd all hunker down on the beds, laying on our tummies with our feet kicking in the air as our eyes grew round with wonder at the screen. Of course we knew all the programmes were set in the Gorja world. But it was just entertainment, never a life we wished we had. To us the outside world of Gorjas was full of 'the Others', where people lived in the same brick houses, sometimes for their whole lives, never travelling except for holidays, maybe even working for decades in the same job. Our way of life, with its emphasis on family, travel and getting work where you could find it, made us feel free – because we *were* free most of the time. We weren't touched by rules and regulations, well, not until later on.

Sometimes we'd also play games. If Dad was back early he'd pull out a set of Monopoly, although we could never let Tom be the banker as he was a terrible cheat. We also played endless games of Connect Four and cards. Although Mam hated cards, she was dead superstitious about them. If I ever got a new packet she'd stand over me straight away. 'Get that joker out and rip it up,' she'd say. 'Go on, quick now. Quick, get rid of it out of the trailer.' She thought jokers were the devil's work and very unlucky.

If we weren't playing games Dad was playing music. As a child I remember being surrounded by tunes and lyrics. But I'm not talking about twee Gypsy guitar songs around a fire or anything, it was proper music like Elvis and Motown. My dad loved the mournful songs of Sydney Devine, songs like 'Long Black Limousine' – they were miserable but even now they bring me right back. As far as Dad was concerned, Elvis was a god. Well, there is only one God and that's the one above, but to Dad, Elvis had a voice *sent* from God it was so other-worldly. When Elvis died, Dad believed he was being punished because he hadn't used his gift properly as God had intended, as he had turned to drink and drugs.

All Gypsies love Dolly Parton too, and in later years Tracey Chapman became the Gypsy pop poster girl. When we heard her belt out those songs about oppression, like 'Across the Lines', we always thought you could take out the black connotations and replace it with Gypsies. Everyone absolutely loved her and her cassette tapes were like gold dust.

In later years it was quite annoying as the lads used to nick our Tracey tapes if they heard one playing. If they could lay their hands on one you'd never see it again. The boys were especially bad for coming over to say hello and leaning inside the window. 'Oh right, so that's Tracey in there, is it?' they'd say and the next thing you knew they'd whipped a hand in, pressed eject and pinched it.

I was thrilled when I got my first car with a CD player, quite early on before everyone else got them. The first lad who stuck his head in to 'hear' my Tracey album and tried to eject it got a shock when he found a CD not a cassette tape. 'What am I supposed to do with this?' he said. But that was how much we all loved her music.

Living in such close proximity might seem like hard work as most Gorjas live in houses and have doors to close shut for privacy when they need it. But we grew up used to being around family members at all times. No rooms were closed off, no one could 'own' any space. I grew up sharing a bed with my brother and sister. I was used to having a warm body next to mine. It made me feel safe and secure.

It's still a mystery to me how Mam and Dad managed in such a confined space sometimes. At Christmas we were all led to believe Father Christmas was true, until quite an old age, and it was a big part of the magic. On Christmas Eve we'd go to bed in an empty trailer and by the next morning literally all the floor space would be covered with toys wrapped in sparkling paper. Who knows where they hid them as space was at a premium for everyone we knew.

I also have no idea how my parents managed to have any privacy of their own but they had three kids so they obviously managed it somehow!

And our parents didn't worry when they shooed us out of the trailer for the day. They knew we'd look after each other and play together until lunchtime, when we would come in briefly then go back out again. We spent hours roaming around whatever area we were staying in. And we did stay all over, going to visit family members wherever they were. This was in the days before mobiles and we didn't have a landline anyway, so everything was arranged at the last minute or by word of mouth. Dad would hook up the trailer and off we'd set, asking around the town for where the nearest Gypsy site was and then asking passersby if they'd seen whichever aunt or uncle we were pulling to. It could take hours to find someone, but no one minded. Time didn't matter. Of course my choice of playmates also depended on where we were staying. Maria and Tom were always with me, of course, and quite often there would be Dad's sister Aunt Ninna's daughter, Martina, and Aunt Winnie's girls, Joanne and Sarah. Sometimes their big sister Violet would babysit for us all.

Martina and Joanne were loads of fun. The pair of them were very loud and outgoing, and they were always up for some mischief or adventure. Martina had a thick black plait like a horse's mane that hung right down to her waist, with huge brown eyes. She was a really pretty girl, and I always felt a bit jealous of her delicate features, so different to my own.

Joanne had similar hair to mine, but in tight corkscrew curls, which she hated. She'd pull them straight and always held them at bay with a big plait. She was tiny at 4'10" and she never grew any taller even in adulthood, like a lot of Gypsy women. Sarah was quieter than her sister, but we'd spend hours drawing together.

Tom would hang round more with the lads. He loved playing with Auntie Mary's (Dad's sister's) boys: Ben, Tommy-Joe and Martin. But with thirty-four cousins there was always someone close by to have a laugh with. You were never alone.

Every time we arrived at a new site, while the adults worried about boring things like where to get water and source food etc., us kids always rushed to build what every respectable Gypsy site needed – a handmade rope swing.

Normally the bigger lads such as Jimmy, Billy or our Tom would take charge, but it was up to us girls – often me, Maria, Jolene, Joanne, Martina and Sarah – to supervise loudly from the ground.

First we'd go and find a sturdy, long twig or log about a foot and a half wide, then we'd look for some rope. Our dads must have lost so much rope over the years, hacked away with penknives in order to entertain us kids. Then one of the lads would climb up the highest tree or find one overhanging a river or stream. The added fear factor was always a bonus. They'd tie strong rope at the top and bottom and the biggest person there, usually Jimmy, would check it, bouncing up and down, pulling the rope, seeing how the bough of the tree fared under the strain. Finally when the nod was given, we'd all pile on, jostling for a place in the queue to test our newfound source of fun.

My favourite game was to twist the rope as much as possible and then, when you felt the strain in your hands and risked losing the skin off your fingers with the pinch from the twist of the twining, you jumped on board and let it go.

The sensation of gazing at the green canopy above while spinning out of control, legs dangling wildly, was wonderful. It was a sense of abandonment mixed with dizziness, a feeling that you could fall at any minute, but knowing you trusted the swing and your cousins' ability to tie knots and find unbreakable logs. We felt invincible.

We grew up to think that the outdoors was our indoors,

the grass was our carpet and the sky was our ceiling. The sun was an alarm clock and the moon our night-light. Being sat inside all day just didn't happen.

Surrounded by so much nature was par for the course and we simply didn't know any different. It was only years later when we moved in to a house, with walls, that we realised how much it meant.

I grew up to love wild flowers with a passion. They were so delicate and pretty, hard-wearing beauties rather than things people bought to plant in their gardens. Places like Bentham, in Yorkshire, where we regularly went to fairs, were covered in my favourite flowers, bluebells. Walking – or more likely running – across a sea of bluebells in bare feet, with the sounds of my cousins' and friends' voices screaming with laughter behind me, are precious memories. We loved teasing each other with 'wet-the-beds': if you touch a dandelion you'd supposedly wet the bed that night, so we'd chase each other trying to brush the other person's arm or back with the vivid yellow petals.

I loved sitting among red poppies, their heads gently bobbing in the wind, and patches of grass full of white daisies, spending hours studying them and sometimes picking them for Mam. We weren't just playing outside; we were part of the outdoors.

Making 'perfume' that smelled like nothing of the sort was another pleasing pastime. We were taught that if a flower overhung a garden or wall, it didn't belong to anyone and was free for the picking. I'd walk for hours, scouring walls for the scent and sight of scarlet red or heavy pink blooms, before snatching a few and running back to the site with them. First we'd pull their soft-as-sand petals apart, squeezing them to stain our fingers, breathing in the heavenly scent as we went. Then we'd fill an empty bottle of pop with water and drop all the petals in, giving it a good old shake. The mix was left to ferment, for the 'perfume' to develop before being dabbed lightly on the inside of our wrists, as we pretended we smelled lovely.

We loved buttercups too, shoving them under someone's chin to see if they liked butter or not. Or we'd peel an apple in one long strip – it had to be all in one – then throw it over a shoulder. Whatever the initial of the flower the apple peel fell on was the initial of the person you'd marry. The fact it landed on a different letter every time didn't matter!

Every night-time, after the dinner pots were washed, Mam would shoo us out of the trailer to play outside so she could convert the bunks in to our beds. Quite often, when evenings were warm enough, we'd congregate by the road near the camp and tell each other stories. Most of the kids would take part, from the age of six right up to early teens. Sometimes it would be fairy stories, other times it was ghost stories, or sometimes one person would say a line and then the others would follow it on. We'd often be in stitches laughing by the end.

All too soon, Mam would holler us back in and we'd say goodnight. She'd flick on the kettle to make smooth malt-smelling cups of Horlicks for us as she finished fitting the sheets and plumping the pillows.

Just after our drinks, I'd lay down with Maria on one side and Tom on the other and we'd give each other a quick kiss on the forehead before the lights went out. 'Night night, sleep like good little children or the Muller Mush will come and get you!' Mam would laugh. Muller Mush was our Gypsy term for devil, but we all giggled too rather than feeling frightened.

Quite often Mam and Dad would watch a film after we'd gone to bed. One night I stayed awake to listen in. As the lights dimmed and they settled nearby I peered over the formica top to see the flickering screen. Imagine my horror when I saw a werewolf howling on the screen. Transfixed with fear, I watched for an hour until the werewolf transformed in to a priest. Shaking, I lay back on the bed, unable to sleep a wink. Later, Dad switched off the generator, Mam dimmed the lights, and within moments the sound of Dad's rattling snore filled the trailer. But I wasn't usually awake at this time, and didn't recognise this unfamiliar growl. In my child's mind there was only one explanation.

Oh my god, me dad's turning in to a werewolf!

My imagination worked overtime and I shivered and quaked, snuggling closer to my sister for comfort. But I knew if I woke the Babby there really would be hell to pay, so I lay in silence, hoping my dad wasn't going to start howling at the moon. It took a while before I could look at him in the same way again.

But really the dangers lay outside the home. By the early eighties my dad owned a tilt cab lorry and we'd all pile in with the trailer on the back and move around quite often. It was during one of our short trips to Manningham Park fairground in Bradford that a family tragedy was narrowly avoided.

I was in the back of the lorry cab with my brother and Mam was holding Maria on the front seat, a bag of candy floss in her chubby hand. As Dad turned the wheel to go round a roundabout, somehow the handle of Maria's plastic bag got caught on the door handle. As she tugged it, the lorry door flew open and Mam and Maria disappeared, screaming, on to the tarmac below.

I can still see them now, mother and baby, clasped together, falling on to the ground, knowing how much it was bound to hurt them both. Dad slammed on the brakes, screeching to a halt, before he leaped out, ordering us both not to look. Scared witless, Tom and I huddled together for a few seconds, before leaping to the front seat to see. Passing people stopped and screamed as they spotted Mam lying on the road, covered in blood, with a seemingly lifeless Maria in her arms.

Afterwards people said there was so much blood on the road they presumed both were dead. But Mam soon stirred, Maria still cradled in her arms.

Somehow she'd shielded Maria from the worst of the impact by holding her tightly to her chest. The pair of them were thrown across the road and Mam had scraped all her arms and one side of her face.

After recovering from a shaky start in life, Maria found herself back in hospital again with a badly broken leg. She spent six months in traction but she was to survive and make a full recovery, which in itself seemed a miracle. Mam insisted she stayed with the Babby in hospital so Dad moved our trailer on to Granny Winnie's site a few miles away in the outskirts of a leafy village called Heckam Wyke. She lived on a couple of acres of field, near my dad's youngest brother Peter and his four kids. It was close by some woodland, hidden by trees, and as kids we loved visiting. So while we waited for Maria to get better, this became our new home.

Chapter Six

Another Day, Another Dollar

Granny Winnie, Thomas Cannon's wife, was from the Varey family. A tiny thing, she couldn't have been more than 4'9" in her bare feet, and if you put a sari on her, she could easily have been mistaken for an Asian lady. Her hair was jet black when she was younger, and she was very olive skinned. She was from a very traditional Romany family, and she was very quiet and kept herself to herself. She was so concerned about drawing attention to herself she wouldn't even dye her hair when it went grey as she didn't want neighbours to gossip, although I'm sure people had better things to talk about.

Whatever the weather she'd wear the same outfit. A long-sleeved turtleneck jumper, usually pastel pink or green, with a cardie on top, and a dark-coloured skirt skimming to the ground. In the summer, we could all be sweating under a hot sun and she'd still be all covered up, perhaps just with her sleeves rolled up, but never anything more.

In many ways she was almost Victorian, believing children should be seen and not heard, although she loved her grandchildren to pieces. But she just needed to give me one look, a flash from her piercing blue eyes, and I would stop whatever I was doing in an instant.

Granny's trailer was a very ornate space packed to the brim with china and porcelain dolls. Granny was also a big fan of Mary Shortle newborn baby dolls and had many of them piled on her bed, all looking at me in their own unique dead-eyed way.

Granny Winnie liked what she liked and that included the colour red. Everything and anything had to be red. When Royal Crown Derby brought out a new pattern, every respectable Gypsy lady bought gold as this was the colour to have. But my granny bought red and didn't care when people laughed at her for it. Her trailer was also always filled with the smell of cigarettes as she smoked like a dragon.

During this time I grew much closer to Granny Winnie and took a real interest in all the doilies and things she'd crochet to sell. She had already taught me how to finger knit, but later, as I watched her one evening with her funny hook flitting in and out of her hand, I asked her what she was doing.

'Crocheting, pet,' she said. 'Do you want a teaching?' And so she did.

The other thing we all adored about Granny Winnie was her cooking. She loved to bake and would spend hours every day whipping up the most wonderful array of pies, biscuits, cakes and buns. Every day before we even saw her trailer we could smell its warm, mouthwatering aromas emanating from the door, curling in to the air like a finger beckoning us to come in.

Once inside we would be sat down with a bottle of pop and handed a plate of tempting, delicious sweet things, with Granny Winnie always insisting we took one. There was nothing she loved more than feeding us. I'll never forget the amazing taste when I sank my teeth in to her shortbread. Or the sweet, tummy-rumble-inducing smell of her freshly baked bread. There was nothing like it. She'd have made a very talented professional baker.

On one visit, years later, we couldn't smell anything when we arrived.

'Is your oven broken?' I asked her, feeling a tad disappointed.

Granny Winnie shook her head, her mouth set firm. 'Nope,' she said. 'I just can't stand the way the dough feels beneath my nails, and I am never baking anything ever again.'

So that was that. She never did. The next time we visited the freshly baked goods were nowhere to be seen and instead out came a packet of Jammie Dodgers. Although we all took one and nibbled it politely, it was never the same.

I was taken to visit Maria every day in hospital, and although I felt sorry for my babby sister, trapped on her back all day, I was also rather heartlessly amused by her poor legs stuck in the air with ropes and pulleys in such a comical manner.

I loved the hospital toys though, especially a wooden horse with pedals. With poor Maria eyeing me with envy, I'd furiously pedal, laughing my head off, pretending I was the world's fastest horsewoman.

As she grew stronger Maria wanted to have a go, pointing her finger and begging. I reluctantly had to get off the horse and let my little sister take a turn. She was told that when she was strong enough to pedal herself she could come home, and eventually one day she managed it.

Although Mam was relieved to have Maria home she was also very upset that my sister had developed a bald patch where she'd been laying down all that time. Once again my mam had the nightmare of a daughter with bad hair.

Despite living a fairly simple lifestyle, Mam and Dad still needed to keep working throughout our childhoods. While Dad carried on his rag-and-bone and scrap metal trades, Mam sold trinkets and charms door-to-door. Then, more through accident than design, she became a clairvoyant.

Such is the stereotype that Gypsies can tell fortunes, people asked her that many times she decided to start doing it. Admitting to us she had no real clairvoyant skills at all, she grew able to read people's faces well and once invited inside their homes she could pick up from their expressions who their loved ones were. She never told anyone anything harmful and saw it as a decent service of giving hope to people and making them feel better about their lives. My sister Maria and I would join her on her doorstep visits.

First she would 'Gypsy' herself up, putting in gold hoop earrings, pulling a scarf around her head, and putting a pinny over her long skirt. Then she'd fill her basket full of wares. These included gold charms, such as a horseshoe, wishing well or horse's head, which she'd lay out carefully on her outspread fingers at the door, selling them at £5 a pop. Or you could buy a key ring for £10. Sometimes she also hawked round pebbles she'd picked up from a river bed and washed, selling them as 'lucky' stones, blessed by Gypsies. If people didn't want any of that she'd offer them something 'useful' instead, such as a packet of sewing needles, hairbrushes or combs. Then if they still didn't want anything she'd offer to tell a fortune, but more likely only did so when she was asked. She always asked to come in and sit down in order to call on her powers and this was so she could spot photographs of loved ones on the walls or any other clues about the person's life.

Us kids were told to go and sit somewhere quietly while Mam carried out her theatrics. First she'd pull out a large old glass paperweight wrapped in silk from her basket, explaining this would help her see in to the past and future. With a flourish she would slowly unwrap it and asked her customer to open their hands while she laid it carefully down. Then she'd asked the person to gaze intently in to the paperweight and we'd see her quickly scan the room for clues about what to say. She'd look out for pictures of deceased elderly relatives, who always passed on their good wishes, or any sign of a husband, who was always about to get that unexpected promotion at work. For these services she asked people to cross her palm with £15.

More often than not, though, when we knocked on a door

we were told to go away with the usual derogatory names for Gypsies ringing in our ears. Once a woman opened the door, took one look at us and said: 'No, I don't want you to read my fortune, but I'll give that monkey a banana,' cruelly pointing to Maria's ears, still exposed where her hair hadn't grown back properly after the accident. My poor sister burst in to tears and didn't stop for ages.

Sometimes Mam and Dad would go out to work together on different estates in Leeds. Dad would start at one end with his scrap metal/rag-and-bone business and Mam would tout her wares and read fortunes. They worked five days a week and carried on their habit of saving half of whatever they earned.

About a year later, when I was about five, we moved to a site in Wapping near our school and stayed there for a while. This was a wasteground next to a cliff face, part of a disused industrial estate.

Safety was a little ad hoc in some places and our patch of land in Wapping was right next to a forty-foot drop. Luckily Dad has always been a light sleeper, as once he woke up to find Tom missing from his bed and the trailer door open. Even a pest in his sleep, my brother had managed to start sleep-walking like a zombie towards the cliff's edge, totally unaware of what was happening. Dad ran outside with nothing but a pair of pants on, and managed to grab Tom's pyjama bottoms before he disappeared over the drop.

* * *

School was now becoming an established part of our daily life. Every morning we'd all walk there together in a big group. By now many of my cousins also attended the school, including Jimmy, Joanne, Sarah, Emma, Joe, Garner, Kelly and of course Tom and Maria, so there was no need to feel alone.

It was in infant class when I realised a little Asian lad had taken an instant dislike to me. He was one of the first kids to start picking on me just for being who I am.

'Gypo,' he whispered, as I sat down next to him. 'Gypo,' he grinned, as I ran past him in the playground. After a few more times, I told him to stop. Shut up. Or I was telling.

But he didn't and on and on and on he went. He just liked the word. It clearly sounded strong and powerful to him, and I knew it meant he had no respect for me. So I turned to him. 'Paki,' I spat back. That stopped him, and his face dropped and he went off sobbing. As soon as the word was out of my mouth, I felt bad. I knew it was wrong, I'd never called anyone that before or since. But somehow I needed to get him back. And 'Paki' was the word I knew would do it.

Within minutes I was hauled up in front of my new teacher, Miss Timpson, who gave me a good telling off.

'But Miss,' I pleaded. 'He called me a gypo!'

She shook her head. 'There's a big difference, Violet.' And she carried on telling me how racist and terrible I was. This was a turning point for me. I knew I couldn't be friends with some of these Gorja kids. I decided to stick with my own.

Sometimes I was caught unawares, though, when my group

wasn't there to protect me. Once Joanne and Sarah were both off sick and the others happened to be elsewhere, so at the start of a break time I found myself in the playground alone.

There was a big agricultural tyre wedged in the tarmac for us to play around but when I walked towards it this particular day, some kids started on me.

'Get out of there!' one screamed. 'You don't play here.'

'Yeah, go on,' another jeered. 'You can't walk through here.'

'I can play where I like,' I shouted back, and promptly made my way in to the tyre – even though I had no particular need to go there. But I didn't see why this lot should tell me what to do.

Out of nowhere one of the lads gave me a sharp shove on the arm. I fell in to the hard inside edge of the tyre, scraping my ear.

'Owwwww!' I yelled, rubbing the side of my head. I looked at his smug, pleased-with-himself face and, despite feeling hot with anger, I thought better of it.

I needed my cousins there, that'd show them, but they were scattered around. Deep down I knew why they'd done this. I was a Gypsy. I was different. And places like the tyre, where every pupil ran through, was yet another place I wasn't welcome.

Later that evening I realised one of my dollar earrings had come off during the scrap.

'Where did it go this time?' Mam sighed. I was forever losing them.

I shrugged. I knew if I'd told her what had happened she'd be down at the school in a shot, and maybe make things worse.

Regardless of the ups and downs in the playground, essentially I fell in love with learning. I loved reading and writing and was a clever child. Mind you, sitting in the classroom all day for any Gypsy kid is hard work. Not being able to run around or be outside for six hours a day was a trial. If I wasn't completely absorbed in a particular piece of work, I would find myself gazing longingly out of the classroom window, at the sky and passing clouds, wondering whether to go roller skating or biking straight after school.

As much as I loved learning, Tom hated it, right from a very young age. He just wasn't interested. Also my dad, who was his ultimate role model, was an example of a man who'd lived and worked very successfully while being completely illiterate his whole life, so from a practical point of view he didn't see the point of learning either.

My dad was born on 3 November 1955, one of four kids. He had two sisters, Ninna and Mary, and a brother Peter. His father, by Gypsy standards a fairly wealthy horseman, soon drilled the work ethic in to his son, all without ever picking up a book or a pen.

By the age of eleven, he'd given up on school and went out to work with his sister Ninna (her real name was Winnie, but she got the nickname because her younger sister Mary couldn't pronounce it properly), then aged fourteen. The pair of them would drive a horse and cart, collecting scrap metal and rag and bone. Everything they earned before 2 p.m. they had to give to their parents and everything after that time and at weekends they could keep as their own.

From a very young age my dad learned the art of making something out of nothing and selling the unlikeliest object for cash. He'd strip motors and gearboxes, selling the parts, and then in winter he sold horse manure, seven bags for £1 or three bags for 50p. Unlike Mam's family, my dad's didn't live off the land. Instead they considered themselves horsemen and wheeler-dealers, always finding something for nothing. For generations Gypsies have recycled goods and fixed things, long before it became trendy to be 'eco' and 'green'.

Not having learned to read was not an issue for my dad. He worked hard and made a reasonable living wage from patching up machines, selling on scrap metal, buying and selling horses and the rag-and-bone trade. The reality is, though, modern life has changed very quickly in the past generation and now our centuries-old way of life is under threat. Being illiterate today, in the age of computers and the internet, gives you a real disadvantage.

For example, I know a man who has never learned to read or write but had a successful career shoeing horses. Now in his forties, he's been doing this job since he was eleven years old, and riding schools from far and wide came for his efficient, professional service. Then in recent years, the RSPCA brought in new legislation meaning he needs health and safety qualifications to carry on with the trade he's been successfully doing for three decades. Unable to read, he can't complete the paperwork and therefore can't carry on legitimately, although some riding schools still use his service on the black market thanks to his amazing reputation.

This rapid change is hard for some Gypsies to deal with. But then again, we've always been a naturally savvy people. Common sense is born in to us. Living on a roadside, it's the only way it can be. You can't walk around with your eyes shut or you wouldn't last long.

Mam was certainly quick to adapt to the changing times; in fact when we started school she started working as a home liaison officer after helping to set up the Bradford Travellers' Education Service. This was a bit of a groundbreaking move: it's very rare for a Romany to work in a Gorja place. But Mam had met some education officers during a school visit and they were impressed by her manner and level of education. They were looking for a true Romany to help them set the scheme up, and she was perfect for the job. Whatever Mam lacked in academic qualifications she more than made up for with her quick wit, her honest ways and her compassionate manner. She had a big heart, understood what Romany families needed and knew how to speak to them.

After school, Mam would often pick us up and take me back to the offices where she worked. This was an eye-opener in itself. I'll never forget seeing my first computer there, an old BBC basic. It looked like magic, seeing that first tennis game – really just two moving lines with a dot in between. To be able to make stuff on the telly move all by yourself just blew our minds. My favourite game was a word game with a witch on the screen funnily enough. All my previous generations of ancestors may have been illiterate but for this Gypsy girl words were opening up a whole new world – and I loved every minute of it.

Chapter Seven

Playing Mam

Far from the stereotype of the oppressed Romany woman, Mam was now an independent working mother, providing for her family and earning decent wages. She loved her job and believed passionately in Gypsy rights. Once she attended a protest march in London against discrimination. New laws were always threatening us and our lifestyle was constantly in the spotlight for all the wrong reasons, so she felt it was important to make a stand.

During the march, Mam was out the front, waving her banner, when she spotted a man collapse in the crowd. Dropping everything she ran over to help.

'I know first aid!' she cried to the man's wife, who was screaming and asking for help. Mam crouched down next to the man, knowing he needed to get in to the recovery position and have CPR. The woman looked my mam in the eye and said: 'He'd rather die than have your horrible Gypsy lips anywhere near him.'

Mam retold this story for years afterwards. To her this incident epitomised the prejudice we were always up against.

Another accusation often hurled at us is that our trailers are eyesores stuck on the sides of roads and fields. Actually in most cases we park out of sight from the roads, behind a hill, or in woodland or high bushes. What you can't see you don't know about and that's the way we preferred it.

In the 1980s, Travellers were all lumped together with ravers by the Tory government, who seemed hellbent on making our way of life illegal. They brought in the Criminal Justice and Public Order Act, which was originally designed to prevent people from turning up at gatherings and raves in public spaces. These were the days when standing in a field off your chops singing 'Aciiiiiiid' was a favourite pastime of some, although of course it had absolutely nothing to do with Romany Gypsies.

But in effect this law made our lifestyle illegal too. Suddenly we were told that new regulations meant we couldn't graze any animals, have a fire or bring in scrap metal to sites we'd used for generations. The rules purposefully seemed to target every aspect of the way we lived.

From a very young age I feared the police. We all did as kids. Just one glimpse of their fluorescent striped cars sent us kids running to the trailers. My sister used to hide underneath ours. And there were so many reasons for this reaction. They only ever turned up to tell our parents off, or to tell us to move on. They caused ripples of panic and distress whenever we saw them approaching.

Once a group of officers turned up and told the women to get off a site immediately, with no warning.

'But we've got no men to move our trailers, they're away at a fair,' one woman explained. 'We'll have to wait until they return with their cars then we'll go.'

The police refused to listen and started pulling the trailers off the field themselves without even removing the jacks. People's homes were being ripped apart. Some of them were written off.

Once my dad got back to the site and found Mam and our trailer parked helplessly in the middle of the road, after the police had suddenly showed up and moved her on without warning.

On another occasion, Tom and I were out with Dad helping him on a scrap metal job when the police pulled him over.

'What's your name?' they asked him suspiciously.

'Tom Cannon,' he replied.

'Yeah, same as me,' said our Tom, helpfully.

The policeman raised an eyebrow. 'Step outside of the vehicle please,' he said. Then after chatting to my dad, who'd started looking worried by now, they put him in cuffs and arrested him.

'What's 'e done?' I cried, hanging out the window.

'Nothing,' said the officer. 'But we've never met a Gypsy who has not at least got a speeding offence, so that's why we think he's lying about who he is. So a trip to the station is in order.'

While Dad started complaining, asking what about us kids, they locked us in the cab, told us to stay put and took our dad away.

Tom and I sat in the cab in silence for a while, unable to

take in the strange course of events, then decided we couldn't just sit locked up all night, so we jumped out the window and went to find a phone box. We called someone on the site, who told Mam, and she came to collect us. She took us down the station, where the officers insisted they needed to check out Dad's ID overnight.

The following day they released him. 'So if I get locked up overnight for *not* having a criminal record,' he said to the officer, 'what would happen if I punched you in the face and actually got one?'

'You'd be locked up for real and you didn't last very well for one night in the cells, Mr Cannon, so think on that,' the man replied.

Dad was fuming, but left quietly. He couldn't believe they'd got away with it.

Despite our reputation in the Gorja world, Gypsies are actually quite old-fashioned in their ways, with strong family values. My mam was devoted to her family as are all Gypsy women. Training to be a mother and wife starts in earnest for girls as soon as you learn to play. My cousins and I played house with our dollies endlessly.

My cousin Joanne in particular loved to clean, right from a young age. Once I turned up at her trailer and she was boiling bleached water on the hob while polishing the work-surface so hard her arm muscles bulged. Humming a tune, she looked utterly content. Cleaning to her was like a game.

Around this time my first love came in to my life. One day Mam turned up with two dolls she'd bought at a car boot sale. One was a lovely oversized Barbie-style girl doll with long blonde hair; the other was a plain one with scraggy hair and biro scrawled on the face.

Maria took one look and bagged the Barbie-esque one. 'I'm not having that thing,' she grinned, as I was handed the moth-eaten one.

Knowing the Babby always got what she wanted, I sighed, thanked Mam, and took my doll off for a good clean. I decided to cut off all the hair and dress her in boy's clothes. After a good scrub, I proudly named this new 'boy' Andrew Alan. For the next twenty years he went everywhere with me, and I would proudly lay him on my bed every day.

As soon as Maria laid eyes on him a familiar wail formed on her lips. 'I want him! I want him!' she screamed. But even Mam didn't give in to her this time.

Despite my love for Andrew Alan, for many years dolls actually gave me the creeps. It started one night when I was being told off by Mam for something or other and sent to bed. Crying and screaming I was put in the trailer, and the door slammed shut. Lying alone, I sobbed and sobbed, Mam shouting at me to be quiet. As I calmed down I looked around the trailer in the fading light, my eyes stopping on my 'Tiny Tears' doll sitting on its shelf near my bed. This was a plastic doll that cried 'real' tears when you squeezed it. It had been a much-wanted Christmas present, but the longer I stared at my once-loved toy the more her eyes seemed to take on a sinister appearance.

After a few minutes eyeball to eyeball with the doll, I felt so freaked out, I grabbed her and threw her out of the trailer window. Slamming the window shut, my heart beating fast, I hid under the covers, relieved she had gone. Able to relax at last, I fell asleep.

I woke up early in the morning, feeling better, with the sun streaming through the curtains. Then I felt something hard at my feet. Peeking over my covers, I saw that there at the bottom of my bed lay my Tiny Tears doll. Now I was sure my imagination was real and somehow this evil doll had managed to climb back in to the trailer to haunt me.

'Aghhhhhhhhhhhhhhhhhhhh!' I shrieked, waking up the whole trailer.

'What? Whatever is it?' Mam gasped, sitting bolt upright.

I burst in to tears, somehow trying to explain how much this plastic doll had frightened me and was now following me around, trying to terrorise me.

Mam may not have understood my doll phobia but she had her ear to the ground about our school and she soon overheard us talk about kids saying nasty things and the general undertones of bullying. So when it was time for Maria to start nursery, she enrolled us in Tyersal Primary School in East Bowling to see if we fared any better there.

But if Tom hadn't liked school, for poor Maria it was hell

on earth. She hadn't learned to read like me before nursery, and it became very apparent from day one she'd no intention of starting.

Crying every day before we set off, she'd cling to my hands all the way.

'Don't wanna go!' she'd yell.

'Aw c'mon Babby,' I'd coax. 'Yous be OK. Me and Tom are going, look!'

But then the expression on Tom's face said it all too. Glowering like a demon, he dragged his heels on the way to class as much as the Babby did. It was only me who didn't mind school.

My brother Tom was growing in to a fine figure of a Gypsy man, his hair turning a shade darker to be glossy brown and his skin always tanning olive in the sun. He also had the Gypsy temperament. He wanted to be outside all day, with his dad, working yet free, tending to horses and generally enjoying the sun or rain on his back. Being cooped up in a stuffy classroom all day was the antithesis of his being and it was something he had to wrestle with the entire time when he was at school.

On my first day at Tyersal, a Filipino girl who spoke not a word of English latched on to me. She was another outsider, sensing I didn't fit in either. Although I suppose it was obvious. No one spoke to me except when they had to during lessons. At break times, I rushed straight off to find Maria or Tom, my best friends.

Poor Maria was in a different playground, divided by a

fence, so we'd rush towards each other, poking our hands through what felt like prison bars, and walk up and down, chatting to each other. Sometimes the playground monitors would shoo us away, telling us to go and make other friends. But of course we never did.

Within a few months, after witnessing Maria's tears every day, Mam had moved us back to the school in Wapping. We went back and forth a few times over the years, although we mainly attended Wapping.

This might seem a bit strange to the average Gorja, but for us, moving and shifting and being somewhere different was normal. We didn't fit in with Gorja kids anyway, and the only friends we had were our cousins at Wapping and each other at Tyersal.

The schools actually allowed us to do this as well. As far as the authorities were concerned they were pleased we were at school at all. Most Gypsy kids didn't receive any education.

As much as we didn't mix with the Gorjas, they never mixed with us. Often birthday party invites were handed out to the whole class except me. But I didn't care. Gorja birthday parties were not something I'd ever attend, or understood, so I didn't miss them. We had enough parties of our own, thanks.

Maria's reluctance to learn or sit still soon had the teachers tearing their hair out. In both schools she became known as untameable unless she was near her big sister. So they took the easy option and started sending her to me.

I'd often be in my classroom getting on with my work when

Maria would appear. Once I was in my classroom, reading with the aid of a tape machine. We'd pull on these massive headsets and then listen to a tape recording of a book reading, to help us recognise the words. I loved it. I could already read it all anyway, but it reminded me of listening to stories around the fire.

While I was fixated on my book, I felt a tap on my shoulder. It was Maria. She was in year one now, but her reading wasn't progressing any better than when she was in the nursery.

'What's up, Babby?' I asked.

My teacher didn't bat an eyelid. It was a given that Gypsy children were 'different' and Maria's appearance mid-lesson wasn't seen as an interruption as long as she came to me quickly.

'The teacher sent me here, to get you to help me to read,' she whispered.

I rolled my eyes. I wanted to help but at the same time I couldn't get on with what I was doing. But the Babby was the Babby, and she needed me.

'OK,' I sighed, slipping off my headset. 'Come and sit with me.'

Maria screwed up her face in concentration as I slowly and quietly read the book to her, sounding out the letters as I went along. It wasn't long before big fat tears plopped on to the page. Poor Maria just couldn't grasp it.

Teachers tended to dismiss Maria as the spoiled baby of the family, a role she did tend to play up to a little in some respects. But in others it was deeply unfair. She grew to hate the label she'd acquired, of being a failure, of not fitting in. Her anxiety every day before school soon grew in to a phobia.

While Maria stressed about school and lessons, I was growing in to an increasingly self-conscious little girl. My brother Tom, as all brothers do, loved to poke fun at me.

Once he grabbed a Garbage Pail Kids card and shoved it in my face.

''Ere, Violet!' he shouted. 'You look like one of them, you do, hahahaha!'

I grabbed the card off him and squashed it up in my fist as hard as I could.

'No I don't!' I yelled, throwing it at his feet.

Garbage Pail Kids were ugly, bulbous-faced cartoon characters and even as a little child his words stung. I tried to laugh it off, but inside I felt nothing but hurt.

My skin was so sensitive I just needed to touch my face and a spot appeared. Various misadventures meant my mam had grown up with a bad complexion too, so she was sympathetic to my unhappiness. Recalling her childhood, Mam told me how, when she was twelve, her friends were playing with some fireworks. When one didn't set off, Mam decided it was a good idea to open it up, dismantle it and remove the gunpowder. She laid the fine grey stuff on a brick and then lit it with a stick used for lighting a fire. The whole thing blew up in her face straight away. Screaming, she ran back to Granny, who immediately washed it in cold water, whipped up an egg white, smeared it on and sent her back out to play. The egg white was one of many old wives' tales that she swore worked.

Later on Mam was spotted by a group of church workers, playing outside with her scarred face. They approached her and asked Granny if they could take her to their youth club. I think they felt sorry for her.

Granny did believe in God, as did Grandad Tom and Granny Winnie. But they believed it in the way that most people believe in gravity: you know it exists but don't particularly understand how it works. God was something talked about in a book that sat on the shelf and Jesus was a figure who hung on a rosary. You only usually prayed when you were in trouble. Religion was kept to Christmases, weddings and funerals. But Granny let Mam go to the church youth club and she enjoyed it, even praying occasionally when she felt she needed a helping hand, though she never saw herself as particularly religious until later in life.

A year after the firework incident, Mam had been playing with her brothers when they pulled down a giant branch hanging off a tree. They told Mam they were all going to swing off it, but as she sat down, they all let go simultaneously and she shot in to the air like she'd been catapulted, scraping her face on branches on the way up. Then of course as an adult she scraped her face again after the accident with Maria. So she was left with a face scarred and pockmarked, and as sensitive as mine.

I loved hearing stories of Mam's childhood, both good and

bad. There was a profound sense of belonging to our parents and their ancestors. Gypsy family ties are very strong and there is nothing your family wouldn't do for you. However, sometimes the strength of the bond was tested to the maximum.

My Auntie Anne, Granny Suzanna's eldest girl, once asked her mam to help when a terrible tragedy had fallen on her. Her husband, Joe, killed himself and left her with two small children: Joe, then three, and Dawn, a newborn baby. As in most societies, suicide is a taboo in Romany culture and Anne's husband's family blamed her for it, so the police had to investigate and a court case ensued. During this terribly difficult time, Anne asked Granny Suzanna for help, which of course she did willingly, and took in her toddler son and baby girl.

Months later, the court case and all the accompanying stress over, Anne was found innocent and returned to her mother to take back her children. Joe was handed over straight away but when she asked for Dawn, Granny Suzanna simply shook her head. She'd grown too attached to the baby, now eighteen months old, and that was that. Ignoring her own daughter's cries and pleas for her baby, Granny Suzanna held firm and sent her on her way. From then on Dawn called her granny 'Mam', and although later she was told that Anne was also her mammy, for years she told friends: 'My mammy's dead.'

This might seem cruel to outsiders, but Romanies believe in putting kids first. We always thought about what was best for the child in whatever situation, even if it might not be best for the adult.

A few years later, Dawn did see her 'Mammy Anne' on a regular basis and they always had fun together. But Granny Suzanna remained her 'mam' in the day-to-day sense of the word.

Funnily enough, history sort of repeated itself; my Auntie Margaret (Mam's sister) had a son called John, who married a Gorja girl, but the marriage broke down. John's wife realised how much her son loved my Auntie Margaret, so gave her full custody of him. My Aunt Margaret devoted her life to the little boy, and they went everywhere together, right to the very end.

Chapter Eight

Girls Will Be Girls

Growing up with other family members in such close proximity meant we all became very close. I loved my Auntie Winnie, Uncle Billy's wife, and saw her as a second mam. They lived all over the place, often in the middle of nowhere where no one else could pull up a trailer, but we still often played with my cousins, Joanne and Sarah.

Aunt Winnie was a tiny woman, only 4'8" tall, and she had titchy size two feet, almost the same as my then eight-year-old feet. She loved her shoes and had a collection of high heels that she'd totter around in on site, in all weathers. One pair in particular I fell in love with. They were four inches high and decorated with ornate flowers. Every time I went to visit her I'd end up rooting through the bottom of her wardrobe, digging them out. It must've driven her crackers but she never said anything. Then I'd slip them on and start tottering around on them myself making everyone laugh.

Every time we went to Harrogate or Poole we'd stay on site with them. Their family never settled on one site for long and

were permanently on the road. We often went out
with them, pulling our trailers – Dad in particular liked to c
this. He hates being pinned down; in fact he hates walls in
general. Even today, the most he can manage is a chalet in the
middle of his plot of land, surrounded by horses. Back then,
he struggled with ever staying in a house. We also often stayed
with Auntie Kay and Uncle Bernard, staying everywhere from
holiday parks to waste land in Scotland, Milton Keynes and
London. They didn't have a permanent base either. I think if
Dad had had his way we'd probably have lived a similar life,
but Mam was keen we went to school and both sets of grandparents were based in Bradford, so it made sense for us to stay
in the area.

Mam always encouraged us to choose the jobs we liked
doing the most in the house. So I plumped for cooking while
Maria, who has always had a touch of OCD, loved keeping
things clean. So that's how we allocated our chores. Mam
would show us how elbow grease would polish up a mirror so
you couldn't tell if it was glass, and the best way to get tea
stains out of mugs. Although she was an independent woman,
these were basic household jobs and all girls needed to be able
to do them.

Mam expected us to get married. Most Gypsy parents would
prefer their daughter to marry another Romany. Keep in the
blood, that's the ideal. But my mam was always open-minded,
and I often overheard her telling my aunties as they gossiped
about their girls over steaming mugs of tea: 'Whoever they

just want my two to be happy.' Little

rely this theory would be tested.

, my 'cooking skills' almost killed some of

A group of us were hanging out together while

a week at Bentham Fair, the yearly trip we loved.

The was nestled in the hills of Carlisle and us kids spent hours roaming the countryside nearby. This time we decided to build our own little house, so we raided everyone's trailers, taking a cushion here and a pan there, until we had a decent stash, all set to make a proper home. We piled up some old bricks, balanced some sticks on top, pulled a sheet of plastic across and laid a blanket on the floor for a carpet. Next we filled it with all our household goods that we hoped nobody's parents would miss, including a kettle and matches for the fire we were building in the middle of our 'house'.

Someone had even pinched a tin of peaches, so as head chef, I started stewing them in the can, carefully adding some extras of my own, including a sprinkle of dirt here and there. When it was ready, everyone looked doubtful but, pleased at my role of 'mam' in the house, I insisted it'd be delicious. I didn't give up until everyone had taken a few good mouthfuls.

Later on, it wasn't so amusing when all my friends turned green with sickness and were sent to bed with food poisoning.

Bentham Fair was full of hills and roads. Great fun, but not without risks. Once someone turned up with a couple of 'sulkys' – lightweight, single-seat, metal frames with wheels that men used to train horses.

The girls and I had great fun asking Tom and his friend Robert to pull us around on the hills, which happened to be main roads, though we didn't let such a small detail put us off. We sat on the back and screamed as they pulled us like a pair of Trojans. The wind whipped our hair while we bounced around, clinging on for dear life. It was brilliant fun. When they got tired we just teased them, saying: 'Tom, Robert went so much faster than you then . . .' and vice versa, until both pretty near collapsed with exhaustion.

My baby sister, Maria, had grown from a pretty, delicate baby in to a pretty, delicate girl. Her hair was blonde and straight, her lips a natural ruby red – she looked as if she wore a slash of lip gloss every day, although she was in fact an absolute tomboy and a bit of a rebel. In all the photos we have of her she's sticking her tongue out or pulling faces. I loved her to pieces, though, however much she wound me up. She was the funniest creature around, always the first to laugh (and cry), and she followed me round like a lost sheep – something I loved and hated in equal measure. Always singing and dancing, I remember cracking up as I caught her singing 'Walk Like a Gypsy' to the tune of 'Walk Like an Egyptian' by the Bangles. As much as I loved to tease her she always got me back. She had the loudest scream I've ever heard from a human being, which would send Mam or anyone within the entire camp running to see what'd happened.

As her big sister it would've been rude not to wind Maria up at every opportunity, just like Tom kindly did to me on a regular basis. Maria was so gullible and trusting, it was almost too easy. I hated sharing my Hubba Bubba gum with her so I'd pop them quickly one by one in to my mouth as Maria would look on in envy. Then I'd hand her one, and as she slowly unwrapped it I'd fill my mouth up completely with the rest of the packet before she saw me.

'How comes you've got so much more than me?' she asked, as she chomped on her single piece. 'Why's mine getting smaller while yours is bigger?'

I grinned. 'That's cos you need to chew it fast,' I said. 'Look, like me: chew chew chew, as fast as ya can. Go on.'

Maria closed her eyes and chewed so hard and fast, I thought her teeth would shatter. My sides would split with laughter. She did it for ages after that, never understanding why the gum never grew in her mouth.

It wasn't just my little sister who tormented me sometimes or seemed to attract trouble to my door. My brother Tom, ever the joker, would also drive me crazy.

One Christmas Dad proudly bought us two amazing presents – a mountain bike for me and a BMX for Maria. The following day, both lay broken in a heap when Tom decided to swap our front wheels for a joke. Whatever he'd done to them, no one could fix them back again. It'd be funny if it wasn't so frustrating, but Tom often denied whatever he was doing, even if he was caught red-handed.

Once, when Auntie Mary (or Auntie Sweetshop as she was known) was visiting, Tom was allowed to fill Mam's Crown

Derby lighter up with fuel, something he'd been nagging her to let him do for weeks since she'd got it.

'OK, OK,' Mam relented. 'Just you be careful. You hold the canister and pump in it just so and when it's full you stop.'

His eyes shining, Tom grabbed the fuel canister and lighter, obviously not listening to another word. Sitting on the couch, Tom pushed the can in and the fuel hissed and whistled satisfyingly in to the lighter while Mam and Mary poured tea, chatting. But my brother, being my brother, couldn't resist ex rimenting, so with his thumb he gave the flint a cheeky little flick.

Instantly the whole lighter blew up in to a fireball and with a scream Tom dropped it on to the carpet. Mam and Mary yelled and leaped up from the couch. In her panic Mam threw her cup of tea over the burning fuel.

'What were you doing, son?' she cried, stamping her feet on the sodden patch of carpet.

'It wasn't me!' Tom yelled back.

My parents didn't have much spare money and as kids we weren't spoiled but we also never went without. Once I went to a friend's house who had a baby doll that grew teeth when you pulled her arms. As soon as I got home I begged Mam for one. She didn't immediately rush out and buy me it but made sure I got one for Christmas. Tom was harder to please as he insisted on having all the latest computer gadgets. Once he'd got a Spectrum computer he wanted an Atari, then it was a Nintendo and so it went on.

Once Mam put her foot down. 'No, Tom,' she said. 'You'll just have to play with what you've got.'

The next day Tom handed her his latest console. 'It's broken, Mam,' he said, looking very sorry for himself. 'Can you take it back to the shop? It should still be under warranty. Then you can get your money back and I can get the latest version.'

Mam returned from the shop hours later looking extremely cross.

'Well, I insisted the shop man change it as it was a fault with the product,' she said, giving Tom her scary look. 'But after giving it the once-over, he said he wasn't surprised it was broken as it looked like a fork had been forced in to the opening . . .'

After that Tom had to wait a long time for the latest console.

Birthdays were a big deal for all of us. Not only did the person whose birthday it was get an expensive present, usually a piece of jewellery or a bike or a computer, Mam and Dad never forgot the other two either. Sometimes we just got a box of Maltesers and a bottle of pop and other times an actual present. I used to collect metal stick men who balanced on a frame, like seesaws and swings, and when it was Tom's birthday I'd often get one of those.

Tom's birthday landed in July, so he often got taken to a theme park, whereas Maria got taken to the Blackpool illuminations. I'd often have a party outdoors with all my cousins and family invited. Dad would blow up balloons, Mam would prepare some food on tables and I'd have my favourite music blaring from a cassette machine.

Living in trailers and moving on all the time meant we always had somewhere new to explore. But as we were outside all day, every day, and often visited the same place more than once, we got to know the different areas too.

One time we went to our 'local' shop in Bradford to get our 10p mix. The lady in the shop was always nice to us Gypsy kids, but we weren't so keen on her. She had long fingernails with crusty bits underneath and we always winced when we watched her pick out the 1p sweets we wanted with them. Once we spotted black Hubba Bubba bubble gum and got dead excited. Buying a few packs, we stuck it all round our teeth then sat on top of the trailers, waving at people going past, pretending we didn't have teeth.

We were always hanging around the roadsides if we weren't out playing on bikes or skipping. Watching the world go by was a favourite pastime. Joanne, Sarah, Maria and I loved singing songs and 'performing' to passing cars. Dressed in our leggings and long T-shirts, maybe with a fluorescent sock or two on, pure 1980s stylee, we'd choreograph what we thought were sophisticated and cool dance routines. 'Nathan Jones' by Bananarama was one firm favourite. It's a wonder we didn't cause any crashes.

We'd make up stories about people who passed us by too. Once we stayed on a site near where an old lady would appear every afternoon. She'd stand on the other side of the road, by her house, smiling as we screamed with laughter chasing each other round with 'wet-the-beds' dandelions, or riding in circles with our bikes. To begin with we talked about how she must be lonely and how it must cheer her up to watch us. Then Sarah grew more imaginative.

'Maybe all her children died,' she whispered in a hushed tone, 'and we remind her of them . . .'

'Oooh,' cried Joanne. 'Don't! Maybe one of us looks like her dead daughter.'

We all fell about giggling.

Our stories grew more macabre as the months wore on.

'Maybe she's a ghost!' I suggested one day. 'Maybe she's not real at all.' We all screamed again, shivering as we laughed. This theory was 'confirmed' one day when a car drove past as she stood on the grassy bank . . . but when it drove off she had disappeared. We refused to believe the car had just picked her up. She must have vanished in to thin air. I was right: she was a ghost!

The poor woman must've thought we were crazy kids, whispering conspiratorially and erupting in to peals of laughter all the time. But we always made sure she couldn't hear what we were saying. In fact we were always very careful to be super polite to Gorjas at all times. Mam had drummed it in to us.

'They think Gypsy kids are terribly behaved, so it's up to you three to show them otherwise,' she'd say.

Another character who often went past was a man wearing Jesus sandals with a long beard. He wore a rough, sack-like shirt with a leather belt. None of us knew who he was, but he'd come close to the campsite and we'd always wave and say 'hello'.

Eventually Mam would invite him to her steps and offer him cups of tea. No questions were asked as to who he was. He was just someone who came nearby and was obviously some kind of religious man. He seemed gentle and friendly so he was welcome on the site. We didn't need to know anything else.

We had total freedom most of the time, and this was an important part of growing up as a Romany. None of our parents wanted to wrap us up in cotton wool; we were here to enjoy the outdoor world. But that didn't mean Mam didn't put her foot down sometimes. One day everyone was going off swimming in the nearby river. Somehow she caught wind of what was planned.

'My Violet, you're not to go swimming in that river,' she said, carefully. I shook my head. I was a good girl at heart and if Mam ever told me specifically not to do something I wouldn't.

'I promise I won't go swimming, Mam,' I repeated back, looking her directly in the eye.

So later on, as I followed the others to the river, I sat on the bank watching jealously as they all splashed each other, shouting with laughter.

'Come on, Violet,' my cousins Martina and Joanne cried again. 'Come in! Stop being so boooring!'

I shook my head. 'I can't. I promised Mam I wouldn't go swimming.'

Joanne's face lit up. 'Oh well then, Violet. You promised you wouldn't go swimming but never actually promised you wouldn't go in the river, so you'll be OK, won't you?'

I grinned. She was right! I could legitimately have a splash around without breaking my promise to Mam. Wicked!

Within seconds I was pulling off my socks and shoes and wading in. The water felt deliciously cool around my sticky feet and soon I was kicking the water in my cousins' faces, happy to be joining in. Then within a few minutes my legs began to burn and tingle.

'Ow, ow,' I cried, jumping back on to the grassy bank. Sitting down on a nearby rock, I started examining myself for the damage. I'd no idea what I'd done.

Already, angry red blisters had formed all over my legs and feet. Tears stung in my eyes not only from the pain but from the guilt. I felt like this was my punishment for going against what I knew Mam had really meant. Deep down I knew 'swimming' also covered going in to the river.

When I got home Mam took one look at me and whisked me to the doctors. He declared I was allergic to water, and that was added to the list of my allergies. But of course he meant just river water.

Despite being allowed to run free outside, little girls were still expected to dress and behave like little girls. This was especially important when we went to fairs, like Appleby, when all the mams were putting their little daughters on show.

I'd usually be in a white or pink puff-sleeved dress, with a matching hand-knitted cardigan over the top. The chest area would be hand-smocked and quite fitted down to the waist, with a belt going round it and tied in a big bow at the back. Laced underskirts would give it some volume.

Every Appleby, we'd also be given an 'Appleby Doll'. This was so we'd have something to play with and keep us entertained to stop us from running round, getting covered in grass and mud stains.

Often the other mams would come and pat me on the head. Supposedly they were being friendly but swiftly they'd give my curls a squeeze to see if Mam had used hair lotion to set them.

Maria was a horror when it came to getting her dress dirty. Sometimes Mam would haul her back in to the trailer three or four times a day to get her changed. Neither of us was to be seen with a speck of dirt on us. Not at fairs at least.

During the evenings the men would sit around fires on fallen logs to chat, and in the mornings we'd go and sit there ourselves to play. Once a little younger girl I didn't know was playing alongside myself, Maria, Joanne and Sarah. As usual we were playing mammies and dollies, pretending to feed and burp our crying babies.

The other girl, aged about five, grew bored and picked up a stick to poke the fire. As she pushed her stick in to the ashes, she slipped, so that the palms of her hands landed on the sooty ground.

We all looked on, collectively breathing in a little.

'She'll be fer it . . .' I whispered to Joanne.

Without thinking, the little girl wiped her sooty hands all

over her pink summer dress, her fingers creating streaks covering the fabric.

She didn't seem to notice, so we didn't say anything to her. But it didn't take long for her eagled-eyed mam to spot the disaster.

'Eh, what the hell have you been doing?' a woman's voice raged from a trailer. Like a bullet her mam shot from the trailer, scooped her up, and took her inside, slamming the door behind her. About five minutes later she emerged pristine, a brand-new dress on, her hair curled to perfection in ringlets. She ran out to play, giving the fire a wide berth.

Among the sounds of the horses braying, the men bidding for horses and children laughing was the unmistakable sound of frantic mams shouting at their girls to keep their frocks clean. It was just one of those things.

Chapter Nine

Gypsies Meet the Gorjas

Every year we'd travel to Manchester to stay at sites in the Blackburn and Bolton areas, and stop there for a while with my Aunt Mary and Uncle Ben. Nearby was a cheap Italian store and Mam loved to get us discounted but good-quality clothes from there. She saw it as her mission to always keep us kitted out in the best clothes, something I think we all carried in to adulthood.

Aunt Mary's kids, Ben, Tommy-Joe, Martin and Mary, had proper small motorbikes for us to rev up and scoot around on, making our trips out extra exciting. The boys were always munching on crab apples all day long and Tom and I would look on jealously.

'Can I have one?' we'd ask at different times, but they kept saying we wouldn't like them. Later I asked Mam and she told me not to eat them either. 'You won't like 'em,' she repeated. Of course this meant we were like moths to a flame, thinking how amazing it would be to get our sticky hands on one of these forbidden crab apples.

After a few weeks of this we got right fed up, so when I found the branches they grew on, I grabbed a handful. 'Here!' I yelled to Tom. 'Found them!' Chucking him one, we grinned at each other. At last! Biting in to them was a nasty surprise. They were hard, like a turnip, with a hideous gritty texture.

'Urgh!' I yelled, throwing it on the ground. Straight away I felt it rising in my throat as vomit.

Ben laughed. 'Told ya!'

How the boys could stomach them I didn't know.

We spent the whole time together as a little gang, roaming over wasteland, the partially demolished factory or brownfield sites. The area we stayed in was the site of an old pit village that had been left to overgrow, making it feel like unexplored territory, a secret world only we knew about. One day as we ran around playing a breathless game of chase, a boy called Sid – whose family had just pulled up with us – fell over, throwing out his hands to break his fall.

When he stood up he looked white with shock. Something was sticking out of the palm of his hand.

'What's that?' he said. We all crowded round. It was made of plastic with a spike on the end.

'Don't pull it out,' I said. 'Let's go and find our mams.'

We ran off back to the trailer, Sid sticking his hand out to the side like a traffic policeman.

As we arrived, my auntie was coming out of the trailer and when she spotted Sid I don't think I've ever seen any of our parents move so fast.

Grabbing him by the shoulders, she screamed at him. 'Oh my God! Oh my God! Come here. Don't touch it.'

Instantly all us kids were surrounded by our mams grabbing at us, crying, screaming and all saying the same thing: 'Did you touch it? Did you? Did you? DID YOU?'

My mam's face was trembling and white with horror. Just looking at her put the fear of God in to me. I'd never seen her like this.

'Mammy,' I started sobbing, feeling guilty but not sure why. 'What's Sid got stuck in his hand?'

'It's a nee-dle,' she said, pronouncing every syllable. 'A dirty needle from a druggie and you can pick up all sorts from it.'

I had never heard of 'druggies' or 'needles' and really had no idea what she was talking about. But I learned that day that just playing on some wasteland could kill us, and that there were things in this world, outside the safety of our Gypsy site, that we didn't understand.

Poor Sid had to go to hospital every six months for tests for HIV and hepatitis. He had a lucky escape, as we all did. The words 'needles' and 'drugs' were something from the Gorja world, but now they had entered our language.

Despite the external dangers that occasionally crept in to our world, most of the time Mam was mainly concerned about the kind of universal worries that mams have about their children the world over. One of her constant battles was getting enough food in to my sister. In fact it was Aunt Winnie who solved the problem, and we always joked that it was she who helped keep Maria alive. Maria, as with most things, was very fussy with her food and despite Mam trying to cook all kinds of tempting dinners, she'd shake her long hair and refuse.

How she grew at all was a mystery to us. Then one day Aunt Winnie served up some of her homemade rice pudding and within minutes Maria had not only cleaned her bowl but she was asking for more. We all stared agog and Mam asked Aunt Winnie if she could take some home. After that, Maria lived off the special rice pudding and Mum says it kept her going from the age of five until about seven.

Later on, Tom and I started to have to bribe her with £1 coins to eat her dinners, a device that Dad had dreamed up. One of the few things she'd reluctantly allow on her plate now were sausages. But one day, after school, she shook her head as Mam put down her dinner.

'Why you not eating your sausages, doll?' Mam asked, wondering if she was ill.

'I'm not eating no meat!' she cried. 'Our teacher showed us a video of what happens in a slaughterhouse and it's horrible!'

It turned out Maria's lesson from her vegetarian teacher was all about the horrors of animal welfare and how meat ends up on your plate. Mam was incensed. Meat is a huge part of the Gypsy diet, so to tell a child a bunch of propaganda, as she saw it, was a slight on our way of life. The next morning she stormed down to the classroom to give the teacher a piece of her mind.

Mam might not have always agreed with the teachers, but as a parent of a pupil she always took a keen interest in how we were getting on. She never missed a parents' evening, always listening carefully to what the teachers said.

'Violet is a studious child,' my school reports always seemed to read. 'She has a vivid imagination and when she actually wants to do something she will do it incredibly well. But when she doesn't she rushes it . . .'

Tom's report was pretty much always the same too. Terrible.

'Tom doesn't lack the ability but his attitude and attention span mean he never achieves his potential . . .'

Every parents' evening, Mam would turn up on time, politely listen and then leave. She never spoke to the other parents or spent longer than was necessary. I always sensed an underlying discomfort at sending us out to the Gorja world to learn, but Mam thought this was for the best, even if we only attended school for a short while. After all, she'd learned to read very quickly during her few months at school, and in her eyes literacy was a gift worth having.

Now she was working as a home liaison officer, Mam was able to get a mortgage in her own right. My dad still worked selling scrap metal and doing other odd jobs so wasn't able to put his name on a bank loan without a regular wage, although of course he contributed to all the bills.

My parents wanted us kids to enjoy as much of the free life as they had led as children, so we often went off travelling for weeks or sometimes months, staying on wastelands all over the country. But when I was nine, the changes in the law meant that finding decent and suitable sites became much harder. So eventually Mam made the decision to buy a house.

Dad was very reluctant to do this. He'd openly state how he 'hated walls' and just the thought of living full-time in bricks and mortar made him feel claustrophobic. He was a full-blooded Romany man and the concept of buying a house and staying put was an anathema. His family was very much of the same opinion. Years earlier, Grandad Tom had also bought a house with money saved from his horses. But the whole family found it suffocating and within months they'd rented it out and were back to living in their trailer.

However, even Dad had to agree that day-to-day existence was getting harder for Romanies. We were often being moved on, and the quality of sites was growing worse. Mam begged him to consider a house as she wanted the best for us kids and, as with our attending school, she thought it was the sensible solution. In any case she insisted on buying a place with a yard so we could still own a trailer.

'Any time we need, we can just jump in and go,' she'd reassure Dad.

So off she went and signed up to buy an old woollen mill that needed a bit of renovation but could be a good two-bedroomed house for us. It was the first time we had set down proper roots. Moving in was an eye-opener. For the first time we had a whole house and a yard. But on the day we moved in, I remember being shocked at the size of the kitchen. 'Mam, is that it?' I said, looking at the sink and a door leading to the cellar. I imagined if we ever ended up in a house, it'd have to be a massive one. There had to be some advantages of living in a house rather than a trailer.

On one side of the building, there were lots of small windows, as it was a mill, and on the other a couple of beautiful stained-glass ones in the bedrooms. As soon as Dad clapped eyes on them he nodded. 'Those windows will be coming out and sold,' he said.

Tom and I didn't quite grasp the concept that playing indoors is slightly different to outdoors, so being stuck in a bedroom meant it didn't stop us trying to play a rowdy game of football. With him at one end of the fairly small room and me at the other, we ran about and kicked the ball as hard as we would if we were out in the fields.

And so the inevitable happened. With one big kick, I watched the ball sail over Tom's jumping head and like a demolition ball smash through the stained-glass window Dad had his eye on.

'Oh bugger!' I yelled. 'Oh no!'

We both stopped and stared, our minds whirring quickly to think up an excuse. Within seconds Mam and Dad were running up the stairs.

'Whatevers the heck happened?' Mam gasped, although it was quite plain to see.

Tom started jumping up and down, giving me a wink. 'Oh God, Mam you would never believe it. There were three of

them, all Gorja kids, all taunting us outside. It were terrible.'
I shot Tom a look, quickly cottoning on to what he'd quickly
thought up.

'Were it now, Tom?' said Mam, looking upset. 'What
happened, son?'

'Well we were just playing nicely in our room and then they
all started on at us, and there were so many we couldna take
them on,' he continued.

'And just while we were minding our own,' I butted in,
'they threw a massive ball at us, right through the window,
and my God, what a shock we got!'

Tom nodded sagely. 'It were so scary, Mam.'

Mam nodded, frowning and leaning in. 'That's terrible, son.
But do you know the worst thing?'

Tom and I glanced at each other, hardly believing our story
had been swallowed but thrilled we'd managed to avoid any
trouble.

'The worst thing . . .' said Mam, her voice slowly rising in
volume, 'is YOU TWO *LYING* ABOUT IT!'

Full of fury she gave us the biggest telling off, banning any
TV, any games and any pocket money for a whole week. And
she made extra sure we knew it was because we'd lied, not
because we'd broken the window. Lying in Mam's book was
the lowest of the low. She always says, 'You can watch a thief,
you can't watch a liar.'

Luckily we only had one neighbour as our house was at
the end of the street and quite isolated. I say luckily as most

Gorjas wouldn't welcome a family of Gypsies living next door. She was an old lady called Maeve, and very kind to us. We must've driven her mad noisily skating up and down the road like maniacs, screaming with laughter, fighting and carrying on. A few times she asked us to hush, but mainly she left us alone. As time wore on, she'd chat to Mam over the fence and I think after getting to know us she was genuinely fond of us.

After buying a house came Mam's next big purchase. A brand new E-registration Fiesta. We all couldn't believe our eyes when we saw it. It was like she'd bought a Mercedes Benz home. Dad was so proud of her too. I suppose it was unusual for a Gypsy man to have a wife who earned so much at the time, but he was never jealous or put out. Maybe they were ahead of their time, but Mam and Dad worked as a unit when it came to money and work. Yes, Dad fixed things and Mam cleaned, but everything else was done together. It's always been like that, one for all and all for one. As long as one of us is 'getting ahead' we all reap the rewards.

Around this time we also had our first holiday abroad. Mam's wage was a good one and along with Dad's work too, the pair of them were bringing home more than ever. We'd had loads of holidays in England, but never saw them as such, as we travelled around all the time anyway. So the prospect of going on a plane and seeing another country – Spain – blew our minds. Dad hated the thought of flying so stayed behind with Tom, who didn't want to go without his dad.

We went with Mam, Aunt Kim (Mam's sister-in-law), Sheila, her sister, and their kids. I remember being amazed at the weird little tray of food we were given on the plane, tasting of nothing. When we arrived at the hotel, I was astonished and impressed in equal measures that you could get banana split ice creams every day.

Mam was much less impressed by some of the Gorja folk sharing our hotel. On the first day we all ran down to the beach, dressed in our fitted swimming costumes. We were never allowed to wear bikinis and actually to this day I've never worn one. Shows far too much flesh!

As we skidded on the sand, dashing in to the sea, something caught our young eyes and our mouths fell open in shock.

There on the beach, bold as brass, were Gorja women walking around, sunbathing, even eating ice creams, with nothing but a pair of bikini bottoms on.

'Maamm?' I asked, trying not to look but unable to tear my eyes away. Growing up I'd never seen a woman's bare breasts before. We weren't allowed to get changed in front of each other, even as kids. Now they were everywhere we looked, bouncing and hanging, nipples big and small.

Mam's face said it all. 'Don't look,' she hissed. 'It's disgusting but just what some Gorja people do, so just ignore them and pretend they are not there.'

I'd no idea that ladies' chests came in so many shapes and sizes but I did what Mam said and averted my gaze.

Mam bought me a pink lilo, and there was nothing better

than lying on it in the pool, after a day's play. By then I was a confident swimmer. Mam insisted we'd taken lessons as we were always hanging round rivers and streams.

After much struggle to get on the damn thing, I relaxed, laid back and closed my eyes, feeling like I was living the life of Riley.

The next thing I knew, I could feel someone pulling me off, and dragging me to the bottom of the pool.

I barely had time to open my mouth to scream. Panic rising, I could see my flailing limbs in front of me, as my cousin Garner's nine-year-old face looked on in determination as he held me firmly by my shoulders.

My chest started to ache as I struggled to resist the urge to breathe. Kicking and shoving at my cousin, I didn't know what was worse, the feeling I was dying or the anger he could do this to me, in the name of 'fun'.

Just as I thought my lungs would burst in my ribcage, I gave him one final shove and he let go, setting me free so I could push myself to the surface, gasping for air.

My hair plastered on to the side of my face like a seal, I gulped and coughed, chlorine burning my nose.

'Maaaaaaaaaaaaaaaaaaaaaaaaaaaam!' I wailed, like a banshee. 'Garner tried to kill me!'

For the rest of the holiday I steered clear of the pool. And in fact it triggered a lifelong nervousness of the water. Even now I'd take a sunbed over a pool any day, and the thought of drowning terrifies me.

On the way back, Dad picked us up from the airport in the new Fiesta. As we all piled in I grabbed my nose.

'Urgh Dad, it stinks in here!'

Mam wrinkled her nose, too. 'What's been going in with my brand-new car?' she started. 'I told yers I wanted to keep it nice. Why does it smell worse than a farmyard?'

We all started grumbling as Dad looked nervously at Mam. 'Well, no wonder it smells really,' he said. 'Tom's been keeping a goat in the boot.'

I started laughing, but Mam didn't see the funny side.

'You what?' she cried.

And so Dad told the story of how he'd gone to a horse auction with Tom while we were away and had handed him £3, to keep him quiet, thinking he couldn't come to any harm with that or buy much. At the end of the day, Tom met Dad with a tethered goat in his hand. Now we were living in a house with a yard, Tom was keen to make the most of it. This started an obsession with pets and animals of all kinds. After he got bored of the goat, Tom sold it on and got a Shetland pony, then a sheep with her lamb. Then he was desperate for an aviary so Dad, being Dad, built him one a week later and he filled it with goldfinches.

Tom loved his birds and was very precious about who he let feed them. Happy to show off to his friends, the cage was a banned place for his little sisters, much to our annoyance.

One afternoon, after enviously watching Tom go in to the cage to feed them, I thought I'd sneak in and have a go when he left. Pulling open the cage door, I stepped inside, but as I did so, a bird flew right at me.

'Arghhh!' I screamed, ducking and running out again, leaving the door wide open in my panic. As I looked up in to the blue sky I caught sight of one of Tom's precious goldfinches, soaring away, never to be seen again. Quickly I slammed the door and ran inside.

Hours later Tom was storming upstairs shouting.

'What the heck's happened to one of my finches? 'E's gone missing!'

'I dunno,' I said, looking up from the TV. 'Don't ask me, Tom. Go blame someone else for a change.'

Mam looked up. 'Ooh Violet, wasn't you outside this afternoon?'

'Not me, Mam,' I said, shrugging.

'Yes, you were,' she insisted. 'I saw you nipping out of the garage . . .' And so the cat was out of the bag, or rather the bird was out of the cage, and Tom knew exactly whose fault it was by the look on his face. I was pleasantly surprised though that he appeared to take the news quite calmly. He didn't try and hit me, or make a fuss. Perhaps Tom was maturing a bit, I thought.

I went to bed as usual that night, hoping perhaps the gold-finch would find its way home and vowing never to go near those horrible squawking birds again. Soon I fell soundly asleep.

Later on, when my bedroom was dark, I woke up to feel something brush against my face. My heart thudding, I opened one eye and listened as the sound of something beating against the duvet sent a chill in to my heart. I told myself I must be dreaming or imagining it. Then something else batted my cheek, sending me bolt upright, hugging my knees with proper fright. On the ceiling, shadows flitted to and fro, and the terrible sounds of a bird cheeping loudly filled the room. All of a sudden, they all seemed to move and the entire room was alive with beaks and wings and screeching noises, harsh enough to make your ears bleed.

'Heeeeeeeeeeelp! Arghh! Get off! Maaaaaaaaaam!' I screamed at the top of my lungs and within seconds, my door flew open and Mam was standing with the light from the hall streaming in.

'Violet!' she cried, as she batted birds away. They were everywhere, circling the room in panic, battering my head and side lamp with their wings. Grabbing my hand, Mam pulled me out of the room. Quickly we realised what had happened. My lovely brother had set around twenty birds free in to my bedroom at night, to teach me a lesson. It worked. I never went near his nasty birds again.

Chapter Ten

Lessons of the Day

After moving in to our new place, Mum sent us to Buttershaw Primary School. I am not entirely sure what the reasoning was behind this, but I think she wasn't ever really happy with any of the schools, so thought she'd try them all. I didn't say goodbye to any of my classmates, as we were always moving on anyway.

This time we felt like we were on our own as none of our cousins were coming with us, and from the start it was tough. This was the third school we'd been to. Maria and Tom came with me of course, but we were all in separate playgrounds, Tom in the seniors and Maria in the infants. Suddenly we found ourselves alone and in our own different ways we all hated it.

Once again, as was normal at school, I had almost no friends. I'd be polite to people in the playground, I'd share if I needed to, but most of my focus went on learning and trying hard in my lessons.

I did make my first non-Gypsy friend around this time

though. Her name was Amanda and we had one powerful thing in common. We were both bullied mercilessly.

Amanda stood out because she wore thick glasses, had a frizzy mane of hair and lived in the worst part of Buttershaw Estate. She was the girl who everyone picked on and the cruelty was dreadful to watch.

Once I caught six or seven girls cornering her, taunting her, telling her she was a nasty, speccy little bitch. Her hands were over her face and she was sobbing like a baby, but still they wouldn't stop. It was like watching an injured animal having stones thrown at it. Without thinking of the attention I'd bring, I shoved past them.

'Oi!' I shouted. 'Leave her be. What's your problem? If you want to fight someone, come on then! I'm a Gypsy, you try me.'

After giving some lip back, the crowd melted away and I was left with this poor girl, who immediately clung on to me, her wet face soaking my shoulder. My heart really did go out to her. So we started a friendship of sorts, where we chatted and played around a bit, generally avoiding all the other girls.

Then one Saturday morning Amanda turned up on my doorstep. I was playing inside with Sabrina, Lina and my cousin Martina. Now, nobody outside our group had ever called on us before, and she'd turned up uninvited, which was wholly unexpected from a Gorja kid. We didn't know quite how to react.

Seeing her smiling face, all expectant and friendly behind

her specs, I didn't have the heart to turn her away, so I let her in, as my friends and cousin gave each other sidewards glances at this funny-looking little girl.

We were colouring in, so I gave her some pens and let her get on with it. We all chatted politely, feeling a bit like Amanda was spoiling it somehow, but not understanding why. About an hour and a half in, after chatting about her parents, Amanda looked up.

'I'm not allowed to play wi' pens at 'ome,' she said. 'Because once I coloured my arms blue and grey and it got my mam and stepdad in to trouble for hitting me. I nearly got took off them.'

Martina looked up and pulled a face. I could tell she was wondering who my weird friend was.

When Amanda went to the loo, they all started on at me, laughing and teasing, saying we needed to get rid of her.

'OK, OK,' I said. 'But don't do anything too mean. Let's just put the clocks forward so she thinks it's time to go home.'

When Amanda returned I gave them a wink, and glanced over at the clock. 'Come on, Amanda,' I said. 'Let's go down-stairs and get a drink.'

When we came back I saw the clock. Instead of just putting it an hour or so ahead, Martina had changed it so that it was three hours ahead.

'What time do you have to be back home, Amanda?' she asked.

'Half past four,' she said.

'Well look at the time now,' Martina said, pointing at the clock. 'It's quarter to four, innit, better get going then.'

Amanda's face dropped. 'It's gone so fast,' she cried. 'Oh. I was having so much fun. I'd better rush or I'll be in trouble.'

And so she left in a panic, the others falling about laughing as soon I closed the front door to her. I felt so mean. I knew Amanda would get home and realise what we'd done. The worst thing was, the next time I saw her, she never said a word.

I couldn't stand the head teacher at this school either. He'd insist on sitting next to me every single lunchtime, his big bald head glistening as he loudly chewed the horrible school meals. He always called me 'Flower', never my name. I don't know what he was thinking, whether he felt obliged to be nice to the Gypsy girl or what, but it was embarrassing and made me stand out even more with the other kids.

'Teacher's pet!' 'You all right, Flower?' 'Hi Flower!' It made a change from 'dirty gypo', I suppose, but it was just another thing to taunt me with. Bizarrely another teacher often just called me 'Pearl'. I think it must've been the name of another Gypsy girl he'd taught before. Sometimes it did seem like teachers lumped us all together and didn't get to know us or view us as individuals.

Sometimes, though, the Gypsy stereotypes worked very much in my favour, so it seemed a bit silly not to make the most of it.

For example, it was around this time that I found myself in class with a boy called Edmund. He and his two brothers and sisters all had exactly the same bowl haircut, and were seen as being the class swots. But for some reason he really had it in for me.

Our teacher at the time was called Miss Potomus and she had long, highlighted hair. She ruled the class with an iron rod, but we kids soon made the observation if her hair was down she was in a good mood, and if she had tied it up in to a bun with two Chinese wooden hairpins sticking out, it was a day not to mess with her.

In this particular lesson, Edmund wouldn't leave me alone.

'Dirty Gypsy,' he whispered, while sat next to me. 'Dirty Gypsy . . .'

He just kept chanting it, while staring at me. I tried to ignore him and listen to the lesson, but every time the teacher turned her back or moved to help someone else he would say it again.

'Oh give up,' I hissed. 'At least choose summat else, like tell me I'm a redhead or fat or something, *anything* else.'

'Stinky dirty Gypsy,' he spat back.

I felt my cheeks burning red. I was so fed up of this little boy, but sat in class there didn't seem a right lot I could do about it.

'Just. Shut. Up.' I snapped back, really feeling angry now.

'What?' Edmund smirked, glad he'd finally got a rise out of me. 'Are you getting angry now, dirty gypo?'

I glared at him, wishing I could make people stop in their tracks with my expression alone, like my Granny Winnie. 'Get lost!'

'Ooooh,' Edmund continued. 'What you gonna do? Put a Gypsy curse on me?'

For a split second my eyes lit up, then I slowly smiled.

'Yes,' I said slowly, turning to give him my best hard stare. 'That's precisely right, Edmund. If you don't stop calling me names I will put a *curse* on you.'

Then before he opened his gob to call me a gypo again, I spat out the words: 'Shimmerdimmerflabbertygabji!' Of course it was sheer nonsense I'd made up as I went along but by closing my eyes as if half possessed and holding out the palms of my hands, it seemed to do the trick.

Now it was Edmund's turn for his cheeks to start burning. 'Wha-at did you just say?' he stammered.

'Find out when you get home,' I shrugged, now desperately trying not to laugh.

A look of panic flitted across his once smug face. 'You've placed a curse on me!' he cried. 'Take it off. Take it off!'

Hiding a smile behind my hand, I flicked through the pages of my book to return to whatever work I needed to do. Edmund was such a fool. They all were.

By now Miss Potomus was standing over my desk asking what the fracas was about and I found myself standing by the blackboard at the front with thirty pairs of eyes straining at me.

'Now Violet,' she said, as everyone fell silent. 'Can you take your Gypsy curse off Edmund now please?'

Instantly I saw many little faces turn a shade whiter and I

almost wanted to openly thank Miss Potomus. She'd no idea just how much power she'd given me in that English lesson that day.

Edmund sat back down, picked up his book and buried his nose in it. I didn't hear a peep out of him for the rest of the lesson.

My 'curse' may have put paid to Edmund's jibes, but I still had to fend off so many other sly comments and accusations. Once someone started going on about Gypsies eating hedgehogs. 'You eat disgusting things like spiky hogs, you dirty gypo,' someone laughed.

'Well, you eat dead cows and dead pigs,' I shot back. 'Did you know pigs wallow in muck all day? That's what *you* like on *your* plate . . .'

I soon learned that if I answered back and gave as good as I got, sometimes that would get me off the hook. Some of the kids started leaving me alone, not knowing how to respond to the torrent of quickfire replies spouting from my mouth.

After a year living in our house, with little moving around, us kids were desperate for a break. We felt the claustrophobia of the four walls. Although not as much as Dad did. He hated living in the house, and struggled to settle. Mam and Dad never argued in front of us; rows were always kept well away from children's hearing. But I am sure they felt the strain. Dad seemed to work longer and longer hours, and often went 'away' for work, finding scrap metal further afield. Sometimes he didn't come home at night, which he always had done in the trailer. But I think Mam accepted that he needed the open road like a bird needs wings.

Then one Saturday we were packed in to a pickup and taken to see Baz, the man who had sometimes sold us trailers in the past. We couldn't stand the excitement. This must mean Mam and Dad were ordering a new trailer and we'd finally be escaping the four walls.

Baz had a business making trailers, doing them up and selling them on. The scent of Baz's workshop always smelt good to us kids. The sawdust and the harsh chemical glue reminded us we were hitting the road again.

After our visit we overheard Mam on the phone to Baz every day for weeks. 'No, no, Baz,' she always started, insisting she knew exactly how he should furnish the inside.

'I want a stripy one . . .'

'No, Baz, you're not listening. I said that had to be pink. Yes, pink . . .'

'Yes, Baz, I want the bedroom doors to be pink plastic, but I want them engraved like the mirrors . . .'

The trendy carpet of the time was proudly emblazoned with a pattern of ribbons and bows, and Mam insisted she wanted the doors and mirrors to match. Baz was obviously amused, but agreed. The outside was to be vinyl stripes, to replace the chrome, which had become unfashionable. But Mam being Mam, she also had strong opinions about what the stripes should look like.

'I want them to be salmon pink,' she ordered. 'But with a twist to them – not straight stripes. They have to be shaped and bent.'

We could hear Baz hooting down the phone. He called Mam crazy, and her stripes were known by our friends and relatives as the 'crazy stripes' for a while, until they started copying her new look themselves.

The day the trailer arrived, we rushed out of our house to greet it like an old friend. We weren't moving from the house, but the trailer would stay in our yard and be our escape route when we needed to get away. Opening the door we stepped in to a world of salmon pink, with ribbons, bow etchings and crazy stripes, so unlike the inside of our boring, uniform house. Peeking inside the squeaky new cupboards I took in a deep breath, smelling the lovely sawdust aroma.

A few days later we set off for a three-day fair in Stowe. It wasn't a long time away, but after being cooped up for so long, we felt like birds that had been set free.

While away, a fellow Traveller asked my dad if he could pop in for a coffee. As he sat down, he praised the interior to the hilt, admiring the colour, the patterns, telling Dad it was amazing to see, so innovative. The next day, he bought his wife to see it and she agreed with every word.

On the third day, we overheard a conversation between Mam and Dad. 'I asked him stupid money . . .' Dad was saying.

'You never!' cried Mam.

'I never thought he'd slap my hand,' Dad replied. 'How can we refuse a profit like that on a second-hand trailer?'

And so our hearts sank. The trailer had been sold to the first man who bid on it, all thanks to his wife falling in love with Mam's pink pattern-fest colour scheme.

Not only that, but the man wanted to drive off with the trailer that day. We were asked to pack up, although we did it at a much slower pace than moving in. Clothes were shoved in carrier bags, pots and pans wrapped up and quilts and duvets shoved in front of the lorry. We swallowed down tears, knowing our long, hot, Gypsy summer was being replaced with another dreary Yorkshire housebound one.

Around this time Mam had resigned from her job too. She had worked as a home liaison officer for five years, initially loving it, then starting to feel things were not changing as fast as they could be. Mam was a big advocate for change and had made a huge difference in narrowing the gulf between Gypsy families and their educational needs. But she'd also spent years fighting ignorance and felt the school systems were still letting Travelling kids down enormously. Watching her own kids complain about being picked on, singled out and bullied hadn't helped.

Maria was regularly coming home in tears. One teacher at school especially had it in for her, always calling her 'lazy' and a 'baby' instead of actually finding out why Maria wasn't learning as fast as she should be. Now she was seeing how the system was failing her own kids, despite her best efforts to change it from within, Mam's faith had been shattered.

On her last day in her job, she threw down her pen and simply walked out, telling them they were all racists, and never to darken her door again.

'You won't change them, Violet,' she always said, when years later I got a similar job to her.

Having persevered with school for several years now, Maria's learning still wasn't improving. In fact she appeared not to have made any progress at all and every morning before 9 a.m. she'd work herself in to a terrible state.

'Why do I have to go, Mam?' she would sob. 'The teachers think I'm stupid!'

Whatever comfort any of us tried to offer Maria, it was never enough.

With Mam losing faith in the school system, she decided to take us out for good and home-educate us. This is still completely legal as long as you can prove you will carry on giving lessons yourself, which Mam had every intention of doing. After all, she wasn't against education, just the way the system was wholly geared towards Gorja folk, as she saw it.

In the end the educational authorities didn't seem to mind and happily let her take us out of school. I am guessing they were even relieved three Gypsy kids had been taken off their hands. Mam told the authorities that she'd sent us kids away to live with the grandparents, although all the teachers knew full well our Granny Suzanna and Granny Winnie both lived within walking distance. No one ever questioned her or inquired about her decision to home-teach.

Tom and Maria were predictably thrilled. I was slightly less so, as I'd miss some of the more interesting lessons. But as soon as Mam made it clear we were still going to be taught lots at home, I didn't mind. I'd always felt a bit envious of Gypsy kids who didn't go to school. They got to stay at home, cooking and cleaning with their mams, which I also didn't mind one bit.

So lessons were now with Mam in the mornings, usually in front of the TV. Tom refused to learn, playing his role as stubborn, lazy brother to a tee. Exasperated with trying and failing to attract his interest with books, Mam gave up and used old copies of *Autotrader* to tempt him to read.

She gave us lessons in everything she saw fit, sometimes teaching us things straight out of the *Sunday Times*. We watched many of the educational programmes on BBC2 and Channel 4. Now we were living in a house and not a trailer, Mam was also very keen to teach us all about Romany culture. She knew our childhood was turning out to be fairly different to her's and Dad's but she was desperate for us to feel the same pride about our people. She taught us how oppressed Gypsies have always been but also how proud we were, and how respect means everything in our culture. I think she feared we were moving further away from our roots than ever and was eager to redress the balance. But in many ways it was a needless fear as we were always on a Gypsy site every day, visiting one of our grannies or our cousins, so it was still very much part of our life. We just went to bed and ate our meals in our house down the road.

One day she gave us library cards and took us to Wibsey Library, which could have been no bigger than our old trailer, but looked like a world of wonder to me.

Maria rolled her eyes. 'Do we have to?' she whined, looking bored until she found the video section. I felt like a kid in a sweet shop as I carefully fingered the books, selecting favourite authors, thrilled to think I could read as many as I wanted.

I devoured Roald Dahl, Enid Blyton and all the *Sweet Valley High* books. I loved stories about kids and the adventures they got up to, like the *Famous Five*. But always in my mind they were Gorja kids, not like us.

Then one day I was loaned *The Diddakoi* by Rumer Godden. It was the first time I had read about another Gypsy before and it truly amazed me. The story was about a girl who was half-Gypsy, although 'Diddikoi' means full Gypsy in our language.

Around this time I also discovered the luminous goddess of the silver screen that was Marilyn Monroe. I suppose the way she was always so feminine and immaculate appealed to the way I'd been brought up. I was watching telly and up popped an old interview with her. Marilyn was talking to the TV reporter on the street and, as they walked, the man asked her why no one was following them, given she was such a big star. But she said she wasn't being Marilyn Monroe at that moment, she was being Norma Jean. Then she said: '*This* is what Marilyn does . . .' and showed off her unique way of walking. She described it as walking as if she was balancing a dime in between her butt cheeks.

I was amazed for two reasons. Firstly you could be a size sixteen and still stunning, and secondly just walking in a glamorous way turned so many heads. From that moment on I vowed to copy it. To me, Marilyn epitomised what a woman should look like, and even if I didn't have the hair or the face, I could have her walk!

Chapter Eleven

Gypsy Princess

Eventually my little dog Mischief went on to have a baby too and I named him Boxer after he was born with a patch over his eye. I loved my dogs so much that I found it hard when they grew ill and died. When I was about ten, Missy got run over. Dad came rushing in with her limp body in his arms.

'Oh, Violet,' he said, as I sobbed my heart out. 'She won't make it. Best off letting her go gently now, my love.'

Grabbing Dad's sleeve, I cried, 'Please Dad, please give her a chance and take her to the vet!' So off he went and, after spending a small fortune, returned home with a listless Missy with her ear missing. I had to give her tablets and eardrops several times a day just to keep her going. Previously a friendly, sociable dog, she became morose and started snapping and barking at all the other dogs on the site. Eventually she grew so nervous and unhappy with the other animals we had to let her go. Dad found a lonely old woman who lived in a quiet house to take her on.

While I lived for my tiny dogs, Tom went for the other end of the scale and had an Irish wolfhound called Shep. He followed him absolutely everywhere including to our old school. No one messed with Shep and, despite being as big as his boy owner, Shep clearly worshipped him. The feeling was mutual. I rarely saw Tom cry but the day Shep died of old age when he was around fourteen, I'd never seen such devastation. Tom ended up throwing himself behind the sofa just to avoid anyone looking, such was his grief.

Aged eleven I shot up to 5'2", and although I am still that height, at that age it was dead tall. As a red-headed, slightly dumpy, spotty middle child I started to feel more and more self-conscious about the way I looked and whenever I spoke I held my hand in front of my face.

I always felt worse meeting new people, which of course we did constantly when we travelled to fairs. I used to hold my hand up and fiddle with my fringe, trying to block out my face, especially if I was with a girl I thought was smaller and more delicate-looking than me.

I'd felt self-conscious about my face ever since I can remember. I also suffered from constant nosebleeds, which didn't help me to feel feminine or attractive. I have no recollection of this but at the age of two I went with my dad to the scrap yard. As he threw the bits of metal in the van, we were told to sit on the wall and wait. I'd grown bored and stood up, toddling along the wall. Before Dad had a chance to sit me down again, I slipped, bashing my head and nose on the way down. The front of my nose was squashed and blood vessels were broken. For years afterwards I suffered nosebleeds and eventually had to have it cauterised. Until I was about twenty, every time the scrap yard manager saw me he'd ask: 'How's Miss Bloody Nose?'

Not only that, but I looked just like my mam, bless her, and whenever people said this she'd always reply: 'Yes, but I was an ugly child.'

I always misunderstood her meaning and heard 'you are ugly too', when actually she meant the opposite. My eyebrows and eyelashes were so light they didn't exist and I had a frizzy mane of hair that even Mam struggled to manage. I looked in the mirror and saw an albino.

Compared to my slip of a sister with her poker-straight blonde hair, I felt such an ugly pug. And with my gorgeous, dark-haired, dark-skinned brother on the other side I felt like the pig in the middle.

I suddenly filled out as well. Once Mam took us to a market and I tried on a pair of trousers but couldn't even squeeze in to the size twelve.

'Hahahahahaa!' Tom cried. 'Look at you, Fatty! You're a size fourteen now!'

I glared at him, my temper rising. But I also bit my lip as I felt tears pricking my eyes.

'Shurrrrrup!' I yelled, throwing the trousers on the floor.

Mam sensed my upset, and grabbed the trousers herself. 'They are rubbish, cheap trousers,' she said, ignoring the expression on the face of the market trader, who was standing right next to her. 'Come on, we'll find you smaller ones elsewhere.'

To add insult to injury, Tom loved teasing me. His favourite saying was: 'You're adopted, you are.' Maybe he picked up on my weakness, my sense of not being comfortable in my own skin, but whatever it was, as my brother he certainly knew how to wind me up.

In fact it was Tom who kindly coined my nickname, 'Princess'. It was based on Aveline, a character from one of our favourite sitcoms, *Bread*. I had the red hair and the loud voice, so it was perfect in his eyes. The nickname stuck and to this day he calls me this sometimes.

I might not have especially liked the character Aveline, but as a family we loved *Bread*, never missing an episode. Aside from the four walls they lived in, the Boswell family could have easily been Gypsies living in a trailer. With their devotion to Catholicism, their pot of money in to which everyone contributed, their strong work ethic and dominant matriarch, it was like watching one of our own.

About this age, I was playing with Mam's make-up and discovered the joy of mascara and eyeliner. Blinking at myself in her dressing-table mirror, I just couldn't believe how open and defined my eyes looked. Suddenly I noticed their pretty blue colour and, wiggling my eyebrows, I could see them properly for the first time. It was a revelation. After that I begged Mam to let me buy some cheap mascara from Superdrug and, bless her, she did, even though Dad hated it. I never wore any other make up, though, just on my eyes. Immediately my tube of mascara became one of my most precious items and I carried it around with me in a velvet pouch with any little pocket money I had at all times.

That Christmas we went shopping down in Bradford. The roads were so packed we had nowhere to find a parking space for the van, so Dad drove a bit out of town and found a space on a side street. When we got back, tired and laden down with bags of presents, we walked down the road where our van had been left, thinking we'd forgotten where we'd parked it.

'I am sure it were here,' said Dad, blowing out his cheeks.

'It were,' said Mam. 'Someone's pinched it.'

We all stood, freezing, with heavy arms, talking about calling the police. Many of Dad's tools were inside, which he needed for work, and with no contents insurance he'd be losing hundreds if not thousands of pounds. For a family disaster this was fairly big in the scheme of things. Except in my young eyes, it didn't take long for my own personal disaster to dawn on me.

'My mascara and eyeliner!' I cried. 'I left it in the van! Oh no, oh God. What am I going to do, Mam?' Mam shot me one of her infamous looks and I fell silent. How she didn't clobber me I don't know.

Although I wasn't the most confident child, I had a big gob on me and from an early age felt very principled about things. Just like Mam, I suppose.

For example, Granny Winnie smoked like a dragon at all

times, and every birthday and Christmas me, Tom and Maria would be asked to buy her a pack of forty Rothmans as her present. But one year I suddenly refused, as I'd discovered how bad smoking was for you.

'I'm not doing it,' I said to my dad, arms folded. 'I am not helping Granny Winnie kill herself no more.' So he asked me what I was going to buy her.

I quickly wracked my brains. 'A plant!' I said brightly. 'That's what I'll get her.'

Granny Winnie had shown as much interest in plants as I had in cars but, determined not to get her the stinky fags, I went to a shop and found a pot plant.

It was an Amaryllis but it hadn't flowered, so it looked like a simple stick. As Granny happily took the boxes of cigs from my brother and sister, she looked puzzled as I proudly handed her my stick in a pot.

'It's an Am-ar-yl-lis . . .' I said, pronouncing the syllables carefully.

Her tiny wrinkled face broke in to a smile and she politely said thank you, before shoving it on the sideboard and lighting up a fag. Then a few weeks later the stick grew an amazing flower and she couldn't have been more grateful. Every time we went to visit, she pointed at the bloom, giving me a wink. So every year after that I bought her another plant.

In later years, my other granny also showed a stubborn disregard to her health. In her late fifties, Granny Suzanna had a stroke and was subsequently diagnosed with insulin-dependent diabetes. She was told she had to avoid sugar but she refused to do anything of the sort, and ended up in a wheelchair. For company, following Jimmy's death and all her children leaving home, Granny Suzanna decided her new companions would be two Yorkshire terriers, Tiddles and Trixie, which she kept in her home in defiance of the Romany tradition.

Granny Suzanna refused to be housed by the authorities, so she lived on a site in Mary Street, three or four miles away from our house. It was small, with concrete floors and concrete walls, and a simple trailer. If you refused the house you were given, you weren't given a lot else and most local authority-run sites are basic, run-down places. The window of her chalet was as wide as the structure itself and she'd sit slap bang in the middle of it, in the middle of the room, queen of all she surveyed, with a dog either side.

These dogs became the apples of her eyes and she spoiled them rotten. The love between them seemed to be mutual as both dogs died of broken hearts two weeks after Granny Suzanna died, even though my aunties looked after them well.

They lived off boiled ham, which Granny Suzanna made for them specially. I cannot eat it to this day as it reminds me of dog food. They also loved Polo mints, but because they got stuck in their teeth, Granny insisted on 'helping' them eat by chewing them up herself and spitting them in to her hand for them to lick off.

As much as she loved her grandchildren, Granny Suzanna

perhaps loved those blessed dogs a little bit more than us. Once we were all out for the day – Mam, Dad, Granny, Tom, Maria and myself – visiting Whitby, North Yorkshire. As we passed an arcade, Tom was really excited, as there was nothing he liked better than to have a gamble, his expectant face glowing with flashing lights. Maria and I were less bothered and preferred the beach, but Mam promised Tom a visit later. That afternoon, after nagging Mam all day, Tom spotted an arcade across the road and we all nipped over, including Granny in her wheelchair, holding the two dogs' leads as she was pushed along. Always eagle-eyed, Granny spotted a sign: 'No dogs'. And if her dogs were not allowed in then neither were her grandkids, according to Granny. Seething with annoyance, Tom knew better than to argue. Mam tried to placate him with a trip to the fish and chip shop up a nearby hill.

'Wait outside with your granny and hold her wheelchair while we nip inside, would you?' asked Mam.

As we waited for our fish and chips, my dad suddenly let out a yell and, pushing past the customers, raced out of the shop as if it was on fire.

'Stooooooooop!' he screamed, running in to the road. Panicked by his reaction we all pressed our faces to the window to see poor Granny's wheelchair disappearing at breakneck speed down the road as if a rocket was attached to the back. Running after her, Dad just managed to grab hold of the wheelchair handles and jerk himself backwards, pulling Granny to a sudden stop and almost throwing her out of the chair in the process. In a flash Mam had cornered a red-faced Tom outside the shop to ask him what on earth had happened.

'The handles just slipped out of my hands,' he spluttered. To this day he insists it had nothing to do with her not letting him have a go in the arcade.

As children we also secretly got our own back on the poor dogs. One game we loved to play was placing Granny's wheelchair on its side, sitting on the wheel and then spinning ourselves round as fast as possible. Occasionally, when she wasn't looking, we would try the spinning game on an unsuspecting terrier, falling in to helpless laughter as we watched it totter around dizzily for a few seconds afterwards.

Eventually Granny Suzanna decided she hated her wheelchair and got rid of it. She'd sit all day in a high-backed, comfortable chair, slap bang in the middle of her trailer, giving orders to whoever came to visit, often relying on her surrogate daughter Dawn to help fix her meals or get something out of the fridge to eat.

'That big lass [meaning Dawn] hasn't showed up yet,' she'd sigh. 'I am wasting away here! Look at me, sat all by myself, unable to reach the shelves.'

She loved watching us make a fuss of her, diving in to the fridge to get her something to satisfy her sweet tooth. Once I turned up and she was complaining as usual. 'Where's Dawn?' she asked. 'I'll die of starvation before anyone cares.'

Then I spotted a telltale piece of cream still stuck to the side of her mouth.

'So where's that cream from then, Granny?' I laughed, as she quickly tried to wipe it off. 'From the éclair in the fridge, by any chance?'

Like Lou from *Little Britain*, sometimes my funny old granny would leap from her chair when no one was looking to get something tasty to eat.

Later on in life, Granny Suzanna became deaf and blind, after consistently ignoring her doctor's advice on how to handle her diabetes. She lived off bread and diabetic jam, usually smothered with sugar.

But although old age robbed her of her sight and sound, Granny was still a force to be reckoned with. Once when my Uncle Wally complained about the smell of her beloved dogs, she grabbed her zimmer frame, struggled up and shoved him out of the trailer backwards before he'd had a chance to even turn round.

'If my dogs are not welcome then neither are you,' she yelled.

After she died we shared so many funny stories about Granny Suzanna before her funeral, we were crying with laughter. One classic was when she visited the opticians after diabetes had worsened her vision.

'Don't worry,' said the optician, kindly. 'After we've found you the right glasses you'll be able to read again.'

Unfortunately Granny didn't hear the word 'again'. Having never learned to read at school she assumed the glasses would magically enable her to 'read' for the first time. She left the opticians very impressed, looking forward to getting home and picking up a book. When she proudly put her glasses on, her disappointment was heartfelt when the lenses didn't help the words on the page to make any more sense than before.

'Oh, I felt so fobbed off,' she complained.

Her somewhat difficult and bolshie reputation almost hid her other side: the fierce love she had for us grandkids, the way she always found something to laugh or tease about. I can never hear the song 'Respectable' by Mel & Kim without thinking of Granny Suzanna. It was a number one hit in the eighties and Dawn and her friend Mary were singing it one day as they got ready to go out. 'You'd better behave respectably,' Granny had shouted, laughing at their funky moves. Afterwards they'd tease her for years, whistling or humming the song to wind her up.

Chapter Twelve

Boxing Clever

From the age of eight years old my brother Tom was sent to boxing classes by my dad. Although a difficult toddler, he'd grown in to a quiet, unassuming, popular lad who – despite winding up his sisters – generally stayed out of trouble just like his father. But my dad saw it as his job to make sure Tom could look after himself, as all Romany men had to. Like we were taught to cook and clean, Tom needed lessons in fighting man to man.

In the Gorja world of course, aside from professional boxing and wrestling, fighting is frowned upon – and usually when it does happen alcohol is involved and it's dubbed domestic violence. In the Gypsy world, however, bare-knuckle fighting is the way we mete out justice and settle disputes, cleanly and fairly in front of a crowd who can act as referees. There is no need for us to get the police involved. After the fight is finished there is always a clear winner and a proper line is drawn under the dispute.

In fact all of our Gypsy world is so self-contained, there is virtually no crime. Of course in later years some people have got involved with drugs on some sites, but on the whole crime is very rare in our community. If any serious crimes are suspected the consequences are very severe.

For example, if a man was discovered to be a paedophile not only would he be banished and probably reported to the police, but his entire family would be ostracised too. Years ago, we heard how one young lad took his five-year-old cousin in to a field and raped her. Within hours of it happening, he'd been reported and banished for good.

Sexual assault on any level is not tolerated. Once I heard of a teenage girl who'd gone with her boyfriend into his trailer. Left alone he'd shoved his hands down the front of her under-wear. Scared of being found 'impure', she pushed him off and ran away screaming, locking herself in a nearby shed until help arrived. Straight away the men on the site dropped everything and gathered to find out what had happened, then went to find the boy, whose mother had been in another part of the trailer when the incident took place. But when they finally got inside both mother and son had already left. His mother would have known instantly how serious the consequences would be for her boy and she made the snap decision to run away with him, leaving the site and all her belongings forever, rather than face the beatings he'd get.

It was also seen as serious if a boy touched a girl 'down there' – even as an accident. Once a lad aimed a kick at a girl near me and it caught her groin. In those instances it was down to the mother to beat her son and tell him off soundly so he knew never to do it again.

We watched, wide-eyed, as the poor boy was dragged away by his hair, his screaming mother telling him she'd have his hide inside the trailer.

For boys, fighting, justice and a sense of honour were instilled at a young age. So naturally Dad was keen to make sure his only son was able to defend himself and become a proficient boxer. Surprisingly my brother took to the sport like a duck to water and was soon training three times a week. At his peak he even won the Yorkshire School Boxing champion competition, something my dad was hugely proud of.

Having an older brother in to boxing meant I often found myself on the wrong end of his fists. But not really living up to my nickname, it was something I certainly didn't shrink from. Quite often I'd be sat watching television when he'd suddenly take a dive at me, pummelling his fists wherever he could.

'Toooom!' I'd scream. 'Gerrrofff!'

One day I was lying on the bed, my legs half in the air, when he launched himself at me. After quickly leaping to my feet, I gave him the most almighty shove, kicking like a mule, and very satisfyingly he landed in a heap on his back on the other side of the room.

'That'll teach ya,' I laughed as he grumbled that he was only messing.

My thoughtful brother was happy to pass on what he learned

at boxing. By the age of ten I knew it was best to throw a punch with your thumb on the outside in case it got broken, that you should aim to use your top knuckles so you didn't dislocate a finger, and you should always keep your other fist up on guard.

Tom had the power in his fists and ability to dive whereas I relied on my fierce temper to scare him back. He'd often run away, locking himself in the bedroom or bathroom just to get away from my rage. By the time I was fifteen almost every door we had in our house had holes punched in where one of us had smashed a fist through it. The upside of having a boxing champ for an older brother was that I'd learned to look after myself. I was twelve when I first knocked a boy out cold.

Coralina and Alan – the couple who got married on the same day as my mum and dad – had a son John, who was then around fifteen. He was always teasing me about my fights with Tom.

'I've heard you're a bit of a hard nut, Violet,' he laughed. 'If you fancy yourself so much, why not have a free shot on me?'

A free shot is when someone stands with their arms by their sides and 'lets' the other person punch.

'No,' I said. 'You're all right, John. I won't bother.'

Perhaps slightly different rules apply between brother and sister, but it certainly wasn't seen as ladylike to be going round throwing punches at other boys.

'Aw, go on, Violet,' he wheedled. 'C'mon, let's see what you're made of.'

I said no a few more times and then, when he wouldn't give up, I made him a promise.

'All right then, John. Just keep your back to the wall as maybe it'll come when you least expect it,' I laughed.

One day I was cleaning the outside of the trailer when he wandered over, giving me more gip about my punches and how his free shot was still open. He started walking round the trailer, laughing at me and poking fun. Just as he came round the other side, I found myself throwing down my cloth, launching myself at him and punching him square on the jaw without a second's thought.

Like a lead statue he fell backwards, landing on the grass out cold. Within a few seconds, he came to, pulling himself up as fast as possible as he shook his head, his cheeks wibbling like a cartoon character's.

I couldn't help giggling. 'You had enough now, John?'

As soon as his eyes focused on me, he shook his head again and tried to laugh himself. 'Ha ha yourself, Violet. I'm only messing. Got you real good, didn't I, pretending to be knocked out like that?' Except we both knew he really had been.

He quickly disappeared, knowing that the shame was on his head this time.

My fights with Tom never hurt me very badly although he used to wind me up endlessly. Thankfully Maria always managed to stop us before it got too serious.

As the Babby, the one with the hole in her heart and the one who had broken her leg, she was always seen as a fragile doll. Woe betide anyone who so much as breathed on Maria. So when she started bawling as Tom and I chased each other up and down stairs, slamming doors and pummelling each other until we yelled, it was our baby sister who put a stop to it. One scream from her, and we would forget all about who was getting back who, and rush to her side.

'What's up Maria? Don't cry, Babby . . .' It was a race to calm her down before our parents heard.

When she was a little older Maria changed from being the person who would stop the fighting to being the one who actually caused them.

As we grew older, as part of our freedoms as Gypsy kids we were allowed to go off every Saturday with our gang. We would buy a Day Rover travel card for £1, which meant we could jump on any bus and go anywhere in Bradford. One day, I went to surf the buses with Joanne and Maria, getting off wherever we fancied. For some reason that day Maria decided to wind up Joanne, telling her she hated her shoes and how she always had nicer clothes than her. By the time we'd reached the bus stop Joanne had not surprisingly had enough and was in a foul mood, but Maria, the little minx, kept on at her.

'I'll punch you if you don't shut it,' said Joanne, after Maria made another sly and unnecessary comment. As Maria's big sister I had no choice but to step in and defend her, even though I could see Joanne's point completely. Maria had been a right little madam that morning.

'Oi Joanne,' I said. 'You can't be saying that to my babby sister, you know she's delicate.'

And within a few moments Maria's goading had set off World War Three between me and Joanne – my cousin and one of my closest friends. For a few minutes we mouthed off at each other, our noses almost touching, and then suddenly we were off, rolling around on the concrete bus-stop floor, punching fists in to each other's arms and shoulders, dust filling our mouths with every shriek and squeal. The bus could have stopped, let people off and driven on and we wouldn't have noticed.

After a few minutes, both panting for air and sore all over, we got up. I grabbed Maria's hand and marched away. 'You little cow,' I shouted over my shoulder, not knowing if I was aiming it at Maria who'd caused the fight or Joanne who had almost certainly left a couple of bruises. I didn't speak to her for three weeks, which felt like the longest time.

Perhaps the most serious fight of all was when I was thirteen. My cousin Martina, my Auntie Ninna's daughter, had moved with them from Bradford to Darlington.

Around this time Bradford had begun to get a reputation as a destination for 'wannabe' Travellers who just wanted to live the lifestyle, but would never be true Gypsies. They were called wydos.

I felt put out about Martina moving, not just because I missed the family but also because she seemed to look down her nose at me now. People who did this, especially those who came from the Darlington area, were known as 'Darlington trotters'. So we went from being good pals to almost blanking each other at family get-togethers in the space of twelve months.

Our paths crossed during another get-together at a Gypsy convention and this time things came to a head. And once again my babby sister was unwittingly the touchpaper. Maria had been excited all morning about wearing her pink candy-striped trousers but they'd somehow managed to get ripped after we arrived on the site.

Maria's eyes immediately welled up with tears. I was trying to soothe her when Martina spotted her.

'Oi, babby Maria,' she teased. 'What you crying about now, eh? Those stripy trousers look better with a good rip in them anyways.'

I shot her a look. Who did she think she was, taking the mickey when Maria was clearly so upset?

'Give over,' I shouted. 'It's none of yer business.'

Martina squared up to me, her chocolate-brown eyes flashing with fury. 'You what, Violet? How dare you!'

Just like that, all the unspoken tension between us exploded like a pressure cooker and like two cats we descended on each other, tumbling on to the floor. On principle I never fought like a girl, grabbing hair or clawing at eyes, so I just stuck to walloping her as hard as I could.

'You wydo!' she screamed, as she punched my arms and shoulders.

'You Darlington trotter!' I spat back.

At the back of my mind, I knew this was the worst thing we could be doing. Gypsy girls did not fight, especially not in front of others. It brought shame on the family. But right then, getting my own back on this Darlington trotter was far more important. Despite her clutching a fistful of my hair in her hand, I managed to roll over, so I ended up victoriously on top of her. As I raised my clenched fist to deliver my final blow I paused for a moment.

'Don't hurt her, don't hurt her,' a voice was saying loudly in my mind, as she screwed up her face to brace herself for my punch. Whatever was said or done, Martina was my cousin and I loved her dearly. Plus I knew if I bruised my cousin's face there would be enormous trouble, even more so than already.

At that moment, her fingers slid out of my hair and instinctively I dropped my fist too. Already other relations had spotted us and I was being dragged off. I knew Mam and Dad would go mad, but I just felt like I had to defend Maria's honour, and maybe settle an old score or two in the process.

Chapter Thirteen

Back to School

If I thought primary school was a rocky road for a Gypsy, nothing compared to the complete horror of moving up to secondary. When I was twelve years old, Mam made the decision to send us back to school as Maria still couldn't read properly, and Mam decided it was worth another punt, despite the bullying. In all honesty, none of us were happy about this decision.

'Mam, why are you making us do it now?' cried Maria, horrified at the thought.

'I just want to give you all the chances Violet and Tom had to learn to read,' said Mam. As hard as she tried to teach her, Maria was simply not picking up the words as well as Mam knew she should be doing.

So amid much grumbling and grouching, we all got new pencil cases, bags and a date to start back at school.

On my first day I was seated next to a girl called Kerry. As the teacher pointed me to the desk, Kerry's eyes rolled and she shuffled her chair away from mine in preparation. Straight away I realised exactly how things were going to be between us.

'Where do you live, stinky gypo?' she said by way of introduction.

'I live over by Wapping,' I said. 'And I am not stinky.'

'Yeah you are, my mum says all gypos stink and you're just the same. Give us nits and all.'

'I've never had nits . . .' I began.

'Then why've you got your hair tied back?' she said, pointing to my plaits.

'I only have it done like this at school so I *don't* get any nits . . .' I sighed, knowing it was pointless even trying to explain to someone like her. It was clear she hated me from the moment she laid eyes on me. I tried to avoid her, but I was set aside from everyone else from the start and making friends seemed impossible.

Once the lesson started, I was moved to the front, next to a boy called Michael who had severe educational needs. For my first English lesson I was handed a *Janet and John* reading book. My heart sank. I could devour several books in a weekend by now, so sitting with a copy of this felt patronising and humiliating.

'Please, Miss Bernett,' I said, raising my hand. 'I can read better than this, Miss.'

'Just sit there and be quiet, Violet,' she replied, dismissively.

For the maths lesson, while everyone else had algebra, I was told to fill in a simple worksheet adding up pairs of socks with Michael.

'Please, Miss,' I said again. 'I know how to do fractions and algebra . . .'

But once again she cut across me, saying I should just get on with what I'd been asked to do. It took a good few weeks before any of the teachers could be persuaded I wasn't stupid. No one wanted to consider that a Gypsy girl might be just as smart as the other kids.

A few weeks later in a science lesson, some of the girls were messing around with Bunsen burners and I ended up getting soot smeared all over my face. It was a rare moment when I could join in so I didn't mind playing the clown and letting people cover my face. Our teacher, Mr Davis, spun round on his chair to see me suppressing giggles with a face as black as a coal miner's.

'Violet!' he yelled. 'What have you done to yourself now?'

I stopped smiling and looked puzzled. 'Er, Sir,' I said, pointing at my face, 'I didn't do this to myself. Some of the others were having a laugh. Why would I smear my own face with soot?'

He frowned and moved closer. 'Get yourself to the head teacher's office and you can explain it to him then!'

So off I went and when I arrived the head teacher, Mr Gray, whose office I'd never been sent to before, shook his head.

'I suppose it was inevitable really, wasn't it Violet? You ending up in my office . . .' he began.

Straight away I took it that he meant it was inevitable because I was a Gypsy.

'So tell me, Violet, why did you do this to yourself?' he asked, leaning back in his chair, his fingers making a tent-like structure. By now I was so fed up. As if I'd cover my own face in soot! How ridiculous.

'Why would I put soot on my own face?' I said. Then – and I am not sure where this came from – I blurted out: 'On your way home may the Lord have you run over by a bus!'

All the injustice of the last few weeks, all the anger and the irritation seemed to spill out, although it probably wasn't the brightest thing to let rip at the head of the school. I bent my head and closed my eyes, wanting to take back every word and waiting for the head to give me detentions for life, or threaten to tell my parents. But instead of meeting my anger with his own, the head looked surprised.

'Calm down,' he said. 'Why don't you go to the canteen and get yourself some juice?'

I looked up again, one eye open. Was he for real? But he pointed towards the door, looking almost worried, nodding his head. So I stood up, smiled and walked out. For the first time I realised I had to stick up for myself and sometimes it was better to show your anger. And maybe, just maybe, he realised I hadn't meant to get in to trouble.

Meanwhile I was still running the gauntlet of the school bullies, spending my days trying to avoid the taunts from Kerry and her mates. I was savvy though and decided to make friends with the tallest boy, a popular guy called Lance. I purposefully targeted him, following him around, being cheerful, telling him how great he was at football and how much I admired him. Within months we were good friends. And when people saw me hanging out with him, they thought twice about calling me names.

But Kerry, determined to make my life a misery, was looking for any way possible to get at me and during one hockey lesson she found the most painful way. Although I am convinced the teacher knew full well we were worst enemies, I was paired with Kerry for hockey practice. This involved whacking the ball to and fro to each other in a bid to make us better players. I could see a sly smile on her face as she started hitting the ball, harder and harder, sending me running all over to get it.

'Dirty gypo,' she chanted through gritted teeth as the ball landed at her feet and she smacked it back with full force, not caring how close I was. After ten minutes or so, she changed tactic. This time, she ran towards me ever closer as she hit the ball. But after I managed to whack it back, the ball having narrowly missed my shins, she stopped it dead with her stick and came up with an even better plan. Now she started dribbling it towards me at full speed. Like a thunderous hippo, she charged at me, her face twisted with concentration.

When she was around five metres away, my heart seemed to pause momentarily. She was running towards me at full pelt, the ball was gathering speed and her devious eyes shone like a fox fixed on its prey . . . Raising her hockey stick high above her head, she met my eyes briefly then walloped her stick downwards as hard as she could, the veins in her forehead and arms bulging with the effort.

Crack!

The last thing I saw was the stick inches from my nose and the hard tarmac looming in front of my eyes. I came to, feeling sick to my stomach, my head absolutely killing me, with the faces of all my classmates peering at me and their hot breath hovering over me. In an instant I remembered Kerry's look of hatred and I struggled up on my elbows despite the spiky pain across my eyes sending me spinning.

'Kerry!' I managed to yell. 'You *object*!' (This was my worst insult as I almost never swear.) As I scrambled to my feet, the teacher grabbed my shoulders and held me firmly.

'Now now, Violet,' said Miss Tyler. 'It was just an accident. You can't go blaming Kerry.'

My face red with fury, my head pounding like a pulse, I wanted to scream. Of course the teachers would believe her over me, there was no point in even trying to persuade them otherwise. The injustice hurt me more than any bruise on my head.

Twenty minutes later I was walking back in to the hushed classroom, a proper egg of a bruise having developed on my forehead like a badge of shame.

As I sat down I was sure I heard a tiny giggle from Kerry and I wanted to kill her. I really did.

Months passed at the school and I tried to fit in best I

could, but it was hard. However hard I found it though, Maria had even more trouble. She's since been diagnosed with dyslexia but at the time she was branded a lazy and stupid Gypsy girl. At a loss as to what to do with her, the teachers started putting Maria in with me again, despite our age difference, as they thought I could teach her myself. Again, even at secondary school, it appeared Gypsies had different rules to everyone else. When Maria insisted she wanted me, they didn't argue.

If I couldn't have been less thrilled about this decision, Maria was beside herself with joy. She hated school and hated the teachers and if Maria hated something then there was no persuading her otherwise. She'd do anything to try and get out of lessons. Once our class was asked if we wanted to volunteer to read to the younger ones. Everyone's hand shot up – including Maria's, she was with me at the time – and somehow she got chosen. Later on, I went to find her. I turned up in an infants' class to see Maria sat with a five-year-old boy, telling him a story using the pictures as she had no clue what the words said.

'And then the teddy bear ended up a tree . . .' Maria was theatrically 'reading'.

'But it don't say that . . .' the little boy began.

'Yep it does,' Maria snapped. 'I promise you it does, you've got it wrong.'

I stood over her until she realised it was me. 'Oh Violet, can you come and help?' she grinned.

Most days we'd turn up to school and Maria would

immediately throw up and get sent home sick. I had no idea what she was doing until later when she admitted to sneaking in a bottle of Dad's Old Spice and drinking it so she'd vomit and get out of lessons.

Tom hated school possibly even more than I did. He'd come home so wound up, Mam would warn him: 'Don't you go throwing punches at people, Tom. You'll really hurt someone.'

But driven to distraction, Tom started to get in to regular fights. He found it hard being treated as a child at school. My dad was training him to ride and sell horses, treating him like a proper man. Then back in the classroom he was getting patronised and told off. He started getting suspended on a regular basis and then one day confided in me he'd decided to go a step further. 'I always get told off for starting it,' he said. 'So now I am going to start *and* finish it, good and proper.'

'Oh no!' I said, not wanting to see my brother get in any more trouble. 'What have you got in mind?'

He just smiled. 'You'll see.'

A few days later someone told me Tom had been taken to hospital. He'd grabbed a lad, held him up against the wall and was drawing back to punch him square in the face. I don't know if the boy moved, or as I'd like to think, Tom changed his mind at the last moment, but he ended up hitting the wall with full force, cracking his wrist instead.

When he had to return to explain himself to the teacher he openly said he'd wanted to clobber the boy and, just to really make sure he was in the supreme amount of trouble, he gave the teacher a mouthful of abuse for good measure.

The next day he was expelled. Now that Tom wasn't going to school, Maria and I refused too.

Mam sighed as we explained our decision. 'Can't we just stay back at 'ome?' Maria begged.

'Please!' I added.

Knowing she'd tried for many years, Mam finally agreed to take us out of school for good and to educate us at home again. She had tried by sending us back but things seemed worse than ever. Maria was more upset than ever and Tom was now getting a reputation as a thug. Desperate to protect us, she decided the best course of action was to cut our losses and keep us safe at home.

The effect of the trauma of school stayed with poor Maria for years. Even when she was a married woman and a mum of three, I was with her recently in the kitchenware section of a department store when she suddenly stopped dead.

Looking like she'd seen a ghost, she started sniffing and going pale. 'Oooh Violet,' she said, her hands tightening around the buggy she was pushing. 'Can you smell that?'

I sniffed. I smelled nothing except for department store and perhaps a faint whiff from the nearby café.

'School dinners!' announced Maria, pulling a face and puffing her cheeks out. 'Brings it all back.'

Chapter Fourteen

The G-Word

All of our family believed in God but none of us believed in any one religion. Although it was important to get wed in a church and attend at Christmas, regular worship wasn't a huge part of our lives. However, many Gypsies are religious and are either practising Roman Catholics or part of the 'Light and Life' movement, a Travellers' Evangelical church that holds conventions up and down the country. Previously all I knew of Jesus was the fluorescent rosary beads I saw above Mam's bed, which looked like a pretty fashion accessory to add to my collection.

Then my dad's sister Ninna split up with her husband, a huge trauma that caused shock waves throughout her family. My poor auntie was a broken woman afterwards, totally devastated. So when she announced a few months afterwards she'd been 'saved' and found God, Dad was pleased for her at first. 'It's a good thing for her,' he said. Religion was seen as something to keep her mind occupied so she wasn't dwelling on the break-up.

But Ninna had joined the Light and Life movement and had started regularly attending meetings and conventions – and Dad, like many Gypsy men we knew at the time, was deeply suspicious of the organisation. There were whisperings that it ripped people off and was cult-like. When Ninna asked Dad to take her to a convention, because she needed the trailer pulling, he was happy to do so, but wanted to leave us kids at home. We were less than thrilled with the idea, as any event with lots of other kids attending in a big field only represented fun to us.

'Aw, it's not fair, Dad,' I whined. 'You're taking Aunt Ninna and her kids but not us.'

'Yeah, we're missing out,' joined in Tom.

But Dad insisted on leaving us behind. He didn't want our heads filled with whatever 'religious nonsense' was on at the convention.

The day before he left, all us kids whined and complained, saying how unfair it was, until Dad agreed to let Mam and the rest of us go with him.

The night before we heard him having some stern words with Mam in the kitchen. 'If you go to this you nor the kids had better not become one of them nutters. No one is going along to be saved. Do you hear?'

Dad was frightened by how deeply Ninna had become involved and he didn't want Mam to go the same way. After all, Mam had always believed in God and prayed in times of trouble, so Dad thought she might be open to the idea.

Off we went, excited to arrive in an enormous field bustling with activity, full of Romany families. We spent all day running round, meeting other Travellers and generally having a laugh while the parents wandered in and out of circus-sized tents to listen to sermons and prayers.

Our parents only had a monochrome old-style trailer – the one bought after Mam's crazy pink striped one was sold – and they didn't update it as regularly because we had the house. Maria and I were embarrassed as it looked old and shoddy, a bit like a New Age Travellers' caravan. Mam and Dad had attached a piece of awning to Ninna's posh Buccaneer one and we would dive in and out of the awning via their front door, so people thought it was our place instead.

On the third day, Mam attended one of the bigger meetings where people were being saved. This was what Ninna had experienced the year before: it was when people felt they were 'touched' by God and subsequently decided to embrace Christianity.

After running round the field all day, our noses burned by the sun, we were exhausted, so we decided to stick our heads in to the huge tent to see what all the fuss was about. There in front of me were hundreds of Travellers all quietly listening to a man singing.

'If you're tired and weary . . . Jesus understands how it feels to be alone . . .' he crooned.

The words mesmerised me. Standing there, transfixed, I started to well up, not knowing why. His song just sounded so emotional and seemed to make sense. I left the tent, brushing away the tears, but his voice echoed in my head. I had no idea why this man's words had touched me so profoundly.

Later on we went to bed back in our trailer and Mam and Dad started rowing. Usually us kids were protected from this sort of thing, but this time we could hear every word. We'd never heard my dad sound so furious.

'I fucking said don't listen to those psychopaths!' he yelled. 'It was the *one* fucking thing I said to you! The *one* fucking thing!'

My dad had never used such bad language before, turning the air blue. Mam, in contrast, sounded very calm as she tried to appease him. Then Aunt Ninna turned up. She's one of the most elegant and peaceful ladies I've ever known and would never be the sort to swear, let alone be sworn at, so I wondered what she'd make of this.

'Calm down,' she said to Dad quietly.

'Will you fucking shut up!' shouted my dad.

We all gave a collective gasp. 'Oh my God,' I whispered to Maria. 'I bet she'll punch him or summat now.'

It was unheard of to speak in that way to someone like Ninna. She was such a proud lady who people naturally respected. We waited with bated breath to see what she would say but instead she turned on her heel and stalked out of the trailer. We knew this was really bad.

We fell asleep to the sound of Mam crying quietly in the

trailer after Dad had stormed out. We found out later he had gone to the pub and spent every penny he had in his pocket, something else that was very unusual for our usually sober father. In later years he'd describe this episode of his life as the time when the devil entered him.

All of a sudden, Dad started going to the pub constantly, smoking more heavily and generally acting out of sorts. He was deeply suspicious about the Light and Life movement, as many Gypsy non-believers were. In his eyes the religious organisation had targeted poor Ninna when she was vulnerable. To have his wife suddenly turn religious after his sister had was too much to bear. And not being a big drinker normally, Dad couldn't hold his booze very well.

Meanwhile Mam's decision to become a practising Christian was never discussed with us. She'd always believed in God and was one of the most moral people I'd ever met, but she had also had her Gypsy ways, like her 'clairvoyance' and superstitions, and often used her charm to get by. Now she became serious about following Christ. She seemed calmer and prayed more. She started reading the Bible and taking us to church on Sundays and Thursdays. We loved this as it was a chance to meet other Traveller kids even when we were staying at home. She also completely stopped fortune-telling, stating it was wrong to try and meddle with such dark forces.

There was another change in her though that I wasn't so keen on. Up until that point we'd been the best-dressed kids on any site with an ever-changing array of new designer clothes, giving us a taste of the very best. Mam loved to make sure we looked immaculate. Her main source of the clothes was a man who came to the door with a bagful, a definite 'ask no questions, get no lies' sort of offer.

Now, overnight, Mam decided it wasn't honest to buy such clothes.

'But Mam . . .' I said, thinking of all the beautiful designer numbers we'd had over the years. Like my purple all-in-one shirt and short set from Moschino that I almost lived in, or my Moschino handbag to die for, or my Dolce & Gabbana jeans or D&G T-shirts. Lots of the clothes were also from Boutique and other niche British brands, all highly cool in the early 1990s. The thought of going without a constant new supply of these designer labels was a terrible one.

'Where we gonna get our nice clothes now?' I complained.

'BHS and C&A like everyone else,' Mam replied.

'Aw, what?' I cried. 'Mam, you're having a joke! We don't want our clothes from there.'

As kids we'd lived like catwalk queens, carefully choosing our designer labels and looking resplendent in our outfits. To be condemned to shopping at BH 'Bloomin' S was not something we aspired to. But Mam stood firm. Living a good and honest Christian life meant turning down people who turned up at the door with bags of clothes and a wink. She was no longer prepared to turn a blind eye about where they came from.

Dad most definitely didn't view this in the same light as

Mam did. Every night he rowed with her, although at the time much of this was hidden from us, as protecting us kids always came first. He started chucking her Bibles in the bin, telling her to stop reading all that nonsense, even though we'd been brought up to respect Bibles as a holy book. One night he grabbed a copy and held a lighter against it, telling Mam it was just nonsense. He watched as it hissed and crackled in to flames, while Mam sat on the sofa in tears, praying silently for God to forgive him.

Us kids could barely recognise this man our father had become. He'd gone from being our quiet, sober dad to an angry patriarch who rowed constantly and went off to the pub to drink whenever he could. He was already a big smoker, puffing on around sixty a day. He just seemed so unhappy. His wife's newfound religion threatened him and his way of life. He couldn't envisage a life of church and God and Bible reading. He wanted Violet Hall, the woman he married, back.

With all this going on, of course it affected us children. Although the worst of the rows stayed behind closed doors when we were out playing, we knew something wasn't right and could see our parents had changed. I became convinced there must be something in God and religion if Mam had found such a dramatically different course. So I started to take more of an interest in church myself. Six months later Mam took us to another convention.

'Please can I come to the front with you and pray?' I asked Mam.

'Of course you can, love,' she said.

'But what about me dad?' I asked her.

'We'll deal with him later,' she smiled.

Listening to how Jesus could be my friend and accept me for who I was sounded very appealing. It was like a lightbulb going off in my head. It's hard to explain to non-believers what being touched by the Holy Spirit is like, but for what it's worth that's what I believe happened to me that day.

Back home, nobody told my dad about my conversion. The realisation just slowly dawned on him. Thankfully it didn't seem to make him more angry; instead he just avoided the issue, ignoring it. I think as time went on he was becoming more resigned. Also he learned things about the Light and Life movement that softened his stance. It wasn't a cult, it was a Travellers' church run by Travellers and for Travellers. That meant all groups including us Romanies. The leaders also didn't get paid for their time; they gave it voluntarily. No one was making pots of money or ripping people off.

Granny Suzanna was the next to join, then Maria did. We were all happy to go along to the conventions, which were just like fairs. Tom, naturally, couldn't have cared less.

Like Mam, I felt a lot calmer and I found it curbed the excesses of my temper. Although strangely around this time I took up an act of rebellion too, and started smoking. My friend Jolene had already become addicted to the terrible weed, and offered me a Benson & Hedges.

As I hesitantly lit it up, Jolene watched on, smiling.

159

'Right, now you inhale, deep in to your lungs . . .'

I felt myself go slightly green then started coughing and choking like an old woman. But with Jolene looking intently I took another drag, and blew the smoke in to a neat thick stream above my head. I was smoking. This was nothing but cool.

Within weeks I was smoking more and more, sneaking off with Jolene whenever we could, after my school lessons with Mam finished for the day. I loved snapping open the lighter and taking that first drag. It didn't take long to get hooked.

Before long I was a twelve-year-old with a forty-a-day habit, earning me a new nickname among my friends: 'Benson'. Mam would've killed me if she'd found out as she'd quit the habit when she'd found God, but as Dad was still puffing three packets a day, she didn't notice the smell on me. It lasted until I was fourteen, where luckily I realised what I was doing and gave up.

After a few more months Dad softened slightly towards the religious conversion of our family. He even attended a Christmas Extravaganza show we put on in church as he was never one to miss anything his kids took part in. But he was still adamant he wasn't signing up for the Christian life.

Then a year after my mum first attended the convention my dad said he would come with us again the following July. A few months earlier my poor Granny Suzanna had had another stroke and she was going to come with us. But Mam had other ideas about Dad's attendance.

'Me mam thinks very highly of you, Tom,' she told Dad. 'If she sees us rowing like we have been it'll really upset her.'

Dad shook his head. 'There'll be no rowing,' he said. And he was right. Over the months, Dad had rebelled against us finding God, but he could see his family were still the same loving people as before. He just saw how much calmer we were and in some respects happier since we'd been 'saved'. Gradually the rowing stopped.

Dad went along to that convention and strangely, a year to the day after Mam was saved, he got saved too. To this day I am not sure what changed his mind, aside from God. I think he saw his family opened to the Lord and decided to let him in as well. And he's not looked back since.

Although I felt calmer after finding God, I still didn't feel entirely happy with myself. The way I looked still bothered me and as a reaction to that I started wearing even frumpier clothes. Mam would joke that I dressed like a forty-year-old. If anyone spoke to me I held my hand in front of my face.

I decided to say a prayer, to ask the Lord to help me feel better about myself.

As I lay on my bed, eyes squeezed closed, I somehow instinctively knew what His reply would be. It was like a silent conversation between us. He said He'd made the world perfect and as He'd intended it to be. And He'd also made me. So therefore I was perfect in his sight.

Almost immediately I started to feel better. Of course I had my moments over the next few weeks, but it was like a veil had been lifted. I started to feel more confident about who I was.

Shortly afterwards a lad said rudely to me: 'Blimey, you've got a big nose on you, haven't you, Violet?' And in a blink of an eye I shot back: 'Yeah and you're not Brad Pitt, sunshine, are ya?'

I didn't know where that came from, but he recoiled straight away.

I was baptised aged thirteen. It was such a big day for me. I couldn't wait. I'd carefully chosen my outfit, an ensemble of white cycle shorts, cut-off Joe Bloggs jeans, a white polo neck and long-sleeved chiffon top with pearls down the front. I thought I looked the bees' knees. In the trailer, I started getting dressed. Maria was playing outside and chose that exact moment to start coming in and out of the trailer, giggling with her friends.

'Hey, our Maria,' I said. 'Will you stop that?'

We weren't allowed to see each other naked, so every time the door went I had to dive for a sheet or towel to cover up. It was making getting dressed difficult and time-consuming.

Maria laughed at me. 'Stop being so moody,' she yelled and, laughing, ran back outside.

Then, screaming as someone chased her, she pushed the

door back open and flitted in and out a few more times, forcing me to dive for cover again.

'Maria!' I shouted. 'WILL YOU STOP?!'

I never shouted at the Babby, but boy was she testing my temper that day.

Maria stuck out her tongue. 'Just playing,' she yelled.

All went quiet and then within seconds, the door banged again and Maria's giggling face appeared around it, screaming with laughter. This time, I had one arm in my top, the other out, and a rage took over me. I pulled on my top, leaping out of the door. Grabbing Maria's arm, I drew back my hand, opened my palm flat and with full force sent a slap neatly across her face.

I'll never forget her expression as she withdrew backwards, clutching her face in disbelief. We stared at each other in silence, eyeball to eyeball. Seconds must have elapsed but it felt like minutes. Like a neon tickertape, words ran across my eyes: 'YOUHAVESLAPPEDTHEBABBYMAMISGUNNA KILLYOUNOW.'

'I'm gonna tell me mam you've hit me,' Maria said calmly, before sucking in the deepest breath, like a newborn about to cry for the first time. Then with an almighty wail, she set off to find her.

'Shit, I'm dead,' I thought. 'I've hit the Babby.'

Mam came running across to the trailer, took one look at me, and knew Maria must've really pushed the boat this time.

'Just make up and be friends,' she said, giving me her eye. After a quick hug, I did my hair, and off we went to get my head wet. Clearly I still had a few things to learn about love and forgiveness before I could call myself a true Christian . . .

Chapter Fifteen

Miracles and Discrimination

Now I had been baptised my view of the world changed and I began looking out for the power of prayer and miracles in everyday life.

When I was thirteen, I witnessed one of the biggest miracles when I saw how praying helped my cousin Billy's little girl, Lala-Marie, survive a terminal illness. Lala-Marie was born in 1990 and from the start was the most beautiful little girl you could imagine. With light blonde hair, huge blue eyes, big chubby cheeks and squeezable limbs, she looked every inch a walking, talking angel.

When she was eighteen months old, her mum Joy noticed she started to cry a lot and sit down when she was trying to walk.

She took her to the doctors who dismissed Joy as an over-anxious mother, sending her home. But as the weeks wore on poor Lala-Marie's cries grew louder. So my Auntie Winnie (Lala-Marie's granny) went with Joy to the hospital. Again the doctors took one look at the babby and told them both to stop worrying unnecessarily.

'It's just a spot of constipation,' said the doctor.

At this Winnie snapped. 'I am not leaving these premises until my granddaughter has had a thorough investigation. I shall sit in the middle of the floor and start screaming myself just like she does until you do this!'

Seeing Auntie Winnie's set jaw and fixed gaze, no doctor dare argue. Lala-Marie was whisked off for an MRI scan and X-rays that very day. The results were shocking.

The poor babby had nine tumours all over her body, including her spine and stomach. The doctors apologetically told my family she was unlikely to survive and there was little they could do except try chemotherapy. Two weeks later another scan revealed she now had eleven tumours and when she was scanned again it was thirteen. The news just got worse and worse.

Of course everyone immediately gathered to be close to the family, constantly saying prayers, asking the Lord for some miracle. But none seemed on the horizon. It wasn't looking good and no one knew what to do.

Lala-Marie was taken to theatre for an operation. Beforehand we were warned the tumours were so numerous there was little they could do and her chances of life were minimal. It was absolutely terrible, almost overwhelming. We all rallied together, feeling utterly helpless.

'We just have to keep praying,' said Mam, tears streaming down her face. We all did, constantly. Auntie Winnie even asked God to give her cancer instead of Lala-Marie.

After the operation Lala wasn't expected to survive the night, but after round-the-clock praying she did. Then she wasn't expected to last a week and again she did.

Her father Billy begged the doctors to allow him to take the little girl home and eventually she was released. With a tube in her face and one in her stomach for feeding, she needed lots of care. But of course no one minded, it was just important she was home. She was well cared for and, with more prayers every day, the little girl kept making progress. Aged two she had another scan. To the doctors' and everyone's amazement Lala-Marie was completely cancer-free. It truly was a miracle.

However, the prognosis still wasn't good. It was thought that the cancer would reoccur, and she wasn't expected to live to five years old. But again she did. Her parents nagged and pleaded social services until they gave her a little specialised bike to get around on and she grew in to the most sunny, outgoing little girl.

A few years later, Lala-Marie was taken to live with her other granny, who was a Gorja, so we lost touch. Despite a very difficult start, she has led a full life, rock climbing and all sorts. On Facebook last week I saw her wedding pictures. She's still in a wheelchair but nothing stops her. It's wonderful to see.

My first miracle was something a little closer to home, but I am convinced it still was one. After being spoiled rotten with our designer outfits when we were growing up, I'd definitely developed a taste for flash clothes. I'd recently spotted a pair of black Moschino trousers in some fashion magazine, instantly falling in love.

'Mam, can I get a pair?' I asked.

She went to the shops and looked for them, reporting back she could only find a pair for £400 and there was no way she was buying them at that price. I'd have to forget it.

'Aw, Mam!' I whined. 'I want them so badly.'

'Well go and pray for them then, our Violet.'

I pulled a face. Yeah right, like Jesus was going to grant me my wish for a pair of expensive trousers. But Mam explained if we pray for things we often got given them. So perhaps it was worth a try.

Not really believing anything would happen, every day I prayed as hard as I could for those trousers. I went off to read my Bible and happened to come across the passage that reminds us that lilies are clothed better than any humans, from Matthew 6 verse 28. So I carried on praying for weeks, just in case. Then one day I was looking in the classified pages of the *Telegraph and Argus* and came across an advert for a designer clothing store that had up to 75% off its sale items. Begging Mam, I got her to ring the number.

'It's two weeks' old, that paper,' she said, 'so there's probably nothing left.'

She came off the phone telling me a man had agreed to sell her a big bag of leftover stock for £40.

My mouth fell open at my mam's stupidity. 'What are the

chances my trousers are gonna be in a random bag of designer clothes? Aw, c'mon Mam!'

She laughed. 'I am sure we can use some of what is in there,' she said.

'Yeah, right,' I said sarcastically. 'I bet it'll be amazing, Mother.'

A few days later the man arrived, but I didn't even bother to come downstairs. What was the point?

'Are you coming down?' Mam shouted. 'Or shall I just give the lot to Maria . . .?'

In a flash I was downstairs, not keen on letting the Babby get her hands on whatever was in the bag.

Mam emptied out the contents. First of all out fell a pair of white D&G jeans, then an orange and brown Moschino skirt, then a Versace shirt, all plain with hidden buttons and massive sleeves . . . and then the most beautiful pair of Moschino trousers I'd ever seen, even better than the ones I'd seen in the magazine. They were black and carefully ripped in all the right places.

Tears sprung in to my eyes, as I grabbed them, squeezing them on. I had to breathe in a bit but no matter. 'Jesus was listening!' I shouted.

I wore them constantly for years. A policeman once asked me if I'd been in a fight with a lawnmower when I was wearing them, but I didn't care. He obviously had no taste whatsoever.

Now we were older and had more freedom to mix with people outside the camp, we started to notice what other Gorja people really thought of us, something that Mam and Dad had managed to shield us from to a certain extent when we were children.

Around the age of fourteen, me, Maria, Joanne and Sarah were all going to the cinema. Like everyone else we queued patiently, then asked politely for four tickets.

The man at the counter did a double-take, looked at us all in silence for a second, then shook his head.

'You're not coming in,' he snapped. 'We don't have Travellers in here.'

'You what?' I asked. 'You can't do that!'

'Yes I can,' he smirked. 'Just did.'

My face prickling with rising heat, I bit my tongue. Sometimes you know arguing will only make things worse. And as much as I wanted to let rip this was one of those occasions I had to let it go.

Another time we were all set for a day's bowling one Saturday. There was Joanne, Sarah, Maria, Tom and some other cousins in the group. We met up outside the Doncaster Dome, where there was loads to do like swimming and ice-skating too.

As I approached the counter, the woman started shaking her head before I even opened my mouth.

'You're not coming in,' she said.

'Why not?' I asked. Although I already knew the reason why. This time I felt incensed. Yes, there were ten of us, but we were all so excited. We might be Romanies but we're the same as all other young people, just wanting to have a giggle and a day out. We weren't there to cause trouble, fight or row. We just wanted to have some fun. And I wasn't letting a jobsworth ruin our big day out.

'Please,' I insisted, trying my best to smile. 'Can you please tell me why we're not being allowed in?'

'Because the bowling alley is too full,' she said.

I swallowed hard. 'Okaay,' I replied. 'Then ten for swimming please.'

If bowling was out, at least we could try something else.

'No, sorry,' she said. 'That's full too.'

'Right. How about ice-skating? Or are you gonna tell me that's full too?'

'Yes. It is.'

I couldn't believe my ears. 'You whaat?' I cried, peering through the window at the few skaters going round. 'It looks virtually empty to me!'

'Well it is full for you, as you're Gypsies and you're not welcome here. Please leave.'

Grumbling to ourselves we all walked away, the lads pulling faces and complaining loudly. Being treated in this manner stung us all. We knew we were viewed as social pariahs and in turn many Gorjas we encountered lived up to their reputations as incredibly judgmental people. As free as we felt as Gypsies, we were trapped by other people's prejudices.

Now we were older we seemed to pick up on discrimination everywhere. Even on a trip to the local supermarket, we'd notice security guards mooching round after us. Mam told us later that she'd always suffered with being followed about like this in supermarkets, even when we were little. We'd never spotted the guards as young kids as Mam had hidden it so well.

A few times me and Maria had a laugh at their expense though. As we picked up a basket at the entrance, sure as eggs are eggs, a blue-uniformed guard would start trailing us like a lost puppy, even if we asked him outright if everything was all right. This time, as he followed us aisle by aisle, I grabbed Maria's hand, and leaped behind the end of the next one, crouching down low next to some packets of cornflakes.

'Ssshhhhhh,' I whispered, holding my index finger to my lips.

Maria stifled a giggle as we waited a few seconds for the security guard's shiny shoes to appear. As they did we both leaped out.

'Boo!' we cried, right in front of him.

The poor man almost dropped his walkie-talkie in fright.

Maria and I roared with laughter, throwing our heads back. Giving the annoyed-looking security guard a wink, I picked up my basket and carried on shopping.

Although we'd finally escaped the misery of school days with all the bitchy comments thrown at us by other pupils, we still had to deal with other kids in the real world, who we soon learned could be just as cruel.

One stop-off point we regularly had on our travels was in the village of Keighley in Yorkshire. A picturesque place, we'd pull up our trailer on a piece of wasteland that hadn't been developed yet, on the edge of the town.

Just by walking down the street you can find out within a few minutes whether you are welcome or not and Keighley was a place where we most definitely were not. The teenagers were the most outspoken, shouting abuse and giving us the finger or other unpleasant gestures.

One day, I was buying 'Grandma Wild' biscuits, the best ginger biscuits from the bakers, when I found myself confronted by a group of lads who came out of nowhere. After the usual abuse, most of the boys got bored and wandered off, leaving me alone with just one of them.

'Dirty fucking Gypsies,' he snarled in my face. 'You think you're summat, doncha?'

It was broad daylight, I was in the middle of a typically English village green, but I could have been in a downtown back alley in the dark for how alone I felt at that moment. And if I thought his insults were bad, things were about to get a lot worse. Before I knew what he was doing he pulled something out of his pocket and the flash of silver told me he'd flicked open a knife. My guts were twisted in to such a knot now I could hardly dare breathe. But once again from somewhere I got the strength to keep my features straight and hold his gaze solidly.

'Fuck off back to where you come from, gypo,' he spat.

Noticing I wasn't deterred, he raised the knife higher, pressing it firmly in to my neck. Thoughts of him slashing me, puncturing my jugular and me bleeding to death flitted across my mind, before I pushed them away.

Breathing deeply through my nostrils I concentrated on his stare, until I could almost see my reflection in the dark pools of his irises.

'Go. On. Then,' I said, slowly and deliberately. 'If you think you're 'ard enough. Stab me.'

As my words hung in the air, I could see the bravado drain from his face. I'd done the unthinkable and I could see he didn't know how to deal with my fearlessness. In one movement he snapped the knife shut, shoved it in his pocket and turned and ran away. Finally allowing the tension out of my body, I slumped against the wall, holding my sore neck and realising he'd actually managed to give me a good nick. I pulled up the collar of my shirt so Mam and Dad wouldn't notice and ran home. I knew they'd hunt him down and beat him soundly if I told them, so to avoid trouble I kept it to myself.

Another time, Joanne, Sarah, Maria and myself were walking back from town when we noticed three lads following us. After looking back a few times, we realised the group had grown from three to ten people, so we started running back to the camp as fast as possible.

Panting and puffing, we arrived back red-faced, rushing in to our trailer and slamming the door shut. We listened by the door, as we heard the lads arriving on the site. These guys were certainly determined.

'Have you seen four lasses?' one of them asked my brother Tom.

I sighed with relief. At least Tom would cover for us. But to our shock he replied: 'Yes. What of it?'

'We want to see 'em. We have a fight to pick with them,' the leader replied.

Our hearts banged in our chests so loudly, we could barely breathe. What on earth was our Tom playing at?

He shouted in to the trailer. 'C'mon girls, out yous come. There's some lads here who want to fight yas.'

I mouthed 'Oh my God' to the other girls, as we slowly opened the door. Tom was gonna get us killed!

Standing tall and waving theatrically, Tom continued. 'Right, get your jewellery off. Now, the biggest girl will be stood against the biggest man. Them's the rules. This is to be a proper knuckle fight, so I will stand by and referee.'

The boys' jaws dropped, but they kept listening.

'I'll watch fair play,' he continued. 'Two big 'uns one on one, one at a time. If they start to beat yous no jumping in . . . I'm warning you, though, touch little 'uns, I get involved. And you don't want me doing that because I will kill yous.'

The lads started looking at each other, as Tom shot his eyes back and forth, trying to get us to pick our partners. Even I must admit, Tom did look like a madman, a force to be reckoned with.

The biggest lad eyed Tom suspiciously then held his hands up. 'OK mate,' he said. 'It's getting late, maybe another time.'

The others nodded. Their faces had changed from naked aggression to pure bafflement. Why this Gypsy lad was offering up a bunch of girls to fight they could never guess.

'Oh, shame,' said Tom. 'I would've watched fair play!'

And within seconds they'd disappeared. Yet again we'd learned to avoid a beating. Blagging was better than using your fists as nine times out of ten people chose to walk away.

Chapter Sixteen

Rebels with a Cause

Around this time I was desperate to rebel. But if you're brought up with such freedoms as I enjoyed, being able to roam out all day long with so few rules, then playing loud music or swearing didn't hold much appeal.

My way of rebelling was to stand out from the crowd in the way I dressed. Now I was old enough to resist Mam's daily hair curling, and I didn't miss having my head bashed with the brush to sit still one bit.

Obviously there were different rules for weddings and special occasions when I'd have to dig out some dress or other, but even then I always selected the plainest one I could find.

I wanted to have an identity, away from the girly dolly dresses and the head of ringlet curls. So I decided to wear shapeless sweaters and baggy Joe Bloggs jeans. I also finally got my hands on a pair of Doc Martens boots.

Mam was appalled.

'Violet,' she said, screwing up her nose in disgust. 'What are those men's builders' boots doing on your feet?'

'Don't you like them, Mam?' I laughed.

I knew it was hard for her. For so many years we'd been immaculately turned out, dressed to perfection in an array of carefully selected clothes. Now I could choose what I wore and it was the complete antithesis of what Mam would pick.

As a concession I saved up and bought a pair of DM boots with a floral pattern on them. 'Are they as bad, Mam?' I asked, waggling my feet in front of her.

She sighed. 'Yes, they are. But I suppose that's as good as I'm going to get.'

Around this time, it was my cousin John's wedding. It was a fancy do and Mam was worried about what I'd choose.

'Please don't be wearing those boots,' she begged.

In the end I went shopping and selected a black silk dress with a square neckline and a fitted waist. It was a real concession to the feminine look my mam longed for me to have.

The day before I flicked the iron on to give it a once-over, without realising that using a scorching iron on silk wasn't a good idea – until I saw the fabric frazzle like a crisp.

'Oh no!' I yelled.

Mam came rushing in. 'Oh, Violet,' she tutted.

Without much time to find a new outfit, Mam dived in to my wardrobe, pulling out jeans and jumpers. 'We must be able to find something,' she said, poking her head to the back of the wardrobe. After a few minutes of looking we stared at a heap of baggy dark-coloured fabric without a wedding-esque dress in sight.

Mam grabbed my hand. 'Right, we're going shopping . . .'

We spent the next few hours trawling through the shops in Leeds, Mam holding up dresses while I shook my head.

'Violet,' Mam said, her voice growing impatient. 'You're not going in jeans and boots. The. End.'

After about three hours, with Mam about to pull her hair (or mine) out, an outfit on a mannequin caught my eye. It was a trouser suit, with mustard-coloured stripes. It came complete with a big straw hat and matching scarf around it. The whole ensemble was £120, way beyond Mam's budget. But it was the most feminine outfit I'd shown any interest in all day.

Within two minutes I was carrying it out the shop. 'You'd better get lots of wear out of it, Violet,' Mam grumbled.

I couldn't have been happier with my trouser suit but my very feminine sister Maria wasn't impressed.

'Why's she got £120 spent on her, eh Mam? I've not had that spent on me,' she whined.

'Well, you already wear dresses, Babby,' Mam sighed. 'If I can get Violet in to anything vaguely decent then this is what I have to do.'

Just as I was growing up and gaining my sense of identity, my world came crashing down when I lost someone I really loved, my Granny Suzanna. She'd been ill for a while and ended up in hospital after a massive stroke. There she lay prostrate on the bed, a spaghetti junction of tubes the only thing keeping her this side of life. Mam warned me not to go after my cousins came away shocked at the sight of her. Our big strong, loud granny, who no one messed with, was losing the fight and it wasn't the image people wanted to remember her by. I decided to stay away, and never said goodbye to her. I just remembered her for how she was.

We have big weddings and so of course our funerals are just as huge. Everyone, however distantly related to you, drops everything and rushes to be with the bereaved family. It's caring for your own, that's the Gypsy way.

After any death the body is brought back to the trailer of the deceased, where family comes to watch over and sit with it constantly until the time of burial. It's an exhausting and emotional time but one where everyone gets to pay their last respects and people have a chance to grieve properly.

I was allowed to go and see Granny Suzanna after she was laid out. As is custom, her trailer was covered in white sheets, lent by friends and neighbours and stitched with purple ribbons, and the inside was filled with flowers. These would usually be something strong-scented like lilies mixed with whatever the deceased's favourite flower was. I cannot stand the smell of trumpet lilies now; it's a scent I associate with the smell of death.

Granny was laid out in a casket and looked asleep, her still jet-black hair all combed to perfection, her face covered in a light layer of make-up. I can understand how the body and spirit are separate entities, as when you have seen the death mask of someone you love, you can see that only an empty husk remains. Granny Suzanna's soul – what made her the person she was – had vanished. I kissed her cheek, and felt her cold, plasticky skin on my lips. The unnatural coolness and hardness of it gave me quite a shock. I knew she was gone, but this seemed so final.

Then we took part in another great Gypsy tradition. We set fire to the trailer of the deceased.

First of all Suzanna's surrogate daughter Dawn, who was still living there at the time, went in and took all her belongings and had a last look around. Then we rang the fire brigade to ask them where we could set fire to it safely. Granny Suzanna lived on a local authority site so we knew they wouldn't allow it there.

They advised us to use a patch of nearby wasteland, away from all houses. So we dragged the trailer to the site and stood around watching as one of the men took a billy-can of petrol and splashed the insides with it. Then someone else lit a match and lobbed it through the open door. Within seconds the fire took hold, the window – through which we'd always see her sitting with her beloved dogs either side – shattering in the extreme heat.

I stood side by side with Maria, Tom, Mam and Dad in silence as thick, acrid smoke curled in to the air.

'Goodbye Granny Suzanna,' I whispered, the smoke stinging my eyes and throat. 'We'll miss you.'

I am guessing that for many teenagers the years between fourteen and sixteen can be a tumultuous time, but honestly for me it was totally idyllic in terms of our lifestyle and the incredibly beautiful places we visited. We spent months travelling from convention to convention, from Scotland all the way down to Taunton, seeing all parts of the country and meeting many different people. Looking back I feel privileged to have had such an experience. We usually stayed in the most amazing beauty spots, living a simple life outdoors and meeting up with friends and family. I couldn't have felt safer or happier.

Beforehand we'd spent much of the time in our house, only seeing Granny Winnie or Suzanna and barely seeing my dad, who was always working. Now we were meeting so many more people, always in the fresh air. We mainly stayed with my dad's cousins Uncle Bernard and Auntie Kay and their kids Bernard, Thomas, John, Luke and Aleisha Kay, but the other cousins would come along at times.

This period of my life stands out because for the first time we felt we could let our hair down. For years us girls had carefully had our hair curled and our clothes immaculate, in case anyone had said anything. Now we could run around like savages, wearing old jeans and a jumper, not caring what we looked like. The boys were family and no one cared. It was liberating at an age when appearances usually mean everything – although still being a fashionista at heart I often found myself making the effort anyway.

We were always up to jokes and gags on each other. Once I went on a trip to Topshop with the boys when I dared them to try on a miniskirt themselves.

'Go on,' I grinned. 'Just do it!'

With typical bravado they all piled in to a changing room, and came out one by one, shaking their legs and booty like a bunch of girls.

'Oo, haven't I got the legs for it?' said Bernard in a particularly convincing high-pitched voice.

I creased up laughing, then in the corner of my eye spotted a group of Traveller girls pass by, raising their eyebrows at Bernard and the others. I've never seen a group of Traveller boys move so fast. I literally wept tears of laughter.

Although I was happy in our family unit, the outside world wasn't always as welcoming of course. Now as an adult I can, in some ways, appreciate why. Romany families are a loud bunch: we speak our minds and we have fun, and Gorja people don't always appreciate this.

One evening during a stop-off in Scotland we all went out en masse, six adults and ten kids, all laughing, joking, ribbing each other and being as noisy as we usually are. We decided to go to a pub restaurant. It wasn't especially posh, probably the equivalent of a Brewers Fayre or a Harvester.

Aunt Kay was dressed immaculately as usual in the long black mink coat she always wore. Whenever I saw her going out, I always silently vowed to look like her one day, so elegant and beautiful. As for us kids, we were always very well behaved on any meals out. My mam used to say: 'People expect Gypsy kids to misbehave so you have to be extra good.' So we were. All in all, we were a pretty unthreatening group by any standards.

As we sat down Dad asked if the bill could be split between the adults. The waitress gave him a blank look and disappeared. The restaurant was almost empty but we waited absolutely ages to be served. Finally the food came, at which point Mam cocked her head, listening to the song they were playing on the loud speakers. It was 'Gypsies, Tramps and Thieves' by Cher. Now, half an hour after we ordered the food, it apparently was still on a loop.

Mam made everyone hush up, as she pointed to the speaker.

'Is it just me or has that song been on since we got sat down?'

I nodded. 'Yeah Mam, you're right. It's been on non-stop.'

We all sat and listened. 'Cheeky beggars,' Dad said, laughing.

Ignoring the music, which played on a loop for the next hour and a half, we had a good laugh any road, ate our food and waited for the bills to come.

The waitress just bought one.

'Sorry,' said Dad. 'Could you split it please, like I asked at the start?'

The girl looked at him blankly then threw the bill back on the table.

'You'll just have to do it yourself,' she spat.

The men all looked at each other around the table, in silence, quickly weighing up the situation. Then one by one they stood up and walked over to the waitress. Suppressing his laughter, my dad said very loudly in the voice of a country simpleton:

'I's sorry, I canno' read nor write as I's a Gypsy. So would you be so kind as to do it for us men?'

Looking uncomfortable, the waitress took the bill and pulled out a calculator.

'I's loves your taste in music, though,' laughed my uncle.

They waited patiently for her to sort out a new bill. Then they carefully peeled off the exact notes and handed the pile of money to her neatly.

'And you would've got a tip if you'd been civilised!' Dad winked.

Around this time Dad was desperate to show us his roots. His family were originally from Arbroath, a small town between the ports of Montrose and Dundee, so we all piled in to the car as he set off to find it. These were of course the days before satnav, so we ended up driving backwards and forwards endlessly around country back lanes with Dad determined that his bored kids in the back would see and appreciate the little town his great-great-great-grandparents once lived in.

After several hours of looking, Dad pulled the car up alongside a man walking down the road.

'Excuse me, Sir,' Dad began.

The man stopped, looked at my dad and then, saying nothing, carried on walking.

Dad put his foot down and crept the car at walking speed alongside the man.

'Excuse me,' he said again. 'We're looking fer . . .'

Again the man stopped dead, turned his head slightly to look at Dad and then carried on.

My dad's always been a peaceful and quietly spoken man. But this time he pulled the car up again and in the deepest, brusquest Scottish accent I have ever heard, he shouted: 'Excuse me kind Sir, can yee tell oues whar Arbroath is, pleaase?'

This time the man's face broke in to a smile of recognition and without a moment's hesitation he started waving his hands, pointing in various directions and giving us a detailed explanation. I had thought the man was ignoring Dad because he was a Gypsy, not because he couldn't understand his soft English accent.

Dad gave us a whistlestop tour of this little town, complete with the ruins of its own stone abbey. But the thing that stuck in all our minds years later was the trip to the chippy. There on the menu sat the words 'Deep-fried Mars bar'. Us kids had never come across it before and we urghed and yucked at the idea.

'What?' said Dad, looking baffled. 'It's a delicacy up north.'

Chapter Seventeen

Boys, Boys, Boys

On our tour of Britain we stayed on each site for just a few weeks, before packing up, saying our goodbyes and moving on. Money was never talked about, but of course Mam and Dad had to constantly work during this time, however hard it was. Mam would sell a few bits of clothing where she could and Dad carried on selling scrap metal or doing repairs for people. We bought fresh food at farm shops. We didn't really need much money as everything was bought and cooked in bulk, with families sharing meals outdoors. It was a simple life, as close to living on the land as we'd get as modern Gypsies.

My love of clothes re-emerged with my new-found confidence. After falling in love with the film *Grease*, I decided during one mission in Taunton to attend the services in a 1950s outfit. I carefully chose a pair of black pedal-pusher trousers, a tight cardigan and matching top. I put my hair in a bun and to complete the 'look' I topped it off with a large pair of black specs with plain glass in.

A few people gave me funny looks when they saw them. 'Do you need them glasses, Violet?' my cousins asked, so I just shrugged and said: 'Not really, but who cares?'

Down in the Taunton mission one preacher was a huge American man named Arnold. His booming voice held everyone in a trance as he said the prayers at the end of the evening. He was warm, charismatic and really made the whole event fun. When Arnold spoke, everyone listened.

A couple of nights in to the mission, I was wandering around the tents in the darkness of the evening, with my fabulous new glasses balanced on my head, when I bumped in to a tent pole. The glasses were knocked off and as I searched the grass, the colour of ink in the half-light of the evening, I couldn't see them anywhere.

'Oh no!' I cried out. 'My glasses!'

Arnold happened to be walking past. 'Glasses? Young lady, did I hear you say you dropped your glasses?' he boomed in his unique transatlantic way.

'Yes!' I said, patting the grass, hoping they were somewhere close.

Before I could say another word, Arnold's drawling voice belted out across the field. 'EVERYONE, DO NOT MOVE! THIS YOUNG LADY HAS LOST HER GLASSES AND WITHOUT THEM SHE CANNOT SEE A THING! SHE IS BLIND. LET'S ALL HELP HER FIND THEM!'

Feeling my cheeks turn the colour of red wine, people started coming out of tents or stopping in their tracks and turning to see who needed help. Squatting down next to the canvas, I tried to hide, as Arnold started waving his hands in my direction.

'THIS WAY, GOOD PEOPLE, OVER HERE! EVERYONE FORM A CIRCLE AND LET'S COVER ALL GROUND. CAREFUL NOW, NO ONE SQUASH THE GLASSES!'

I wanted to curl up and die as for fifteen minutes a sizeable crowd gathered, all carefully brushing the grass with their fingers, looking intently for my cheap, fake glasses. Finally someone ended the torture and found them.

'Thank you,' I said, grabbing them and running off.

The next day a few of us, including a group of girls I wasn't too keen on, were all sat round chatting, so I decided to tell them the funny story about what had happened yesterday.

'Are those glasses not real then, Violet?' said one girl called Missy.

'No!' I laughed. 'Made out of plastic.'

'Yeah, right,' she said.

I took them off. 'Honest. Look!'

She picked them up and peered through them. Then she handed them to her friend, Casey.

Casey tried them on, then held them in her hand. With slow deliberation, she opened her fingers, dropped them at her feet, then moved her foot hard on top of them, grinding them in to powdered plastic bits.

'Whoopsy,' she said, staring at me. 'That was an accident, eh!'

Everyone stared at her in horror. It was such a deliberately cruel thing to do.

I felt my chest rise, my temper boiling inside. How dare that little cow do such a nasty thing? But more able these days to keep my temper, I thought twice. So I stood up and said very clearly: 'You really are a butterfingers, aren't you, Casey? Well God bless you, anyway.' Clearly my Bible lessons in turning the other cheek paid off.

After I'd realised I didn't have to look dowdy there was no stopping me on the clothing front and as far as I was concerned, fashion has no rules.

A lot of Gypsy girls are tiny things with ample busts, whereas I was blessed with big rugby legs. However, I did have a little waist. Determined to look good, I made the best of what I had, so with 100 sit-ups every night I earned myself a mini six-pack and biceps. Then I picked a pair of boot-cut skinny jeans from Topshop, size 26" regular, and a fushia pink crop top with beads around the neck and matching beads hanging down the middle. I thought I looked amazing. I lived in that outfit for months, along with two floor-length dresses from River Island. Everyone loved that shop in those days.

As I grew in confidence my clothes became more outrageous. Another favourite outfit was a pair of black cycling shorts worn with a skintight top and a long black crotcheted cardigan over the top. In the summer I had the oddest patchwork suntan.

Changing my hair colour was another big discovery. I went along to get a few highlights put in and when I saw the colour chart with the bright, bold colours at the bottom, my heart leaped.

'Wow!' I said, as my eye landed on the electric turquoise. 'I'll have that, please.'

The hairdresser looked at me oddly. 'You sure, love?'

'Yep!'

Coming home, people stopped and stared at me, some openly pointing and giggling.

'What's happened to your highlights, Violet?' asked Maria. 'They go that colour after you've been swimming?'

I didn't care. In fact it set me off on the path of rainbow-coloured hair, and over the years I had every variation. Right up until Maria's wedding. I was tempted again then, even at nineteen. I begged Mam to let me have one strip of blue, to be tucked behind my ear. It matched the colour of my dress perfectly. Mam's face went white. I got the eye stare so I knew she really meant no. In fact she didn't trust me to go back and get my hair done on my own on the big day, so she insisted on sitting next to me.

Tom, meanwhile, was much more interested in settling down and getting married young. It all happened very quickly. He was always in to riding out on his bike, playing computer games and generally being a bit of a lad, then within six months that all changed and he announced, aged seventeen, he was going to get wed.

The lucky girl in question was Marie, a Traveller girl he'd

known all his life and had been dating for six months. Poor Tom didn't even get a chance to break the news himself. He took Marie out in his car to propose, but on the way back he was pulled over by a policeman.

'What's your name, son?' asked the copper.

'Tom Cannon,' replied my brother.

'Oh, is your mam Violet Cannon?' he asked. This policeman actually often went to Mam's Bible study group and was one of the few officers who was sympathetic and friendly towards Gypsies.

'Yes, that's right,' said Tom.

The copper explained he knew Mam and, shining his torch in to the car, he spotted Marie's new rock on her finger. 'Whose is that?' asked the officer.

'It's mine,' beamed Marie. ''E just proposed.'

Before Tom even got home, the police officer rang my parents to congratulate them.

'I've just met your future daughter-in-law! Congrats!' he said.

'What you talking about?' said Mam.

Embarrassed he'd ended up spilling the beans, the copper made his excuses. 'Oh I am sorry,' he said. 'I thought you knew.'

As his parents they would have liked to have known first, but Tom was always quiet and shy. When he got home Mam gave him an earful. But he denied all knowledge and went to bed.

Although about to have a wife and start a family, Tom was still very much a young lad. Around this time he decided to experiment with a stereo system. Dad had already messed with it, taking off the plug to sell somewhere or patch something else up with, so Tom went upstairs to try and get it to work regardless.

We were all downstairs when a massive bang went off in the bedroom, shaking the light fittings and lampshade.

'What's going on?' yelled Mam, as we all piled upstairs. Wherever Tom was concerned there was always trouble and it was fun to watch sometimes.

Standing with his hair on end like he'd just blow-dried it upside-down, he looked half-stunned, a pair of live wires held in his sizzled hands.

'It wasn't me . . .' he said.

Tom's wedding was held a year to the day of Granny Suzanna's burial. Mam insisted he waited until mourning was over, as she had to wear black every day for a year after her death. This was a fairly strict code for the close relatives of the deceased. It's a formal tradition that began in the Victorian era, when Queen Victoria chose to only wear black after her husband Prince Albert died. It was probably around this period that it was adopted by Romanies too, and has continued to this day.

For a Gypsy wedding Tom's was rather small. His new wife Marie chose a lovely Roman Catholic village church in Dewsbury; she wore an elegant white dress and they had a reception in the pub. Around 200 people turned up to the ceremony, which by Gypsy standards was a small, personal affair. I sat in the front pews next to Mam and Dad, who were dabbing their eyes with both pride and sadness. Mam was openly devastated her babby boy was leaving the family home for good.

It's the man's role to buy the bride a trailer and Tom had saved up money from the horse Grandad Tom had given him when he was born. As soon as they wed they'd be living in their new £4,000 trailer.

As Tom's bride-to-be Marie walked in to the church she was quaking with nerves, bless her. Standing at 5'8" she was taller than most Gypsy women and she looked very young, as young as me and Maria, even though she was also seventeen.

Despite her obvious nervousness, her smile broadened as she walked towards my beaming, suited-and-booted brother, and her happiness and joy at getting married was plain to see.

Her family liked Tom too. They thought he was a solid, practical, down-to-earth young man. A good choice for their daughter.

Afterwards we had a meal, but no speeches, in keeping with Gypsy tradition. Mam gave Tom a set of Minton china, some bits of Crown Derby and other furnishings for their trailer. Maria and I saved up and bought Tom a set of Crown Derby cat figurines. I could barely believe my brother, who still loved playing stupid pranks on me, was going to make someone a husband. Although I had no doubt he'd make a good one.

It's customary for a newly married Gypsy couple to be left completely alone for the first few months of their marriage. Aside from a quick ten-minute 'how are you getting on?' visit, Mam and Dad left them be. As we don't live together beforehand, often those few first months can be fiery as new couples adapt to each other's habits and learn to live with each other. In any case, Mam and Dad had already known Marie all her life, as she'd met Tom as a six-year-old when she lived on the same local authority site as Granny Suzanna, so it wasn't like they were getting to know a stranger.

She'd also gone to Tyersal Primary School and Mam remembered teasing Tom once as he walked alongside her to school with another friend on his other side.

'Which one's gonna be your bride then, eh, our Tom?' she'd ribbed.

Seething with embarrassment, Tom shook his head and pulled a face. 'Neither!' he cried. How little did they know!

Obviously it varies from family to family but I wasn't allowed a boyfriend until I was sixteen. There is this idea that Gypsy women are oppressed but I don't see it like that. Anyone spending five minutes in the company of my mother or any of my strong, loving, no-nonsense aunties would know that to be untrue.

Coming to the question of the s-word (sex), again I feel very uncomfortable even mentioning it, same as with bodily functions. We never talk about it, as before marriage it is unthinkable. The consequences of it are so severe, it's not worth even considering. All girls have to keep themselves 'pure' until their wedding night, which in most cases is aged around seventeen or eighteen. We weren't allowed to attend biology lessons about the birds and the bees at school, and even as kids we never talked about it amongst ourselves for fear of being seen as 'dirty'. So women would not know anything until just before their wedding when a sister or cousin or auntie would take them aside and maybe give them some basics. It took my baby sister to say a few words to me before my wedding day at the age of twenty-two, as she had got married before me.

'Violet, do you want babies straight away after you get wed?' she said simply.

'Er no, our Maria.'

'We best get you to the doctors straight away then,' she said. And that was that. I don't even feel comfortable talking about monthlies or anything like that. All I was told was that I was growing older then directed to a cupboard with 'things to use'. Girls were not allowed to ride horses, in case it broke the skin below. Nobody ever discussed such matters, even when we were in a group of teenage girls. No one wanted to be seen as the 'dirty one' who brought such matters in to the open. It's just not how we were brought up.

For boys, things were seen a little differently. It's never spoken about but silently accepted that Gypsy men might look for 'it' elsewhere before they were married, but woe betide anyone who was caught. Boys were not seen as needing to wait as much as the girls.

For me, on the other hand, I was in no mad rush to get married. I didn't want to sit in a trailer as a seventeen-year-old bride wondering when my life was going to start, I felt like I had something to achieve first. This hasn't always been an easy decision. The pressure is always there or at least implied. I just chose to ignore it, I suppose.

So you're only allowed to kiss your boyfriend. I've spent hours kissing, and doing absolutely nothing else at all. But sometimes boys try to make you a 'grab'. This is when they 'force' themselves on you for a kiss, usually with a bit of play-fighting first. Alternatively a boy will say 'Do you give Freemans?' This is when the girl 'allows' herself to be kissed without so much as a tussle.

A grab is only ever done in jest – it's a bit of role playing that allows boys to kiss girls, even if the girls have pretended to fend them off first. I've seen girls who've been made grabs after pretending to fend the guy off while smoking a cigarette, and not a speck of ash has fallen off the tip during the whole so-called 'fight'. In many ways I think it's a silly performance.

If anyone tried to make me a grab I'd always reply: 'No, don't think so, sunshine.' I personally would have felt like I had lost some of my dignity or my reputation, which should be prized. For what it was worth, I knew my reputation was good. I had a good name, was from a decent Christian family and I'd never allowed myself to be a grab, however much a couple of boys tried.

My friend Jolene, the same girl who gave me my first puppy

dog, Tiny, was also responsible for introducing me to the world of boys. It was right back when we were twelve. She'd started going out with a boy at Appleby Fair and when I turned up with her to meet him, so did his friend, 'coincidentally'.

'Jolene,' I said, 'you are shameful! Who's 'e?'

This guy, brown-eyed and black-haired, went by the dubious name of Buzzby and obviously had designs on me. Within moments of meeting he started asking if we could 'go out' together. He kept asking and asking until eventually I just said, 'Yeah, OK.' Within a split second he had pushed his face on to mine in a clumsy attempt to kiss me.

'Oi!' I yelled. 'Watcha doing?!'

Backing off, he looked confused. 'But I thought we were going out,' he spluttered. My first big lesson about boys already learned.

After that incident, I really did wait until I was sixteen before I so much as looked at another boy again. This time his name was Tomboy and we met in camp in Doncaster. He was the camp's cool-looking dude, with lovely dark hair and a goatee. He certainly caught the eye of a few girls on the camp. I 'dated' him for three months, but it never progressed and felt a little childish.

After Tomboy, another lad called Jon-Paul chatted me up one day while we were in a gang. Like always you only ever 'dated' in a big group and very rarely did you spend any time on your own with a lad. Sometimes if a girl dumped a boy he could be vindictive and spread a rumour she'd slept with him.

Then it would be up to the girl's family to prove otherwise and defend her honour.

I know about five girls who were whisked to the local GP to be examined down below to see if their virginity remained 'intact'. Once the family had got a piece of paper from the doctor to prove this they'd show it to the boy's family. Then the eldest boy, be it a cousin or brother, would be set up to 'fight' the dishonour brought on his sister's head in a bare-knuckle scrap.

Anyway, this lad, Jon-Paul had only been chatting to me for twenty minutes when he suddenly looked very seriously in to my eyes.

'I love you,' he said, trying to hold my hand. I did a double-take. 'You what?' I asked. He kept staring in to my eyes, in a way he probably thought was mysterious or intense. Instead he just looked like a bit of a psycho.

'Well, thanks for that,' I replied. 'See you around.'

When a girl turns a lad's proposal down it's seen as a right knock-back. After that we never really spoke again and just avoided each other.

Another lad, Felix, aged seventeen, who I'd only met briefly at a fair once asked me to marry him. Chatting to him for a while he suddenly blurted out: 'You'd make someone a lovely wife, wouldn't you? Would you marry me? Sure you wouldn't?'

I was totally taken aback and instead of feeling even the least bit flattered or romantic, it just freaked me out. It struck me that so many boys just wanted to get married, come what may, and they were looking at me as a 'wife' not as Violet, a person. It made me even more determined not to make a mistake when it came to finding the right lad for me.

Being a gay Gypsy man is a big difficulty. In many ways our Gypsy life is a few decades behind the rest of society, so it's rather like a 1950s culture in which homosexual men lead clandestine lives. One lad I knew from a young age, called Ryan, was obviously gay even as a little boy, even if we didn't understand what was different about him at the time. I never viewed him as a boy; he was so effeminate and loved playing with girls, seeming more on our wavelength. In his teens he followed convention though and married another girl and they went on to have five kids. But twice Ryan tried to kill himself.

People always say: 'Gosh, whatever drove him to attempt suicide, he's a lovely man.' It's never been spoken about but to me it's obvious. He's a gay man trying to live in a hetero-sexual marriage. It's heartbreaking to try and live a lie.

Another gay lad I knew was tolerated by his family as long as he kept his relationships secret. So he did for many years. Then he fell in love with another man and wanted to live with him so immediately he packed his stuff and left the site to be with him. He could never return. I've seen other men who I suspect are gay just stay single for the rest of their lives. How lonely is that?

If being a gay man is fraught with difficulties, being a Gypsy lesbian is a complete no-no. You'd be completely ostracised. Romany people just cannot understand why a woman and a woman would get it together. Again, you'd have to leave a site for good if that was your choice.

For Gypsies, your family and your culture always play a big part in any relationship. One time I met an American named Chris at a Travellers' convention. We kept in touch via letters and he became a regular pen pal. One day he rang me up and started asking me if I'd like to come to the States.

'Thanks for the invite, Chris,' I said. 'But I am afraid it's simply not gonna happen, is it?'

Not only could I not be seen visiting a boy on my own, it wouldn't feel right to meet his family and stay with them if we weren't engaged, and nothing could have been further from my mind.

'Well, maybe we could change the reason for your visit . . .' he began. 'Maybe we could make it a special reason for you to come over . . .'

My heart started thudding, but not with anticipation. Horror, more like. If this poor guy proposed to me on the phone, I thought I'd die of embarrassment, despite the distance between us.

'Whoops, I am really sorry Chris,' I stammered, 'but I can hear the beeps, my money's running out.' And I slammed the receiver down, breathing a sigh of relief at my close shave. Only then did I realise he'd called me and I was on the house phone.

The older boys in Gypsy families took it upon themselves to 'protect' the younger ones. Tom was always following me round, watching me, making sure I wasn't too 'close' to any particular boys. It was a way of saving my reputation, but also a legitimate way for an older brother to annoy his little sister in the name of 'family honour'.

Once I was out with a group of friends, walking down by a river, when one of the lads put his arm around my shoulder after we shared a joke. Tom spotted me from the other side and started yelling: 'Get ya hands off of her!' I felt myself curl up with embarrassment as the group scattered. The cheeky git only did it to wind me up.

Chapter Eighteen

Tricks of the Trade

Now I was sixteen I wanted to get a job so I asked Mam if that was OK. As long as it didn't interfere with church, wasn't too far away from home and wasn't anything illegal, then she said it was fine. So I went across the road to Tesco and got an application form to be a shelf stacker. When I arrived at the question about ethnicity, I left the box about my race blank. No way was I putting 'Gypsy'. In my mind it was asking for prejudice. After a good interview, I was offered my first job.

I got a uniform and was put in the magazines and lightbulb aisle. Having grown up earning bits and pieces with Dad and seeing my two hard-working parents earn a living, working a long day felt natural and good to me. Every Friday and Saturday, I worked eight-hour shifts. I was fast, efficient and always cheerful, so quickly I caught the boss's attention. Most of the young workers at Tesco were studying for good careers at college or university and I was the only one who had no such plans, so my line manager started suggesting I follow a career path at Tesco.

'You could be manager within a few years,' she said, brimming with enthusiasm. 'You've certainly got the brains for it.'

I laughed. I'd deliberately kept the fact I was a Gypsy hidden, but was quite open about my lack of career plans. After all, why did I need one when I'd be married one day with a child? That was the only plan I needed.

One of the lads I met at Tesco was called Philip. He worked alongside me in the warehouse sometimes. It was soon clear he'd taken a shine to me and inevitably he started asking questions.

'Why do you have trailers in your back yard?' he asked one day.

I shrugged. 'We just like caravanning,' I said.

Once I was singing 'Rotterdam' by the Beautiful South to myself as I heaved boxes up on to the shelves.

'I've got tickets to see the Beautiful South. Do you want to come?' Philip asked.

'No thanks,' I replied.

'Why not?' he said, looking puzzled. He was a good-looking lad, one of the ones the girls talked about. I could see he wasn't used to this reaction.

'Not allowed.'

This seemed strange to him. Most sixteen-year-old white British girls were starting to become very independent from their parents, and going to the odd concert would be no issue. For me, Dad would never let me out alone with a Gorja lad. In fact I wasn't allowed to socialise with any of my work colleagues but it was never an issue. I had my family and all my friends, so mixing with Gorja people just wasn't something I missed.

I also got on very well with Josh who worked on a parallel aisle to me. While I stocked up the magazines and lightbulbs, he did the washing powder. As a Jehovah's Witness, he also didn't go out drinking with the lads after work or mess around teasing the girls. Around this time, I toned down my Marilyn Monroe walk. I'd noticed men started to follow me round the store as I minced up and down the aisles and I didn't want the attention.

Although I got along well with everyone, I tried to keep my distance at the same time. One lunchtime, all the girls were laughing in the stuffy room upstairs that was used as a rest area, sharing crisps and talking about who had slept with who. I sat at the end of the table, nibbling on my cheese sandwich, avoiding all conversation. It wasn't something I ever talked about.

'Hey, Violet,' said one. 'Haven't you got anything to say?'

I shrugged, shook my head and fished around in my bag for a magazine to read.

'Hey!' said another. 'C'mon, I'm sure you've got some stories to tell. I mean it's not like you're a virgin or 'owt, is it?'

Swallowing the last of my sandwich, I brushed the crumbs off my lap and stood up. 'I've really got nothing to add,' I said firmly.

As the door swung closed behind me I caught the sounds

of an eruption of laughter. If they hadn't been gossiping about me before, I knew they'd be doing so now.

The following week, I noticed Josh had become even friendlier. Word must've reached him that I didn't join in the same as the other girls. He probably felt more comfortable around me. Philip started to ask even more questions afterwards, too. 'Are you Irish or something?' he said one day, as we passed boxes to each other.

I laughed. 'No, Philip, like I've told you a hundred times before: I'm from Bradford.'

One afternoon my cousins John and Coralina-Margaret appeared on my aisle to see when my shift finished.

'You coming for dinner tonight?' John asked.

'Yeah, I'll be getting off in a few hours, so see yous outside,' I said.

As soon as they disappeared, Philip popped his head up over the aisle. 'Where're they from?' he asked, nodding at the door.

'Eh?' I said. 'Oh, John's from St Helens in Merseyside.'

'No,' Philip insisted. 'Where are they *from* from? That accent isn't anything like Liverpudlian.'

I laughed. 'Oh, will you give up? He's from St Helens, I swear.'

The last thing I wanted to tell Philip was that my cousins spoke Romanese and their accents were picked up from all over. I was still very wary about letting anyone know about my background.

By the time I was seventeen all the boys knew which girls

were grabs and which ones were not. A few months after I'd ended my short relationship with Tomboy I bumped in to him when I was meeting a friend down a back lane.

'Hello Tomboy!' I said in a friendly way. It was nice to see him again, and we had a chat.

Then he started shuffling his feet and looking down. 'It were nice when we were going out, weren't it, Violet?' he said, looking at me from under his fringe.

'Yeah it were, Tomboy,' I replied politely.

'Shame we split up, eh?' he said, his gaze intent.

'Yeah, shame,' I nodded, again keeping things polite.

Tomboy looked up suddenly and smiled. 'You want to go out with me again then?' he said.

I shook my head. 'No, no, that's not what I meant, Tomboy.'

'Oh, well, in that case,' he continued, moving closer to me, 'let's have a proper kiss goodbye then, you know, just to finish things off nice.'

As he went to grab me I realised he thought I was a grab myself. He ended up accidentally knocking me over and, panicking about being a grab, I flung my arms out, scrabbling at the gravel for something to help as his puckered lips pressed down against my turned cheek. Flailing about for a moment, I blindly felt a rough corner of something and, realising it was a brick, seized hold of it. Then with all my strength I walloped him on the head with it.

He rolled around, clutching his scalp like an injured animal. 'Ow! Ow!' he groaned.

'Don't you ever try that again, yer hear me?' I yelled, scrambling to my feet and running home.

This was the second time I'd almost been made a grab and had fought back. The first incident had happened a year before.

We were staying in Dewsbury with various cousins and some Irish Travelling families. One of them was Marie, the girl who would one day become my sister-in-law. My cousin Joanne was babysitting that night and asked me to join them.

Although we got on, sometimes I think they thought of me as a bit snobby, as I never swore and only went to religious events, and maybe in their eyes they thought that I believed I was above them. But we still got on and I was happy to join them in the trailer when they asked me to hang out.

I was sitting on the bed when Joanne, and her cousin from the other side of the family joined us. They must have given each other a signal behind my back because the next thing I knew they'd grabbed both of my arms and pushed me backwards, pinning me down.

'Eh?' I shouted. 'What you doing?'

A boy, one of their pals, appeared at the door. 'Lemme kiss you then!' he grinned, throwing himself on top of me. Without hesitation I raised my knee and as hard as I could I kicked him in the groin.

'Aghh,' he yelped, and rolled on to his side. I leaped off the bed and eyed the other two. 'Nice try!' I said, victorious. I had spoiled their little plan to make me a grab.

As far as I was concerned, if you let a boy kiss you before he dated you, you'd never get a boyfriend.

My family was still the main focus of my life so when Mam decided to book another holiday I jumped at the chance of going. I was in my late teens now and it was to be my last big family holiday abroad. Leaving it to the last minute, Mam accidentally booked a Club 18-30 hotel, a place where young Gorjas have the time of their lives with booze and members of the opposite sex. Not exactly a good choice for a traditional Romany family, with or without your parents in tow!

Mam was appalled at what she saw over her balcony and forbade us to go out and look.

'There's girls here parading around with almost nothing at all on,' she gasped. 'It's disgusting.'

One of the holiday reps kept giving us weird looks as we went downstairs for breakfast. Eventually she came out with what she was thinking: 'Where yous from?' she asked.

'We're Gypsies,' I sighed. The questioning and stares do get to you after a while, even though they are inevitable.

'Aw, you can't say that,' said the rep. 'Can't call yourself Gypsies . . . that's not nice.'

'Eh? Why not?' I asked. 'That's what we are.'

'Yeah, but the word "Gypsy" is racist, isn't it?' she insisted. 'You shouldn't put yourself down like that.'

I just laughed. Sometimes it's best to quit while you're ahead.

In 1996, my first niece, Margaret Violet – or Marnie as she was known – was born to Tom and Marie. I was thrilled to bits. I adored her and looked after her whenever I could. Mam and Dad were beside themselves with happiness having a grandchild at last. The Cannon line was going to continue, although of course a boy would be needed to carry on the surname.

With me to help spoil her, the little girl didn't want for anything. I was very proud to buy her first designer dress, a pretty Moschino number, a few years later. No niece of mine was going to grow up without a wardrobe to die for.

Although I was older now, and didn't have a man myself, it didn't mean I was short of offers. A trainee preacher called Henry turned up in my life after I met him at a convention in Scotland. He was the youth leader so we would see him at all our sessions.

Henry was a bit of a catch and he knew it. For most Christian girls, bagging yourself a preacher man was like landing David Beckham. He wasn't bad-looking either. A good six feet tall, he was well built, with red hair and just about the right mix of arrogance and confidence to put your head in a spin.

Now I got on with Henry, but we didn't always see eye to eye. He had very set ideas about Christian doctrines and how I should modify my behaviour with regards to them. I'd stopped clubbing on a regular basis at this point, but he said I should publicly denounce it. I refused. It made me feel uncomfortable telling other people what to do. By now I knew what my life was about, but it didn't mean I should judge other people's choices.

Not being able to go pubbing or clubbing meant we were

always thinking up new ways for Christian Gypsy teenagers to have a laugh, so we arranged a string of social events. We had a full-on American-style prom, fancy-dress parties and then – shock horror – Henry decided to hire out a nightclub and make it a Christian night. That made me laugh, that did.

For the fancy-dress party I knew full well all the girls would get kitted out as princesses or fairies, so I had to come up with something totally different. I went to a sari shop in Bradford, bought myself a trouser suit and then covered my face in very dark foundation. Driving to the party, I stopped off for some petrol at a service station, ignoring the funny looks.

While waiting at the counter, someone started nattering away behind me in what sounded like Arabic. When I looked over my shoulder I was startled to see they were talking to me.

'Er, sorry,' I said. 'Can't understand you.'

When I arrived, predictably all the girls were huddled around in groups, looking fancy with their wings and tiaras, and I was pleased with my quirky choice of outfit. Walking past a few of them I nodded and said 'hello' but everyone just stared at me, said a quick 'hi' and turned back to their conversation. Blimey, I thought. What have I done?

I spent the first part of the night chatting to Henry, who was dressed as a punk rocker. But halfway through the evening I felt hot and uncomfortable in my black wig, so I nipped to the ladies' to whip it off.

I'd carefully pinned up my hair underneath the wig so when I took it off I'd have curls again. Shaking them out, I chuckled at myself in the mirror. I did look good even if I said so myself. Just a shame everyone else seemed so moody for some reason.

Back outside I went to get myself a Coke, when I heard Joanne shouting: 'Oh my God! Violet!' I spun around, wondering what disaster had happened, when Maria burst out laughing.

'It's YOU!'

It turned out no one had recognised me at all with my dark skin and wig on. We all fell about laughing. It was supposed to be fancy dress, not total disguise.

Henry and I began to develop quite an intense bond. It was a bizarre mix of our mutual love for our religion, and a jokey, almost competitive, friendship. At one of the social dos I wore an incredible, fitted, red silk dress and he'd nicknamed me Jessica Rabbit after that.

One evening he'd arranged an all-you-can-eat Chinese buffet, and I couldn't resist challenging him to an eating competition. He threw his head back and laughed. 'I could not only eat you under the table but I could eat you too, Jessica Rabbit.'

'Right, we're on then!'

I starved myself all day knowing I was up against it with a man his size. But when we started the competition I was determined to win, slowly eating each mouthful and avoiding things like bread and rice, which fill you up. Every time he patted his lips with his napkin and pushed back his chair to get more, I was hot on his heels, piling up the same amount spoonful by spoonful. We both made it up there and back about five times, before he sat back in his chair, threw down his napkin and puffed out his stomach.

'That's me done,' he said, looking slightly green around the gills. 'Couldn't do another mouthful.'

I felt almost sick to the stomach myself, but with one last push, I stood up, went to the buffet and came back with a single rib on my plate. Eating it so fast, to trick my stomach in to squeezing it in, I nibbled it like a demented rabbit and threw it on the plate.

'You're some woman, Jess,' he conceded. 'You win.' It was a silly thing to do but secretly I was pleased I'd gained some respect from him.

Forgetting once again about his hatred of all things night-club, Henry hired another one out in Edinburgh for a group trip. I asked Dad if I could go and his immediate reaction was: no way. He told us we knew we could never go away for the night, but when I explained that Henry and Jeremy, another church leader, would be attending, he relented and gave permission. After a day of sightseeing we set off for our teetotal night out. At one point Jeremy started giving me a lecture.

'I just wanted to say I don't think you should marry a Gypsy man,' he began. 'I mean, a woman with your talents would be wasted just living as a wife and mother . . .' On and on he went. I just stared at him with utter bafflement. What was this weirdo on about? Only afterwards did it dawn on me perhaps he wanted to ask me out himself and, as a non-Gypsy church leader, he wanted to put his hat in the ring.

Later on, Henry was in the back of the minibus and everyone else had gone in to the hotel, and I found myself sitting alone with him. Throwing an arm around my neck, he spun me towards him, reaching forward with his mouth.

'Hey! Henry!' I said, genuinely shocked. 'What do you think you're doing?'

He withdrew, holding me at arm's length. 'No harm, no harm, Violet. Just giving yous a little kiss.'

I could see he thought I was mental, turning him down. As a young preacher he was a right catch for a Christian girl. Looking back I don't know if it was arrogance on my part or perhaps I was put off by the arrogance on his, but somehow I knew I didn't want this man, however good he was and however much we got on.

All the while this went on, with men coming and going in and out of my life, I was praying to God to make sense of it all. I wanted to know when I'd met 'the one'. Was this too much to expect?

I stayed friends with Henry, but gave him a wide berth from then on, never allowing myself to be alone with him again. About four years later he married someone else. They were married about eighteen months when he died suddenly, aged twenty-nine. It was thrombosis, out of blue.

Around this time, I had a friend of a friend called Barry who had been dating a girl called Desiree. I knew Desiree was a very serious and committed Christian, but Barry wasn't. Whenever Desiree came down to visit him, suddenly he was all spruced up, at the front of the church, singing the loudest and praying the hardest. But as soon as Desiree went home, Barry would be back out with the lads, boozing in pubs, clubbing and generally acting in the least Christian-like manner you can imagine. After a few months of this, word got out he'd proposed and Desiree was beside herself with happiness. Barry was a good-looking lad with a head of tight black curls and a cheeky smile and, as far as Desiree was concerned, a Christian to boot. Watching it all unfurl I could see what was happening and what possible heartbreak lay around the corner for her, post-honeymoon. Desiree thought she'd caught herself a good Christian husband-to-be but the man she was about to marry was very different. His true colours would only show after he'd got the ring on her finger.

I wanted to say something, but it wasn't my place. Witnessing it all happening though was upsetting. After all, I'd been praying to God all this time that a Christian husband would turn up for me, so I feared I'd fall in to the same trap. It was so easy for a man to pretend to be a believer just for a few months until he'd got you up the aisle.

Desiree married and, lo and behold, within weeks of the

wedding, Barry stopped going to church. I never talked to her about it as we weren't that close. But I could only imagine what she must've thought.

Silently I vowed to carry on praying for a Christian husband but I also knew now not to hold out for one. I never wanted to be tricked like that. Desiree's experience served as a warning to me.

Chapter Nineteen

Outed

I'd been at Tesco for around a year when the line manager started insisting she wanted to promote me. First she wanted me to go on the till – which I refused as I didn't want to sit down all day in case I put on weight – then it was counting stock and then eventually she put me in the security section.

That evening I went home and proudly told Mam. The irony was not lost on either of us that they were putting a Gypsy in charge of damaged and stolen goods. Except of course they still didn't know my background.

I started my new job in the Returns department the next week, and Philip seemed to be missing me working in the warehouse as he still kept coming over to chat.

'So where did you say you were from again, originally?' he asked for the umpteenth time.

I put down my pen and looked him in the eye. I was fed up of this; I'd had months of it now. What harm could there possibly be to tell him?

'OK Philip, I'll tell you. I am a Gypsy, OK? A Gypsy.' Then I picked up my pen and carried on ticking the stock check.

Philip's uncomfortable silence spoke volumes and I tried to ignore it.

'Oh, right,' he said, eventually. 'OK, no worries.'

Philip's behaviour really got my back up, but I was quite thick-skinned by now when it came to jibes about my race. If I got really angry every time I'd have died of a heart attack by my mid-teens. So I would just let it wash over me, smile and move on. It's their own ignorance doing the talking, that's what I always told myself. Besides, Philip wasn't exactly a friend, just a work colleague.

Within a few days, the first complaint since I'd joined Tesco nearly eighteen months earlier came through. I wasn't working quickly enough doing a stock check. I'd never had a complaint before, but I took on board what my line manager said, nodded in all the right places and vowed to work even harder.

That day, Philip clocked on a bit later than me. As he walked past I heard him laugh.

'How's the thieving Gypsy today then, Violet?'

I knew he probably didn't mean any harm but it was an insult I could never find amusing when it was said by a Gorja.

'Leave off, Philip,' I said.

Later on my line manager informed me I wasn't wearing the correct uniform.

'Oh, but it's the same one I've had since I've been here,' I said.

'Yes,' she sighed. 'But you're missing your tights. All female staff have to wear tights.'

Apparently a new rule had come in, even though it was the middle of summer.

During this time, a friend of mine, Chanelle, who I'd known all my life, had been involved in a terrible car accident. It was a head-on crash, and folk said the engine of the car was found a quarter of a mile away. Dreadful, it was. She was found hunched underneath the front car seat, all smashed up and lucky to be alive.

She'd been in hospital a few months and then was let out, but she still felt so depressed. A beautiful girl, she couldn't come to terms with having a small scar on her forehead. Although very fortunate to walk away from the accident at all, all she could focus on was this little L-shaped scar. I promised to take her out clubbing one night, to take her mind off it.

I'd taken all my holiday at Tesco already, so I explained the situation and asked for paid compassionate leave.

'No problem,' said the manager. 'Hope you make your friend feel better.'

For the first time in months I saw Chanelle really laughing that evening as we got ourselves all dolled up to go out in a big gang in Wakefield. I didn't drink as usual, but we all danced the night away, having a proper giggle.

I saw one of the girls from Tesco as I waited at the bar in the club. 'Hiya!' I said, as she smiled politely at me.

Back at work the following week I was asked to see the manager.

'Is there a problem?' I asked, as she shuffled papers, refusing to meet my eye.

'You could say that,' she said. 'You're now not going to get paid for your day off last week as you asked for it off on compassionate leave but you were then seen partying in a nightclub.'

'Er, yeah?' I said. 'I told you I was going out to cheer my friend up who'd been in hospital.'

After twenty minutes of going back and forth over what compassionate leave meant and how nightclubbing didn't count, I was told I was subject to an internal disciplinary hearing panel and if I wasn't happy with the result I could ask for an external panel.

'Go on then,' I said, leaving the room. 'Hopefully the panel will listen to my point of view.'

I left the office, walking past the warehouse. There was a metal set of stairs leading up to the compactor and I had to run up there to dump some cardboard boxes, all the while trying to calm myself down.

As I walked up the steps, Philip turned up at the bottom.

'Hiya, thieving gypo,' he laughed.

'Not now, Philip,' I sighed. 'Really, really not in the mood.'

Ripping up the cardboard with my bare hands felt good. Great for anger therapy.

'Hey! Would you prefer to be called "filthy gypo" then instead?' he teased.

Chucking the last lot of cardboard in, I turned as he started walking up the steps I was on, jumping up and down slightly, making them bounce.

'"Thieving, dirty gypo" then!' he laughed, clearly thinking his own joke was hilarious.

This was too much. I stormed down the stairs. 'Seriously, leave me alone, or may the Lord strike you down himself on these here steps,' I snapped, and I brushed past him, stomping back to my security section.

As I walked off, I heard a clatter behind me. I turned back to see Philip in a heap at the bottom of the steps, clutching his ankle, his face twisted in pain.

'Oww, shit Violet, can you get someone?'

I couldn't believe it. I'd only said those words in jest and it'd really happened. It was just a case of bad timing but still!

A few weeks later, the disciplinary panel meeting took place. I felt really uncomfortable sat in front of these people, all making notes and looking me up and down good and properly. As calmly as I could I explained I wanted the day off to cheer my depressed friend up and I had always been honest about my intentions. Being seen in a nightclub didn't mean I was doing anything wrong.

I sat and watched as pens scribbled, eyebrows were raised and small sideways looks exchanged. I couldn't help but feel I was being judged now as a Gypsy rather than the hard-working Tesco employee who'd never set a foot wrong previously.

Afterwards they made a unanimous decision not to pay me.

I opened and closed my mouth in disbelief, struggling to find words. 'But . . . but . . .' The injustice was so unfair. Finally I found my words as they concluded the meeting. 'I want to take this higher,' I managed to blurt out. 'You said I could and I want to now.'

'Sorry,' said the manager. 'We're finishing this here and that is the end of the matter.'

I stared at her agog. Her treatment of me was unbelievable. It seemed that all my hard work counted for nothing and they'd already made their minds up.

'Yes,' I snapped. 'It really is the end of the matter. The end completely as I QUIT!'

The managers all started shaking their heads. Apparently I was contractually obliged to give two weeks' notice or I wouldn't get my performance-related pay.

'You can shove your "performance-related pay" sideways where the sun don't shine!' I said, before reaching for the door handle.

Tears smarting in my eyes, I stormed out of the room, desperate to get my uniform off before I left. News quickly spread I was leaving and Josh, Philip and the girls all ran upstairs to make sure I said goodbye after I'd got changed.

Then one of the girls gave me a hurriedly wrapped present. This made my eyes well up completely, I was so touched. I sat with tears dripping off my chin as I opened my present, all fingers and thumbs. It was a small cup from the homeware section. As I pulled it free, I started laughing. It was a strange present but I loved the sentiment behind it. I can imagine the girls dashing round the aisles trying to find a last-minute 'goodbye' present. In a Tesco food store this was hard to do.

'Thanks so much,' I said. 'I'm sorry I have to go.'

In the end Tesco did cough up the bonus and after saving diligently I found myself £2,000 richer. Instead of keeping it in a bank account or wasting it on make-up and clothes, Mam suggested I splash out on a diamond ring, something that would hold its value. With my Aunt Dawn, I went shopping and found the most beautiful baguette cluster diamond ring I'd ever laid eyes on. I bought it to keep in a box. It's my 'Every Little Helps' ring.

By the age of nineteen I still hadn't had a proper boyfriend. But it really didn't bother me. I was always busy with friends and luckily my family never put me under any pressure, so it wasn't an issue.

Although it wasn't a problem for me, I found out it was for other people. My friend Sabrina started questioning me about it on the way to Appleby Fair in 2000. For most of the year, Appleby-in-Westmorland is a sleepy town in Cumbria, but for one week every June it gets transformed in to one of the biggest Gypsy fairs in the country, with around 30,000 people attending every year. For generations it was a place for people to buy and sell horses, making money for the rest of the year, starting in 1685 with a charter from

James II. Nowadays it's more about catching up with old friends and having a laugh, though it's still the biggest fair on the Gypsy calendar.

As Sabrina and I walked from the field, down the hill to the town, she started grilling me about my love life.

'When you gonna get yerself a boyfriend then, Violet?' she said to me.

I shrugged. 'Dunno. Don't want one.'

'Well, you don't want people talking,' she continued, pulling at a piece of grass as she walked past.

I laughed. 'Well I'm not exactly a loveny,' I said. A loveny is another word for a tart or a slag.

'Tha's not the problem Violet, though,' she continued. 'Not that you don't want one, but you know, that you don't actually like boys.'

I turned to her as she carried on walking, ripping the piece of grass to bits with her fingers.

'You what?' I said, staring at her. 'Do you really think people will think that of me?'

She shrugged. 'Just sayin',' she said, twirling her hair.

So there and then I vowed to get myself a boyfriend. Although I pretended I didn't care what people thought, of course I did deep down. And I didn't have to wait long. This may or may not have been a coincidence, but Sabrina soon introduced me to her boyfriend's friend John.

This fair had been one of the muddiest ever. We spent four days squelching around, calf-deep in mud, chatting to family and friends and looking at horses. John went everywhere with me, and he was OK, friendly and nice-looking in his checked shirt and jeans, but again I didn't feel especially keen. I didn't know what I was looking for, but I knew it wasn't this. Perhaps he was just too soppy, or too keen, I don't know, but I kept him at arm's length. When we said goodbye, I didn't expect to see him again.

By the end of the fair, my parents tied their trailer back on to the car, but what with all the mud the wheels did nothing but spin, splattering anyone nearby. As I sat in the car, my heart sank as I looked in the wing mirror and spotted a familiar checked shirt coming up the road. It was John arriving to give a hand.

He quickly positioned himself behind my parents' car, giving it a shove, gallantly getting covered in mud and ingratiating himself as much as possible.

Now you never introduce boys to your parents unless it is serious, so I felt my cheeks burn as Dad started chatting to him.

'Oh sorry, son,' he said. 'You've got yerself smothered by helpin' us.'

John smiled like he couldn't have been happier, and offered his hand to shake. 'Hello, sir,' he said. 'I'm John. I met your daughter Violet this fair.'

I shrunk down in to my seat, cursing him under my breath. Cheeky beggar.

A few weeks later, John was hanging round my friends again

and we did end up going on a few 'dates'. But it was all very half-hearted, on my part at least.

One day I went off with Ely, a lad who ended up marrying my sister, and a few others, on our way to another fair where we had planned to meet John. On the way there, Ely starting teasing me about him.

''E likes you, you know,' he said.

'Yeah, I know,' I sighed.

'I mean 'e really, really does,' he went on.

I started to feel a bit sick. After just a few dates some boys were keen to propose and this is what Ely seemed to be hinting at.

'Are you working me?' I asked, catching his eye in the rear-view mirror.

'No! I swear!' he insisted. ''E really likes you, I promise. He might even have something to say when you meet again!'

That was all I needed to know. I grabbed my mobile and called John. I had no choice but to finish with him before he said 'owt. Once a lad tells you he loves you, it gets dead awkward. They expect you to say the same and marriage is the next logical step. John was a nice enough lad but he was a serious sort. I was always up for a laugh and a joke: we weren't a good pairing. I waited ages for him to answer, as our car sped towards the fair.

'John?' I said.

'Violet!' he answered, as if he were smiling. 'How lovely to hear from you.'

'Yeah, thanks John, you too. Look, I have something to tell yer . . .'

'Oh, what's that? Sorry Violet, bad reception. Let me call you back.'

Heart thumping, I put down the phone and waited for him to call.

'I am so looking forward . . .' he started. But I cut in. 'Listen, John. I'm sorry. I just have to say . . .'

But before I could finish, again the phone went crackly and he lost his signal.

Over the next half an hour he rang back four or five times, only able to hear a few words – words I was by now desperate for him to hear – before the phone went dead. It was excruciating.

Finally he called back and the line was as clear as if he were sat next to me.

'Right, John,' I said, the words tumbling out at speed. 'I want to finish it with you. I am sorry, but it's not happening between us.'

'Oh.' He sounded so disappointed. 'Why? What have I done? Is it cos I don't earn much money?'

'No, John, it's nothing to do with money or 'owt else, sorry.' And, exhausted by now, I said I had to go and hung up.

While I didn't really hear from John again, I wasn't so lucky with his sister. She ran in to me a few weeks later.

'Violet?' she screamed. 'Who do you think you are, breaking my brother's heart? What are you, a numberplate chaser? Not rich enough for yer, isn't 'e? You little cow! Think you're too good for 'im? He's a broken man now, devastated, will never be the same again – and all cos of you, you little jumped-up bitch . . .'

Three months later I heard John got married. Wasn't *that* devastated then, was he?

Funny how when you look back things seem to make more sense and you can even understand your own motivations for events that at the time you could not fathom. Without a doubt the next man, who broke my heart, led to me getting married later on in life to someone totally unsuitable . . .

But first up was Moses Whitely.

Chapter Twenty

First Loves

The first time I met Moses was through Ely, the boy who was to become my brother-in-law, while we were waiting for our shish kebabs to cook in a kebab shop. Watching the dripping hunk of lamb spinning round on the turnstile we both turned as a flash Land Cruiser car pulled up by the kerb outside.

'Oh, that's Moses,' said Ely, nodding to the car. 'You'll like him.'

I rolled my eyes. Everyone was always trying to set me up.

'Will I now,' I sighed. And my first impression of Moses wasn't good: he emerged from the driver seat blowing a whistle with rave music blaring out. As I stared at him through the window, he was jigging and twitching his body as if he'd stuck a wet hand in to a socket, and although I was fairly sure this wasn't the desired effect, it made me want to laugh.

But Ely was right in the way he was something to look at. He was tall at 6'2", with jet-black hair, a beard and olive skin. He was definitely a good-looking lad. And once he'd taken the stupid whistle out of his mouth and stopped trying to dance like Bez from the Happy Mondays, he looked even better. He came in to the shop and we got introduced and had a chat.

At Ely's brother Franklin's wedding, Moses appeared again. On the way back, a group of friends and I all piled in to a van to be taken home. Moses joined us. Tired out, I laid my head back and felt Moses twisting my hair gently.

Without saying a word, I closed my eyes and let him.

'Hey, Moses is messing with your hair,' said one girl. 'Tell 'im to stop.'

Watching Moses over the past day I'd realised a few other girls had their eye on him too. Standing tall over the crowd with his charming smile, he wasn't short of admirers. And I was finding myself one of them.

'No,' I said, smiling. 'I quite like him doing it.'

A few weeks later, at another convention, a girl called Rosie who I knew vaguely but didn't particularly like, came steaming up to me.

'You're Violet, aren't ya?' she demanded.

'Yes.'

'You do know Moses's after me, doncha?'

I shook my head.

'Well, lessee who can get him first, shall we?' she grinned, pushing past me.

And like a red rag to a bull, I immediately knew I had to make Moses mine. Three weeks later I was his girlfriend. Little did I know I'd just strapped myself in to the biggest emotional roller coaster ride of my life.

Moses drove in either a Land Cruiser or a Land Rover. He always seemed to have money but, as I soon realised, he also didn't really like spending it. I had no clue what he did for a living. He often disappeared for weeks to Germany and once, when I pushed him, he told me he sold pine cane furniture.

'Look,' he said, showing me some catalogues. It made no sense at all, but also seemed to pay very well.

To begin with, I wasn't sure if I even liked him. Once he picked me up on a boiling hot day and I reached to switch on the air conditioning in the car.

'Hey hey!' he said, shaking his head, just as my hand went near the 'on' switch.

'Do you know how much extra diesel is wasted when that's on?'

Later on I told my mam. 'Tha's why rich people are rich,' she said. 'They don't like letting their pennies go.'

Moses wasn't just precious about money. He was also very finickity about his car. To save the seats he'd had Egyptian cotton towels stitched together to make seat covers, and covered others in plastic to keep them 'best'. Every time I sat down on them, I felt like ripping them off his precious car.

So, being a bit mean myself, I was soon looking for a reason to finish with him. He lived with his grandparents and one day, when he picked me up in his car for a date, he took a call saying his grandad had been taken in to hospital.

'I am so sorry, Violet,' he said, looking as white as a sheet. 'I'll have to take you 'ome.' His grandad had had a heart attack and although he was going to pull through, Moses had to rush off to see him.

'No worries,' I said, half relieved. 'Hope your grandad is going to be OK.'

As if sensing I wasn't happy, Moses asked me if I was planning on finishing with him. 'Nooo,' I said. 'You're all right, just take me home.'

Back home, as he drove off, I immediately called his mobile.

'Sorry, Moses, we're finished,' I said. He protested he couldn't help cancelling our date, but it wasn't about that.

'By the way, tell Rosie I got you first,' I said.

Later on, when I went to visit some cousins on a nearby site they told me Moses had been telling everyone he'd never go near me again and he'd had to teach me how to kiss.

What a charmer! However, a few weeks later he apologised, and we got talking again. My mam and all my friends had kept on telling me how good Moses was for me, so gradually I relented. Despite his idiosyncrasies I had grown very fond of him and decided that perhaps our relationship was worth going for after all. We went on lots of dates together and although we never told our parents 'officially', everyone knew we were an item.

They say you should never sit at home waiting for things to come knocking, but in the case of another job, one did. Paul Johnson was a man who'd been given his job at the Bradford Travellers' Education service by my mam years earlier, before she left. One day I spotted him walking up our driveway, wearing a suit.

'Mam, what's Mr Johnson doing here?' I said, staring out the window.

'I dunno,' said Mam, drying her hands on a tea towel. 'Let's see.'

She welcomed him in, gave him a cup of steaming tea and we all sat at the table, wondering why he was turning up out of the blue after so many years.

'I have a job vacancy,' he explained. 'And I wanted to see if Violet was interested.'

Mam's eyebrows shot up.

'You do know Violet is a chip off the old block now, don't you Paul?'

He nodded. 'That's why we want her,' he said.

He explained they had a traineeship going and he'd love me to apply. Maria's ears pricked up: she'd been out of work and was looking for a job too.

After Paul had left we had a chat about it. 'Why don't you go for it too, Babby?' I suggested. 'You could do this job as well, y'know.'

Maria ummed and ahhed and eventually agreed. It might sound strange to persuade my sister to go for the same job, but sibling rivalry or in fact any rivalry in our family was simply not on our radar. We all wanted to 'get on', just as Mam and Dad had done in their early married lives, and if I didn't get the job I'd be just as thrilled if Maria did.

233

We both had our interviews on the same day. Maria wore a pair of jeans and a jumper, whereas I wore grey trousers with a purple high-necked top, made out of lilac denim and silk. I didn't know what you wore for an office, so just chose the smartest thing in my wardrobe.

I spent ages coaching Maria on what to say and how to answer the questions I'd guessed they'd ask.

'If they say what you could bring to the job, tell them you've been a Gypsy all your life and understand the culture. If they say what are your skills, say you can read and write, and that you're brilliant at listening and finding solutions to problems . . .'

She sat nodding on my bed, whilst applying another coat of nail varnish.

'Maria!' I snapped. 'You actually listening?'

Giving me her usual cheeky smile, she nodded again. 'Yes, how can I not, Violet?'

Afterwards Maria asked how it'd gone for me. 'Yeah good, I think,' I said. I wasn't sure about working for such an organisation but the team seemed to have their hearts in the right place and were interested in what I had to say.

'How did yours go?' I asked.

'OK,' she shrugged.

She seemed a bit nonplussed so I wondered how it'd really gone.

'How did you find the questions?' I asked.

'All right,' said Maria. 'What did you say though when they asked how you'd persuade a Gypsy kid to go to school?'

'I said I'd listen to what their problems were and try and work closely with the educational teams and teachers to get them back in the classroom if their mams weren't gonna teach them at home,' I said, thinking that was the best answer I could come up with at the time. 'What did you say?'

Maria shrugged again. 'I said I hated school too and wouldna blame any other Gypsy kid for not wanting to go.'

Funnily enough, Maria wasn't offered the job – but to my surprise I was.

After having left full-time education six years earlier, at the age of eighteen I started a placement as a teaching assistant and found myself enrolling in several college courses to study basic IT alongside it. I taught myself too, buying an old computer for £50.

So now, for the first time in six years, I found myself back in a classroom. This time not as a dirty gypo, but as an adult, to help teach Traveller kids and bring them a better life.

Just when things were all going well in both my love life and working life, we had some devastating news. Auntie Winnie had been diagnosed with cancer. Thinking back to the time she'd once prayed for her granddaughter Lala-Marie, telling God she'd rather have cancer than let her have it, she felt quite deeply it was meant to be.

Of course we didn't. The thought of my poor auntie suffering cut me to the core. Once, after she started what little treatment they decided was worthwhile, I went to visit her in her trailer.

Her tiny, delicate feet had blown up like two painful pink balloons after all the steroids she'd taken. But she stayed as cheerful as she could be. After one visit she asked me for one thing. 'Can you get me a pair of them lovely wedge heels you've got on?' she said, admiringly.

'Yes Auntie Winnie, of course,' I said, thrilled I could do something for her. Her feet may not have been as pretty as they once were, but she still took pleasure in trying to make herself look nice. Who could blame her?

This seemed to come round so quickly, but suddenly it was our Babby's turn to get married. Maria had fallen for Ely and, after a whirlwind year-long romance, they were getting hitched. The selfish side of me was devastated. We had our ups and downs like all sisters, but Maria meant everything to me and was my best friend as well as my sister. Not a morning had gone by without me waking up with her next to me. And we told each other everything.

I begged her to wait until she was eighteen, and to begin with she said she would, but then changed the date to September, a few months before her birthday. When a woman marries she doesn't see her family as much and never hangs out with single women, so I knew things would be changed irrevocably and I wanted to hang on to her for a little while longer. But Maria, being Maria, always did things her own way.

My mam and aunties were utterly thrilled. There's nothing

like a wedding to get the females of the family clucking around, sorting everything out. It's a pinnacle in any woman's life, her biggest day, and no expense or effort is spared. Bradford Cathedral was duly booked and Maria chose the Cedar Court Hotel for the reception.

Maria had chosen the most beautiful white dress I'd seen. Long-sleeved, high-necked and made out of lace, it was gathered at the waist and then flared out in to an enormous cathedral-length train. It was classically beautiful and for my classically beautiful baby sister it truly was the perfect dress. And she would have the full retinue to accompany her, too. Marie had trouble deciding which bridesmaids to pick so she had nine to join her down the aisle in the end.

As tradition dictates we had to go for a hen do so I organised a night out at Batley Variety Club, a place where many Travellers go. It was a great evening.

When the big day arrived, there wasn't a dry eye in our house. The Babby truly looked like a princess and, as she twirled in Mam and Dad's trailer, we all passed tissues to each other.

In the car on the way up there, Dad was almost as nervous as Maria.

'If you've changed your mind,' he whispered to her, 'you can just simply say so and we'll go home and there'll be no fuss.'

Maria smiled. 'I love Ely,' she said.

Dad had had 'the Chat' with Ely, when he'd asked for Maria's hand. He took him for a walk, shook his hand and said in no uncertain terms: 'I wish you luck, but I will break your legs if Marla ever comes home with so much as the tiniest bruise on her body.'

After the service, we all piled in to the reception, ready for the drinking and socialising to begin. Moses came along, of course, and started nodding and winking at me in his unsubtle way, hinting that we should be next down the aisle. He even started singing the Frank Sinatra song: 'If you turn me down once more I'll join the French Foreign Legion.' As the words started to grate, I returned the melody with my own. 'I try to say goodbye,' I sang, the song by Macy Gray.

As people waited in the reception for the start of the wedding, Moses turned up, beaming, clutching a bottle of champagne.

'Fancy a glass, babe?' he said, knowing full well I didn't drink.

'It's not time for the toast yet, Moses, what you bought that fer?'

'Just cos,' he said, a glint in his eye. 'Go on, have a glass.'

'No, Moses,' I said. 'You bought it, you drink it.' And I turned round to chat to my friend.

Later on, after a few more drinks, Moses took my hand and led me to the garden. Wobbling, he went down on one knee, his face shining as he swayed slightly.

'Violet,' he said, a semi-belch slipping out. 'Will you plee-ase marry me?'

I looked at him and despite the fact I knew he was a clown

in many ways, his heart really was in the right place. And if I was being honest in spite of this, that and everything else, I did love him.

So instead of saying no I found something else coming out of my mouth.

'Where's the ring?' I said, looking at his empty hand. 'Come back with a ring and we'll see.'

Ten minutes later Moses disappeared, saying he had to get something. He came back four hours later, having changed his clothes but with no sign of a ring. A mixture of relief and disappointment washed over me.

With Maria married, it was time for the dances. Not only does the bride have a first dance with her husband, she also dances with other family members or friends as a 'last dance'. For the two of us, Maria had picked Shania Twain's 'Man, I Feel Like a Woman'. Neither of us said anything, as we clung to each other, giggling and crying. It was a bittersweet moment, knowing our sisterly love would always be there, but that it would never be quite the same again.

One strange thing happened at Maria's wedding, which led to one of the scariest events of my life. While I was dancing with the family in the big reception hall a young boy, aged around seventeen, came falling out of the toilet having been 'two-ed'. This is when two men set upon another and it is seen as a really cowardly way of fighting someone.

For some reason, my dad was accused of being one of the

men who'd been involved. Aside from the fact my dad would never lay a finger on a young lad like that, he'd been dancing with the family anyway, so he plainly told them they had got it wrong.

'Listen, lads,' he said, gently but loudly, 'it wasn't me.'

A few days later, the male members of the boy's family turned up outside our yard shouting for my dad. He came out and repeated it wasn't him, but this didn't seem enough for the seventeen-year-old involved.

He went on and on, blaming my poor dad. And after a few minutes of listening to him screaming, my own temper snapped.

'Right!' I yelled. 'If you think you're hard enough, come an' fight me then, eh? Go on! I'm more your age, stop picking on me dad!'

Instantly, Dad appeared at the door, dragging me by the elbow. 'Leave it,' he hissed. 'You'll just get yerself in to bother. Now go inside.'

Reluctantly I did, my blood boiling. The look on the lad's face as he stalked off told me it wasn't the last I'd see of him.

Meanwhile, Maria might have then been a married woman but I was worried for her in many ways. She'd been so cosseted and spoiled I wondered how she'd manage as a wife. Sure enough, a few days after she wed she rang me from Tesco.

'What's up, Babby?' I asked.

'I'd like to make a stew. You know, what like you make me. Now how do I do it?'

And so, step by step, I had to tell her how many carrots to buy, how many potatoes and what type of meat was needed. Then when she got home she asked me to dictate how to cook it and all. Just like my mam had had her big sister Anne to help her after she'd got wed, Maria had me.

Mind you, nothing could have been as bad as when my friend Mercedes got hitched. She was only seventeen and had absolutely no clue how to make proper dinners as her mam loved cooking and did it all for everyone.

She rang me in a panic one day.

'The boiled potatoes I put on,' she cried, 'they've got smoke coming out of them!'

'Smoke?' I said. 'What on earth did you do?'

'I just put them in the pan and switched it on,' she said.

'Blimey, Mercedes,' I said. 'Have you let the water boil dry or summat?'

'Eh?' she replied. 'Do you need to add water to boiled potatoes?'

I started laughing. I couldn't believe she didn't even know that.

While my personal life was a bit of a roller coaster, my traineeship was opening my eyes ever more to the needs of our ethnic group and how we are treated.

At first I was worried about being seen as the thick one on my college courses. After all, most of my formal education, aside from the stint in secondary school, had ended when I was nine years old. I didn't know if I'd be able to keep up with all the reading and writing. I always felt paranoid about my spelling and grammar. But I was in the Gorja world now and it was time to sink or swim.

Chapter Twenty-One

A Real Education

I was put on a placement at St Peter's Primary School in Bradford, working alongside kids as well as doing a college course.

One of the first assignments we had was to work with a cup of water, paints and one colour to make an ornate pattern. This exercise was to show us how to look through the eyes of a child or something. Anyhow, the paints were cheap, nasty paints from the school, so when I got home, I bought my own nicer paint and redid the picture myself.

When I showed it to our teacher the next day she called my portfolio amazing. Whatever I had to do, I wanted to be the best.

My favourite thing was to spend time with the kids in the classroom. I discovered I loved it. Watching a child's face light up with recognition when they understood something for the first time was unbelievably satisfying.

I had to sit with the Traveller kids on a table. The tables all had different colours adhering to a code – basically they meant 'thick', 'less thick', 'middle' and 'really clever' – but the colours meant the kids never knew what level they had been classed as.

One day I was sat with a Traveller boy called Tommy. He was a sweet little thing, only five years old, and he appeared to be in something akin to shock at facing a classroom full of Gorja kids all busy learning subjects he'd no clue about. It was my job to teach this little lad to count so, pointing to one tiddlywink, I then pointed to the number one.

Then I pointed to two and so on, carefully, slowly, hoping he'd take notice. Instead of smiling or nodding, or having any kind of Eureka moment at all, he just looked at me completely blankly. Or in fact as if I was slightly mad.

'Come on, Tommy, we'll run through it again,' I said, gently.

Again he looked at me like it was all gobbledegook. Obviously he'd never been taught anything at home or been to nursery school so this really was a case of starting from scratch.

Behind us on the red table full of clever kids, a little boy was loudly doing a sum.

'If you have thirty-seven pence plus twelve pence . . . that makes . . . um . . . forty-eight pence,' he said, triumphantly.

'No, it don't,' said Tommy, swivelling on his seat.

The red-table kid looked up from his sum, frowning. 'Yes it does,' he said. 'And what would you know anyway: you're on the blue table.' So much for the kids not knowing what level they were at.

'It don't though, Miss,' said Tommy, his brown eyes pleading towards me. 'Thirty-seven pence plus twelve pence makes forty-nine pence.'

My mouth fell open with shock. Yet this also made perfect sense to me. This child had probably been taken out to work with his parents all his young life, hearing about money and absorbing how simple addition and subtraction works without him even realising it. I nodded, telling him what a clever little boy he was and I almost flew out of my seat to tell the teacher.

She listened intently, nodding away as I explained what I'd witnessed, but when I suggested Tommy was moved to a different group and given harder things to learn she shook her head.

'The national curriculum guidelines clearly state what a child should be able to do at what age and we have to stick to them,' she said.

I felt like the wind had been taken out of mine and Tommy's sails. What a shame that we couldn't celebrate a child being amazing at solving sums, even if there were gaps in his knowledge elsewhere.

Another big eye-opener was when I met two Traveller girls who were sisters. They were seven and eight years old and the youngest was deaf. They arrived in the classroom with a good report, after being assessed thoroughly by a number of teachers. They always stayed together and went nowhere without the other.

I was sent to work with the pair of them, but it seemed easy as they were so bright and on the same level.

One afternoon, a few weeks after they'd started, I had the seven-year-old deaf girl on her own as her sister was off doing another game with a different group of kids. I got out some Disney pictures to colour in and the deaf girl indicated to me she wanted to stick to the colours the characters were drawn in.

I set out the pens and said to her: 'Do you want to start with red?' I had to speak very slowly so she could lip-read.

She looked a little confused. 'Red,' I repeated, slower. 'Red. Red?'

After not seeming to understand, I wondered if it was the way I spoke, so I said 'blue' instead. Again she didn't know which pen to pick up. It was so strange.

I chose another colour and asked her to point out where the yellow was.

This went on for a few minutes when the penny dropped. The girl had no clue what any of the colours were.

After chatting to the teacher, we tested her in other areas and realised what had happened. Her older sister had been helping her from the start. Despite being assessed by other teachers the eight-year-old had unbelievably managed to help her and do all the work for her.

My next placement was at Usher Street School. Even though I'd had some experience as a teacher by now, I still couldn't help feeling like I was on the 'other side' and a bit of a fraud as I walked in to a classroom there for the first time. But taking a deep breath, I walked in with as much confidence as I could muster. On my arrival the teacher looked up straight away. 'Ah, you must be Miss Violet Cannon. Just in the nick of time – we have a young Traveller here named Toby who has climbed up a tree outside and he needs getting down. Can you please help?'

I went outside to find an angry-looking little boy sitting like a cat in the tree, his arms folded, his mouth obstinately closed.

'What you doing up there, son?' I asked.

He just needed to open his mouth for me to realise he wasn't a Traveller kid at all. He was just a naughty boy, but difficult children were just lumped together with all the Gypsy kids as far as the teachers were concerned.

More and more I realised that's how the authorities viewed Gypsy children: naughty kids with special needs, not individuals. The number of times I heard the cry: 'Violet! Can you please come and take so-and-so now?' and I'd rush over to see a little boy or girl who simply wasn't being as quick as the other kids or was causing a ruckus in the playground. More often than not they weren't a Gypsy at all, or sometimes they were but they had good reason not to be fitting in.

I soon realised every naughty child was seen as a Gypsy problem, and as the Gypsy 'helper' they were my problem too. It simply wasn't fair.

Meanwhile, my love life continued to be as complicated as ever. Over the next few months I split with Moses a few times.

Once was after my friend somehow managed to set fire to his precious car. Lina was smoking a fag in the back, as Moses wound down the windows, pretending to cough. 'Do you have to do that in here?' he moaned.

Lina rolled her eyes and laughed. 'Oh just shurrup!' she said, flicking her ash out the window.

As Moses tore down the road, towards a roundabout, he took the corner a little too fast and the car ended up careering along on just two wheels on the right.

'Everyone to the left!' he yelled, as we all threw our weight on to the other side of the car. With a spine-jarring thud, the car landed upright again, and we all breathed a sigh of relief. I looked behind me at Lina, who was now no longer smoking a fag. Behind Moses's back so he didn't see, she was making frantic hand-pointing signals to show she'd lost her fag and didn't know where it was.

I pulled an 'Eeeek!' face, looked at Moses and tried not to laugh as Lina dropped on to the floor, patting the towels, trying to find her errant ciggie. The smell of burning soon alerted us all.

'What the hell . . .?' yelled Moses, slamming on his brakes and spinning round. Thick smoke was billowing from his floor, as Lina finally found the fag, chucking it out the window.

'Sorry!' she said, trying not to look at me. We were both cracking up, as Moses stormed round opening all the car doors, waving away the smoke from his precious vehicle.

The Shania Twain song 'That Don't Impress Me Much'

always makes me think of Moses. He was so precious about all his belongings; the lyrics were him down to a tee.

This episode led to another of our splits, but they never lasted for long. By now I was in love with him and he was again suggesting getting married. As much as I was warming to the idea, part of me still didn't trust him. He was always 'popping' over to Germany and his phone used to go off at night, and he'd have to take the call outside. I had no concrete evidence he was cheating, but something certainly niggled away at me.

One other thing bothered me too. Moses wasn't a Christian. At one convention I decided to pray about it and as I closed my eyes I said to God: 'Please, if Moses is right for me, let him get saved too.'

As I opened my eyes again I couldn't believe what I was seeing: Moses was taking a seat at the front. He rarely came to any conventions and I thought perhaps the Lord had heard me.

Although we weren't together at that point, the time soon came when I needed a shoulder to cry on. Aunt Winnie had been given a month to live but she'd managed to last six months and now she'd gone. And I'd still not got round to buying her those wedge heels. It felt like the bottom of my world had fallen out. I was devastated and of course Moses was one of the first people I turned to.

'I will come and give you a cuddle,' he said as I sobbed to him down the phone. Within minutes his Land Cruiser had pulled up and I climbed in.

'Aw, babe,' he said, throwing his strong arms around me. I'd never felt so glad to see him. It felt like my insides had been crushed and the tears didn't stop.

'The worst thing was,' I cried, 'I'd never got round to buying Auntie Winnie those wedges. I feel so bad!'

As he rocked me gently, I felt something else move. A phone was vibrating in his pocket.

'Sorry, babe,' he said, fishing it out and jumping out of the car. He moved a few paces away, but as he slammed the door shut it didn't close properly, and I could catch a few words.

'Yeah, babe . . . OK, OK, thinking of you too.'

His words turned my blood to ice. The object was obviously on the phone to another woman. As he jumped back in the car, attempting to put his arms round me again, I glared at him.

'Who the hell was that?' I snapped.

'My dad,' he said, starting to lie. But one look at my face warned him otherwise.

'OK,' he admitted. 'It was Melissa.'

I'd heard about this girl and how she was always waiting in the wings for me and Moses to finish. I couldn't believe my ears. I jumped out of the car.

'Just when I needed you the most you've let me down,' I snarled, wiping away my tears as anger took over.

'But you're different from Melissa,' he shouted after me. 'Because I really love you!'

Chapter Twenty-Two

Losing It

After Auntie Winnie died our whole family was shaken to the core. The funeral was devastating. I had a wreath made in the shape of the wedge heels, so she got them in the end.

I was equally upset for her daughter Annie who was just fifteen and the babby of the family. I told her at the funeral that she could always have a place to stay with me if she wanted. A few weeks later she took me up on the offer. I loved taking care of her, cooking and cleaning and letting her sleep in my bed. It was a bit like having Maria back with me.

Within weeks, after a few pleading phone calls and appeals for forgiveness, I took Moses back. Don't ask me why, but I suppose I couldn't help myself. I was in love, despite his flaws.

Although I was happy to see where our relationship led us, Moses seemed intent on setting the pace a bit more quickly. One day he invited me along to a car dealership where he was picking out a new motor. He sat down with the salesman to decide on the design specifications for a brand-new SLK Mercedes.

'I'd like a lilac finish,' he said, 'with a cream roof.'

I did a double take: these were not exactly normal colours for a Gypsy man's car, but never mind. Then he went on to choose custom-made seats and a tow bar. My ears pricked up again.

'Tow bar?' I said, looking at him. 'But both your cars already have tow bars. Why do you want another one?'

He smiled. 'It's for you, to tow the trailer with!'

I laughed. 'But Moses, why do I want to be towing your trailer?'

'Fer when we get married,' he said.

I stood up.

'But you haven't even asked me!' I spat, angry at his presumptions. We stared at each other in silence, as the car salesman shuffled his papers, not knowing where to look.

'Oh come on, Violet,' he said. 'It'll take three months to get ready anyways.'

I grabbed my coat and started walking away. 'You, Moses, can shove your SLK sideways!' I shouted.

I could not believe the cheek of the man, presuming I was marrying him when I'd not even been asked.

That year I turned twenty-one and, like on all my birthdays, I was spoiled rotten. Mam and Dad bought me a beautiful gold 'collarette', a necklace made from a thin band of dull gold with gold kisses, and a matching bracelet. Everyone made me feel like a princess – everyone it seemed except for Moses.

He showed up with a massive card, about three feet high

with a soppy message: 'To my baby with love from your teddy bear.'

On the face of it this might seem like it was a romantic thing to do, but the reality was different. I'd still not made our relationship 'official' to my parents and to get such an intimate card made things awkward for me.

Although Moses could be tight in many ways I admit I was looking forward to getting my present off him. It was a big birthday, so I was sure to be in for a treat. So imagine my face when I tore off the paper to find a bottle of Fendi perfume and nothing else.

'What's this, Moses?' I asked, looking up at his beaming face.

'It's my mother's favourite,' he said, proudly. 'I love the smell of it on her so I thought it'd be nice for you.'

At that moment I mentally crossed present-giving off the list of Moses's talents.

For my big day I went go-karting with a group of friends, and Moses's sister Isis turned up. She was much younger than him, and bought me a lovely Florentine wash set from M&S. She was a better present buyer than her brother, I decided.

Straight afterwards we all trooped off for another convention. Mam and Dad drove the trailer, but while we were there Dad ended up selling his car, so on the way back me and Moses ended up driving home together.

Reaching across the gear stick, with my family trailer on

the back, he glanced at me. 'This could be me and you one day, babe,' he winked. 'A family.'

That night, once again, I finished with him. And then, once again, he talked me back round and I went back out with him a few days later.

Although my romantic life was more of a roller coaster than a canal cruise, work life was interesting and fun. In the classroom I was still enjoying helping the kids – when they weren't winding me up. One little boy, called Freddie, was from a Travelling Showman family. He was as rude as they come.

On his first day after I was introduced to him, he said to me quietly: 'But Miss, you're not a Traveller like me, you're a pikey, Miss.'

I gasped, feeling my face grow hot. What a little shit! Pikey is one of the worse terms of abuse for a Romany. Probably the equivalent of calling an Asian teaching assistant a Paki.

Holding my temper just in check I smiled as sweetly as I could.

'I am Gypsy, Freddie. I don't like the term pikey.'

'Yeah, but that's what we all call yous. You're a pikey aren't you, Miss?'

'Freddie!' I said, slightly more firmly, feeling the power of my mam's eyes flashing in to my own. 'Really, don't ever call me that again. It's not a nice word.'

In short, Freddie was a bloody nightmare of a child. As sweet as he could be, he didn't fit in at all, had no interest in learning and he hated every second of school. He told me during one break he'd rather be out on his father's stall along-side him, earning money.

A few months after he started, I overheard an altercation between Freddie, of course, and two other boys. I squatted down in between them at their little desks, asking them firmly to stop rowing and be kind to each other. Freddie didn't take his eyes off the other kids, so angry he was almost snarling.

As I stood up to leave, I turned just in time to see Freddie's face contort in to absolute fury. Screaming like a man possessed he'd leaped from his chair and was standing over another boy.

'Call my mam that again and I'll kills yous,' he yelled, his cheeks flushed crimson.

The teacher stopped her lesson and roared like I'd never heard her before.

'Freddie! Leave my classroom immediately! This behaviour is NOT acceptable.'

Tears streaming down his cheeks, Freddie bowled out of the room, knocking in to chairs as he left and slamming the door behind him. The teacher turned and carried on her lesson, so I went outside to deal with Freddie myself.

'What did they say, Freddie?' I asked softly, as he snivelled in to his sleeve.

'It was my mam . . . my mam . . .' he sobbed. He refused to tell me their exact words, so I knew it was something dirty.

Later on I had a quiet word with the teacher. Straight away she'd concluded Freddie was in the wrong and she'd not even asked the boys what they'd said to him. She'd obviously decided that Freddie was just a troubled, naughty little boy who couldn't be tamed. Also the SATS tests were about to be taken and the boys Freddie had shouted at were among the brightest kids. This teacher needed them to perform well in class, and that was the priority at that time.

I was shocked. But this was the way schools worked. Traveller kids were helped to a certain level but ultimately the school put them in a box and they were closed in. The only things that mattered were the scores, targets and league tables. However good the teacher was, however much they cared, the pressure was on them to toe the party line.

Throughout the school I also saw other cultures and religions celebrated at every single opportunity. Religious festivals such as Diwali and Eid were taken seriously and it was seen as important that other kids learned about them. But if a Gypsy child went to a fair, even one as important as Appleby, no teachers ever asked them to talk or write about it. It was seen as 'something they did', with no relevance to anyone else. I felt this sort of discrimination made the Traveller child feel even more isolated.

I left that day feeling very sad. Earlier that month I'd been asked by a visiting education chief about the way 'Gypsy people' lived. He'd actually asked me: 'What do you cook on?' I stared at him, feeling so patronised. What did he think? I sat in my trailer gnawing on lumps of raw meat? And he was supposed to be at the top of the tree, one of the clever ones. Mam's words echoed in my head as I made my way home that evening. 'You won't change them, Violet. It's institutional, their ways.'

Shortly afterwards I resigned and got a job cleaning.

Meanwhile, despite my reservations, Moses always managed to persuade me to take him back. And very quickly his hints about getting wed were becoming less subtle. Once we were walking round a shopping centre when he steered me in to the jeweller's. 'Do you like this ring?' he said, pointing out a beautiful diamond.

Automatically I shook my head. I kept on shaking it as he pointed out ring after ring. 'It's horrible,' I'd say. 'It wouldn't suit me.'

After pointing out twenty or thirty rings with equally scathing responses he seemed to give up.

Shortly afterwards we went to a fairground together. It was fun to be out for the day, our faces lit up by bright lights, laughing as we tried the coconut shy or the strongest man game. Then as we sat down on the Sizzler Twist, a rather scary spinning cart ride that I loved, Moses turned to me with a serious face.

'Got something to tell you, babe,' he said. Moses was always making a big scene, telling me in a grand way how much he loved me. Sometimes I quite liked it, other times it was a bit much.

I took a deep breath, reeling in the desire to roll my eyes.

'What now, Moses?' I said, smiling.

He opened his mouth as if to start speaking and then thought better of it. 'Oh, it don't matter,' he said.

Later on he admitted, just before he dropped me off home, what he'd really wanted to say. Looking at his feet, he ran his fingers through his hair.

'Babe, I am half a showman,' he said. 'I am not a full Romany.'

I looked at him, genuinely shocked. Being a showman was not something to be proud of. In fact, it was the exact opposite. They tended to look down their noses at true Romanies and there was real rivalry in camps. 'That's shameful,' I said. 'Don't you go bragging about that, Moses, do you hear?'

He gave me a hug, whispering how he hoped it didn't matter as lineage is not important. I agreed with him, but deep down it did bother me. And yet I knew if our relationship had been 100 per cent right it wouldn't have mattered to me at all. I still had my niggling doubts. Even on the way up to the fair, Moses's phone constantly lit up.

After much soul-searching, I knew after eighteen months this couldn't go on for any longer. I needed to finish the relationship once and for all.

So when Moses told me he was going on yet another of his mysterious trips to Germany, I plucked up the courage to end it completely. I knew he'd try and persuade me otherwise, so I took the coward's way out, and waited until just after he'd left.

Every time he went away he caught a boat across the Channel and at some point midway we usually lost the signal. That evening he called me as usual and I chatted completely normally until his signal started to get crackly.

'Violet, you're breaking up a bit, babe,' he said. 'I am going to lose you soon.'

Switching my tone somewhat, I cleared my throat. 'Well, that's good Moses because we're finished. Did you get that? It's not a mistake on the line – you've lost me already.'

And with that the line went dead. I sat on my bed and sobbed. I was due to go out with his sister, Isis, that night. Drying my eyes I caught sight of myself in the mirror and made a promise. This man had already taken so much of me. I needed to find another one as soon as I could.

So I opened my sister's wardrobe to find the best outfit possible. Maria was the same size as me, a size eight but athletic, while I was more curvy. But I couldn't resist squeezing myself in to the most revealing outfit she had. A mix of turquoise and lilac stripes made from suede, it was little more than a bra top and a belt.

Checking myself out in the mirror, I decided this was the very best way of 'getting back out there'.

My mam had other ideas. She looked at me in horror as she saw what I was planning on clubbing in.

'Get that off now, Violet,' she said.

'Well, you let Maria go out in it,' I said, sticking out my lip. 'And she's the same size as me.'

'Yes, but she's got a different physique. Now get it off.'

I shook my head. 'I've just split up with Moses and I need some fun,' I said, flouncing off.

In the club toilets people couldn't believe what I had on. 'You're looking well,' they said, admiring my outfit, or lack of it. I felt like a million dollars.

'Don't mind if I say so myself,' I said. 'For tonight I am looking for a new man!'

Isis's mouth fell open. 'But what about my brother?' she said.

'He's finished,' I said, turning my heel. Looking back it was a bit mean to take it out on her, but I was sick of the lot of them by then.

A few nights later, still determined to keep my spirits up, I arranged to go to the cinema, inviting my cousin Annie along. She'd not met many people while her mam Aunt Winnie was ill and I wanted her to mix again and introduce her to my friends. We got ready together, Annie laughing as she smoothed her hair with my GHD straighteners.

When we arrived and met up with the gang, Annie seemed to disappear.

'Where's she gone?' I said, looking round the cinema car park.

Then I spotted a familiar van. The one belonging to Moses. A horrible feeling formed in the pit of my stomach, as I spotted yet another familiar head of dark hair, all sleek and straight from my GHDs, in the front seat next to the driver.

Marching over, I felt myself shaking slightly. My first instincts had been right.

There, next to Moses, was Annie. She had her head turned,

as if she were talking very closely to him. I raised a fist and thumped on the window.

Winding it down quickly, Annie stuck her head out. 'Just give me a minute,' she said, before winding it back up. Completely gobsmacked, I was uncharacteristically as speechless and as meek as a kitten. I walked back to my gang of friends, who been watching the events unfold with interest. Finding Annie and Moses together was so totally unreal I couldn't quite take it in.

'What should I do?' I managed to say, as we all stood staring at his van, with what looked like Annie kissing him inside.

'You go back, girl, and get her out of that man's van!' spat one of my friends, Natalie, who was incensed on my behalf.

Taking a deep breath, a blind rage took over and this time I marched back, yanked open the van door before they'd even had time to notice and shouted: 'Annie, you're fifteen, he's twenty-one, now get out of this motor NOW!'

Grabbing her coat, an open-mouthed Annie knew better than to argue this time and scrabbled out as fast as she could. Moses was sat staring at me, but I wouldn't even give him the satisfaction of saying a word. I glared at him, not wanting him to see how I really felt behind my steely eyes. Inside, I was dying.

With a tearful Annie tripping behind me I stormed back to the group, just daring my tears to fall. The next thing I did was the hardest. Blood is always thicker than water, and I knew

Annie had been young and silly, probably set up by Moses to get back at me, or God knows what.

So however much I wanted to rip her eyeballs out I did something totally different. I politely said goodbye to Annie and told her to go home, walked in to the cinema foyer with my friends and insisted we bought the tickets.

'You what, Violet?' they all said incredulously. 'You sure?'

Staring at each other, the group couldn't believe I was prepared to let it go like that. Digging my nails in to my palm I nodded and asked for the tickets to see a film I can't remember a thing about now.

Like an automaton, I paid for them and took my seat, while Annie went home. And in the darkness, with the surround-sound drowning me out, I quietly sobbed and sobbed. I knew it was finally, properly over between me and Moses, and despite all our ups and downs it hurt like hell.

Chapter Twenty-Three

Picking Up the Pieces

Somehow, I managed to move past what happened and Annie went home with her tail very much between her legs, but still without a confrontation with me.

I knew I had to forget, even if I couldn't forgive. I just had to move past what had happened. It would have decimated my family to do otherwise and family is everything. I couldn't understand why Annie had done what she'd done. It was an immature action, and maybe she'd been manipulated by Moses, who knows? But we never spoke another word about it and a week later I even took her with me to a party. In the physical sense I was present and acting normal, but mentally, I was constantly reliving that moment, her rendezvous with Moses. But the only thing that was important to me was not allowing Moses to split my family apart.

By now, workwise, I was doing relief cover for a cleaning company, mainly offices and schools. I had no airs and graces about getting my head stuck down a toilet with a brush, giving it some elbow grease. For me, as long as I was working, that's all that mattered.

I'd also decided to set up the Northern Network of Travelling People. During my work in schools I'd discovered there was no single body to join up all the separate Travelling groups across the north of the country, in places like Hull, Leeds, Manchester and Liverpool. There were so many small separate groups who could help each other and provide support and information, it seemed to make sense to join forces.

A few months after the cinema trip incident, on New Year's Eve, word got out that the family who'd threatened my dad at Maria's wedding was still seeking revenge, and instead of going after my dad they'd decided to take me up on my offer to fight.

All my friends told me what they'd heard and couldn't believe it when I refused to change my plans and stay in that night. 'If you run once, you run forever,' I said to them, full of bravado, just like Mam had taught me. But I also meant it. If something was to happen, then so be it. We'd arranged to go to Chaplin's Nightclub in Bradford and I planned to turn up with bells on. So I left the house feeling like a right glamourpuss in a pair of tight black leather trousers, a basque and four-inch heels. I looked like something out of *Buffy the Vampire Slayer*. I insisted on dancing all night, even though I was on my own on the dancefloor for some of the time as my friends began to feel increasingly nervous. Word was out that I was a wanted lady that night and no one knew when they'd turn up. But I carried on regardless, necking a few J2Os and generally having a right good time.

Just as a new song came on, I felt someone brush past me. I whirled around to see a girl's fringe come slamming in to my face and before I knew it I was headbutted to the floor.

Kicked and punched from all sides, I could sense the dance-floor clearing around me although the music carried on. Just three words flitted through my head: I. Am. Dead.

Shielding my face from the blows, from deep inside me I got a surge of determination and, gathering all my energy and strength, I managed to roll on top of the girl, pinning her to the floor. Spotting a big fat gold chain around her neck, I followed every instinct to defend myself, and grabbed it with my fist. As fast as I could, I twisted it around and around like a garrote, while all the time she kicked and squirmed beneath me. Her face grew fatter and redder as she spluttered whilst being strangled with her own bling.

'You object!' I yelled.

Just as her chain snapped in two, and I realised my one line of defence had failed, a pair of enormous hands like two slabs of meat grabbed my bare shoulders, and when they couldn't get hold of me, a large male arm swung around my face, the crook of an elbow pinching my nose.

A bouncer had stepped in, just as more girls had piled in looking for me.

'You! Out!' yelled the burly guy.

Before I had a chance to open my mouth, I found myself

spinning in to the street, staggering on my heels, clutching my forehead. Although he'd just saved me, I was fuming.

'But it weren't my fault!' I shrieked, hands on hips, pointing wildly back at the nightclub. 'It were them! They should be chucked out too, y'know!'

The bouncer, who was getting no thanks for almost certainly having saved my life, waved me away. 'Leave or I am calling the police,' he replied.

'It's not fair!' I raged, really wound up now. The injustice of it all stank as far as I was concerned. Various friends and cousins gathered around me and gently led me away as I continued to give the bouncer a gobful.

'Come on, V, just leave it darling,' they said, as I climbed in to the car. As I never drank I was always the driver for everyone. As I flicked the mirror down in the car I looked at my face and gasped. I'd felt my nose being squashed as the bouncer's inside elbow wrapped around my face. Now I realised it had been broken and thick red clots of crimson blood were pouring down my mouth and dripping off my chin.

'Aw, for the love of God!' I cursed, rooting for a tissue. 'I look like a right savage.'

Years later, after I'd become a children's youth worker, the same girl who I'd tried to strangle with her own jewellery turned up at the Sunday School where I was working.

I recognised her straight away and felt my cheeks burn with embarrassment and shame. But I shook away the past and pretended I'd just met her and she did the same with me. I took the hands of her gorgeous little ones and led them away to do some drawing, thinking how people changed and grew up in life.

After what had happened with Moses and my cousin, all sorts went through my head. I couldn't stop crying and wondered if I was a really horrible person for something like that to have happened. With my self-esteem completely crushed, even my friends noticed how depressed I appeared. They rallied round me and one day invited me to a local fun fair, which is what we call the shows.

The lights, sounds and smells of the show reminded me of being a kid. It was a laugh just hanging about, feeling young again. We stayed till it closed then jumped in the car and started driving off. As we pulled away we saw a Romany Gypsy girl we recognised look both ways then dash in to the fairground.

'Hey, it's shutting now,' I said. 'What's she doing here?'

We looked at each other and smiled. Chances are there was a boy behind this and she was having some illicit encounter. Like all Gypsies we love a bit of gossip, so vowed to return and ask around. We had to find out!

The next day, we turned up again, had a chat with a few of the guys on the stalls and generally larked around like we had the previous day. One of the lads, called George, seemed very friendly. A typical showman, he was smiley and a bit arrogant. At only 5'9" he was quite short, with brown eyes and mousy hair hanging over his eyes in curtains. I sensed a twinkle in his eye when he spoke, which I ignored.

Later on, as we stood by the shotgun game, a couple of Asian lads approached us. 'You couple of sexy bitches,' one muttered. With hands in their pockets, they stared at us through dark fringes.

'You want some?' one said, a smirk on his face.

'Look, lads, we're Gypsy girls. We don't date other men,' I said. 'Now clear off.'

'You think I am thick,' said the lad. 'I know a stinking gypo when I see one. I've had plenty and all.'

I glared at him. 'And who exactly do you know?'

He started reeling off a list of names, none of which I recognised, then he said Guy Jason. Now Guy Jason was one man you didn't mess with. Everyone respected him, mainly out of fear. He was one of Granny Suzanna's best pals from back in the day.

'*You* know Guy Jason, do you, eh?' I said.

'Yeah I do, you little whore,' he replied.

'Well, why don't you ring him up now and say you're stood here with his best friend's granddaughter and you've just called her a little whore. Go on. If you have his number I'll ring him myself.'

The look on this lad's face was priceless. Even if he didn't know Guy Jason, which I suspected he didn't, he obviously knew his reputation.

Muttering an apology he started backing away, just as

George came round the corner in a car. It was a new Jeep and he rolled down the window, obviously pleased to have spotted us while he was driving.

'Hey girls, these lads giving you hassle?'

We half-rolled our eyes: talk about too late, mate! But we nodded and quickly the Asian lads melted back in to the crowd.

George leaned over his open window. 'So what do you think to my new car?' he asked, smiling.

I looked it over. It had personalised number plates and was very smart. He looked rather out of place driving it.

'Not new enough for me,' I laughed, trying to wind him up.

'You a number plate chaser then?' he said.

'Very much so,' I joked, turning my heel and walking off. As usual I was wearing my tight leather trousers and I could sense him watching me.

He shouted out a crass reference to my backside, and I spun back round. 'Do you want a punch in the mouth?' I yelled.

Jumping out of the car, he ran after us, spouting an apology and trying to make small talk. He asked to see my phone and, proud it was a new Motorola flip-up, I pulled it out. Turning it over in his hands, his phone started ringing. Then I realised he'd got my number by calling his with mine.

'You're a cheeky one,' I said.

This was the start of a relentless pursuit, something I was both irritated and enthralled by. He'd ring me every day, asking for a chat, or giving me some compliment. I was used to the shy, roundabout ways of Gypsy boys, so I couldn't help but be flattered. After such a rejection from Moses, George was like a breath of fresh air.

Or so I thought. Later on I described it as bullshit, just a different brand.

After months of phone calls and requests for dates, George and I fell in to a friendship of sorts, but I knew that for me, being with a showman wasn't allowed. Besides, I'd told Moses one of the reasons I was ditching him was because he was half-showman. How could I go out with one now?

However, I was older now, aged twenty-two, and Mam had started to make comments and jokes about me always chasing men away. I laughed it off as we shared the same caustic wit, but ultimately I knew this is what people were thinking. Violet Cannon could never hang on to a man.

Other people started to make comments too, comparing me to my Aunt Mary who didn't get married until she was twenty-nine, very late in the Gypsy world. And at the end of the day life without a family or children was inconceivable to me.

Mam also used to have a saying: 'My girls can fall in love with anyone, a black man, an Arab or an alien for all I care, as long as they are happy.'

Well, this was putting her claim to the test. Slowly my friendship with George was evolving in to something more on my side. On his side it had been more from the start. Three days after meeting me he told me loved me, and many of his calls were gushing protestations of how much he wanted me.

It proved irresistible, and I started dating him, albeit in secret from my parents. I soon started to meet his friends and family on the show sites, and even discovered that Frankie – the rude little boy I taught at school – was one of his cousins. He began to join me at church too, although I didn't want to take him to the Gypsy one, so we went to the small Gorja one nearby.

A terrible tragedy befell my cousin Joanne around this time. She'd had a beautiful baby boy eighteen months before who had died of cot death. I went to the funeral, and was so upset afterwards I went to meet George for a hug.

Mam picked up on me not being at the wake. 'If you were not at the wake or at home, where was you, little girl?' she said.

I knew it was time to come clean. 'It's George,' I admitted. 'He keeps asking me out and I don't know what to do.'

Mum sighed. I could see she was sorely tested on this one, but she agreed I could date him. George wasn't my type looks-wise at all, but his relentless pursuit made me feel wanted and special, which was something I'd not felt for a long time. By now I did feel slightly isolated in many ways. I'd lost Maria, my best friend as well as my sister, to marriage. As much as we stayed in touch, she couldn't 'be there' for me in the same way any more. Other friends were also drifting away as they married and settled down. For perhaps the first time in my life I'd started to feel a little alone.

I soon became friendly with the Gypsy girl we'd spotted nipping in to the fairground late at night, Sunshine, who was going out with George's cousin. We started hanging out in a foursome, so when she rang one day and asked if I wanted to go to Party in the Park – a free music festival in Leeds – I didn't hesitate.

I got together a fabulous outfit of black leather trousers, pink cowboy boots and a pink leather basque, all topped off with four-inch heels.

'Let's rock and roll!' I grinned as I turned up for the lift to take us there.

When we arrived though, it turned out that George had forgotten to tell me I'd be serving in one of his cousin's catering units.

'You what?' I said.

'It'll only be for a few hours,' he said.

Eight hours later, I was dripping with beads of sweat, my arms aching with carrying drinks, and I'd had no chance to see any bands.

Boiling hot in my outfit, I'd also attracted so much unwanted attention, I could barely keep up with the insults and compliments. We kept running out of hot water, people complained about paying £2 for a can of Coke and some had to wait forty-five minutes just to get served.

As if this wasn't all bad enough, George's cousin cornered me when I dashed out the back to grab some cordial.

'You look really hot in that pink basque,' he said, leering at me. 'I like what's underneath too.'

I stared at him in shock. I knew I couldn't tell George or he'd go mad. It'd break Sunshine's heart too.

'It's not any of your business,' I snapped, pushing past him.

To make matters even worse all the others smoked, so kept nipping out the back for fag breaks. After five hours, I grabbed a packet off the shelf myself.

'But you don't smoke,' said George.

'I do now,' I shot back.

I stood outside, holding the cigarette in my hand, not lighting it up, but just breathing in some fresh air. Well as fresh as you could get with smells of cooking oil and beery men surrounding me.

Exhausted, we finally finished and had a meal together to celebrate. Not wanting to make a fuss I pretended I'd enjoyed some of it after all.

Later, George told me how another cousin of his, Howard, who I'd met earlier, didn't like me.

''E keeps saying you're leading me on,' he complained.

I wasn't sure how to respond to this. I didn't know what George was getting at. Howard was a fairly successful showman, with lots of units and rides, and he seemed happy in his own skin. So why he'd take against me so vehemently didn't make sense. But I took it onboard, and in my own way, vowed to make an extra effort with him.

It wasn't just on George's side that there were objections to our relationship. Mam and Dad met George early on and both of them were very quiet after he left. I could tell they didn't like him but I didn't want to hear.

Once I was getting ready for a date when my mild-mannered

father, someone who'd never so much as raised his voice at me, suddenly seemed to snap.

'I don't want you going out with the lad,' he growled at me, as I sat in the trailer doing my hair.

'Why, Dad?' I asked. I didn't recognise the look in his face. Real anger and pain.

'I just don't and you're not going to.'

'But Mam said . . .' I began.

A huge row ensued, then Dad said some words I'd never thought I'd hear coming from his lips: 'If you try and leave this trailer to go out with that showman, I will break your legs!'

Slamming my door shut, I threw myself on the bed and sobbed. What had come over him? What was so bad about George? Didn't anyone actually want me to be happy? I waited until Dad took his truck out and sneaked out anyway.

Later I heard that Mam had told Dad to let me make my own mistakes. She'd said: 'We don't want her sat in a trailer by herself when she's older saying we wouldn't let her date the man she'd fallen for. We have to let her do her own mistakes and then we're not to blame.'

Much later on, I'd openly say to Dad: 'I wish you'd broken my legs. It would've been less painful.'

Chapter Twenty-Four

The Next Big Thing

Around this time Maria discovered she was expecting her first child. I was completely thrilled for her. We'd always been close, but of course after her wedding we'd had to grow apart as we no longer lived together. Maria had moved to a site in Bedford with Ely and, although we spoke all the time on the phone, it wasn't the same. It couldn't be. My Babby was a married woman.

I jumped around the room when she broke the news she was having a child. In some ways I couldn't imagine our Babby being a mam, but I also knew she'd grow in to the role and be incredible.

Now we were older and she was a respectable expectant married woman, it still didn't change the way some people treated us, though. Once we went for a wander together around the local shopping precinct. I had a Chanel designer backpack on, one I always wore, and we set off to look at the make-up in Boots. As we stood at the counter chatting to a heavily made-up lady selling pricey foundation, a security guard came striding up behind us.

'You two,' he snapped. 'Come this way, please.'

Maria's mouth fell open as I spun around. 'What the . . .?' I started.

'This way,' he growled.

Our cheeks burning as the heads of other shoppers twisted around to see what the kerfuffle was about, we had no choice but to follow the guard.

'What are we supposed to have done?' I cried. 'We were just looking at foundation.'

Ushered in to a side room, Maria started to well up. Already she was feeling hormonal and tired. To suffer this humiliation was a step too far.

'We have reports that you two have been stealing,' said the security guard. 'Now what have you got to say?'

'Eh?' I said, genuinely confused now. 'For a start, no we have not. And secondly, even if we had, we haven't actually LEFT THE SHOP, so how can it be classed as stealing?'

'Don't you get lippy with me!' retorted the guard. 'I know your sort. We've reason to believe you've nicked a lipstick.'

My temper snapped at this point. I grabbed my bag. 'Do you really think with a £350 designer handbag on my back I'd really steal a blooming cheap lipstick?' I cried. 'Here, look!'

And with one swift movement, I tipped up my bag, spilling the contents on to the table.

All three of us stared at the pile of keys, mirror, sunglasses and tissues, in a silence only broken by Maria bursting in to tears.

'Oh, Babby,' I soothed. 'It's OK.'

I turned to the guard. 'Have you had enough now or shall I make a complaint to the manager about harrassment?'

He swallowed hard. 'Yes fine, feel free to go . . .'

With my arm around Maria's shoulder, I held my head as high as I could as we walked out. Maria was blowing her nose hard. 'Let's go home, Violet,' she sniffed.

'Hang on a minute,' I said. Marching up to the make-up counter, I waved a twenty-pound note in front of the assistant. I bought the foundation, grabbed my receipt and we left.

Once again an innocent trip to the shops was ruined by discrimination.

Christmas was around the corner and it was time for the lights to be switched on at Heckmondwike in West Yorkshire, an annual event for showmen and the equivalent of Christmas lights going on in a high street. We all went along but George seemed to have had a falling out with Howard, so once we got there he asked me to go for a drive with him.

He was in a steaming mood. 'What's happened, George?' I asked.

'Howard owed me some money and when I asked for it he threw it at me, saying you are using me and don't really want me.'

I was shocked. I had no idea why giving George money would involve such abuse. What did it have to do with me?

'OK,' I said. 'Well sorry, but Howard sounds slightly off his rocker today.'

Rain started pattering on the windscreen as George swung the car down country lanes – driving, it seemed, in to the darkest lanes. Eventually he pulled up outside a house and told me he had to pop in. A few minutes later he came out, and we set off again.

Then he started indicating to pull over once more. 'What you doing, George?' I said. It was dark, cold and raining. What was he playing at?

'I just feel a bit sick,' he said, unlocking the car and jumping out. 'Can you get out too, darling?'

'You what? I am not getting out in that!' I said.

He went quiet for a few seconds and then sighed. 'Please, Violet, just do as you're told. Just for once.'

Thinking he'd now lost the plot too, I unbuckled myself, grumbling away. I got out to find George behind the back of the car, down on one knee in a puddle.

'Violet, will you marry me?' he said, his curtain hair dripping slightly with the wet. In his hand he was holding a box with a very beautiful ring inside.

'Oh my God, George,' I said, peering at the twinkling ring. 'Have you stolen that?'

Looking cross, he shook his head. 'No! I bought this good and proper.'

He pulled it out and, jumping back in the car, I switched on the light to see an antique art deco ring with a row of tiny clear diamonds. It was absolutely beautiful.

George was sat next to me, his face filled with a mixture of expectation and adoration. We'd only been seeing each other properly for two months. And this poor boy was taking such a battering from Howard, saying I didn't care . . . and he was so sweet . . . and after Moses, would I ever find a man again?

'Yes,' I cried, welling up. 'Yes! Go on then!'

We had a cuddle and then I told him he'd have to ask Mam and Dad. Mam had a bad heart, so I hoped the shock wouldn't be too much for her. This was all happening a little fast.

One condition of me agreeing to marry George was that he must speak to his mother, Joan, again. At the time he'd lost contact with her and refused to have much to do with her. I never got to the bottom of why, but as a person whose family is everything I knew it wasn't right and I wanted him to make amends. We all have our family arguments but to lose touch didn't make sense. Only later did I change my mind.

In the end, I knew my family wouldn't be pleased when they heard my news, so I went off shopping with Maria to think about how to break it to them. While we were in a department store, I picked out a really pretty knife and fork set.

'Those are nice, who you buying them fer?' she said.

'Myself,' I replied.

'What, for you in the house with Mam?'

'No, I'm getting married . . .'

The expression on her face, one of complete horror, made me wince a little. I also felt put out. I hadn't been thrilled when she got wed but at least I said congrats and managed a smile.

Maria drove back home with me in silence and once inside, I unpacked the shopping bags and went to my room. I overheard Maria telling Mam exactly the way I'd told her, using the knives and forks as a way to introduce the subject.

I called up George and asked him to come over. He went off for a quiet chat with my parents, then my dad took him off for another one, in private. He said the same thing he told Ely, Maria's husband, before they got hitched: 'Good luck, all the best, but if my daughter comes home with so much as a bruise on her, I will break both your legs.'

I knew my dad was a quiet man who steered clear of trouble, but when it came to protecting his girls, a primitive instinct took over.

Around this time Dad was finding life hard anyway. Always a proud man, he'd recently had to face the prospect of unemployment. While working with the horses, one had kicked him hard in the hand, shattering the bones. After wearing a pot for weeks, he'd only gained around 15 per cent of the use of his hand back again. For some reason, I blamed myself for this accident. I knew the prospect of my impending wedding was causing him stress. I knew he didn't like George. Yet I was defying him, ploughing ahead, convinced it was what I wanted and needed in my life. Now Dad was incapacitated I knew he had even more time to dwell on it all and yet he was the last person I wanted to hurt or upset.

However, like any bride-to-be I was excited I was finally getting married, and Mam and I started on the plans straight away. Maria's wedding had been the most perfect day and she'd looked, of course, like the most beautiful bride anyone had ever seen, so I knew I could never compete with that. I tried to go for everything differently, just wanting to keep the wedding venues the same. However it wasn't just the plans that were different. The build-up wasn't the same either.

For Maria's do, Mam was beside herself with excitement and utterly in her element, with my aunties and cousins all fussing round. But the build-up to my wedding felt muted somehow. I couldn't quite put my finger on it so it was hard to complain. I tried to shake off the feeling and carry on with the wedding preparations.

The first thing we needed to do was book Bradford Cathedral. Because it was such short notice we needed special permission and had to pay the canon £200 to go down to London and meet with the Archbishop of Canterbury to get a marriage licence. He came back with an enormous document, on heavy paper, which looked like a royal warrant or something.

Reading the words made me well up a little: 'George Leonard [I didn't know who he was] by Divine Providence Lord Archbishop of Canterbury of all England and Metropolitan by Authority of Parliament lawfully empowered for the purposes herein written to our Beloved Christ George Michael Buckley of Amusement Depot Paley Road, at Bradford in the county of West Yorkshire a batchelor and Violet Margaret Cannon of Bungalow Brow Ward Terrace at Bradford in the county of West Yorkshire a spinster . . .'

Our names alongside the Archbishop's sent a shiver down my spine. We were really going to get married.

The next step was choosing the reception venue. I wanted to have it at the same place Maria had hers, the Cedar Court Hotel in Bradford. But when Mam made the booking she made a slip, telling the receptionist: 'My other daughter had her reception here a few years ago . . .'

'Oh. Right,' said the receptionist. 'Sorry, hang on. I'll just have to check the availability and get back to you.'

An hour later the hotelier rang back. 'Sorry, we're fully booked for the next six months.'

This didn't surprise either Mam or me when she told me. Most Traveller families have to pretend they are not Gypsies to the owners of the venue until the big day dawns, hoping no one finds out otherwise they cancel on you. As if a bride and her family don't have enough to worry about on their wedding day! Of course we had no way of proving this is what had happened in our case but it was very fishy.

So I went for the Midland Hotel in Bradford, Mam being very careful this time they didn't suspect we were Gypsies when she booked it. It's an unusual choice for a wedding venue as it's an ex-railway building and there isn't a garden. But the sumptuous interior made up for any of that. We wandered around to choose a room, and when the door to one big dining room opened I literally gasped. Inside was the most awesome twenty-foot-long chandelier sparkling and winking at me from the ceiling.

'This is the one I want, Mam,' I said. My eyes shining in

the reflection of the sparkling diamonds, I just knew it would look amazing in the background of the wedding pictures that I'd treasure forever. I don't know how much the room cost as I didn't ask, but my dad put down a deposit for it and that was that.

I decided to opt for a little-known dress designer based up in Scholes. A number of Gypsy brides, and all the ones you see on *Big Fat Gypsy Wedding*, choose dressmaker Thelma Madine. Thelma's business started on a Liverpool market stall and she makes the most outrageous, outlandish dresses you can imagine. Of course for the TV documentary hearing about weddings with massive over-the-top gowns makes for better viewing. But the reality is a little different. Only a few Gypsy girls use Thelma's dresses and not all of us have that over-styled, Disney princess taste. We might all want a fairytale, but we don't need to look like a cartoon character to have it.

I wanted something elegant, fitted and above all classy. First though everything would have to come under the scrutiny of Mam's watchful eye. She knew – and hated – my love of all things colourful, so anything I was considering had to pass her own taste test first.

I'd always wanted ivory and purple as my colour scheme. But Mam vetoed ivory because she was worried that people might think that I was only wearing ivory because I wasn't pure enough to wear white (in other words not a virgin). Then my Auntie Mary made a passing comment one day, 'I bet your bridesmaids will be dressed in purple,' she laughed.

Straight away those colours were crossed off the list. Then Mam made it clear it didn't really matter which colour I chose, as really she wanted no colour at all. And although it was my wedding, I also had to think of her wishes.

We spent hours tramping around different shops, Mam pointing out supposedly beautiful gowns, me not liking them . . . Then we stumbled across one dress hanging up in a shop in Scholes and it seemed to jump off the peg and scream at me.

A beautiful pure white, it was covered in silver threads and very similar to the design I wanted. Immediately I could imagine walking up the aisle in it.

I pulled it off the hanger and held it up to myself, twirling from side to side, smiling. 'Oh Mam, have you ever seen such a dress?'

'Nice,' she said. 'Shame it's got a colour in it.'

'But it's silver, Mam, and silver is a metal not a colour, no? I want one like this.'

She paused for a moment and then agreed I could try it, so I whipped it on and immediately felt like a million dollars and a real princess all rolled in to one. I stared at my reflection, turning this way and that, just feeling like I couldn't believe this was really happening. After all this time, after Moses breaking my heart, after all the attempted grabs, the proposals and hanging on to my virtue, I was actually getting married.

I never thought any further that that.

Chapter Twenty-Five

My (Not so Big or Fat)
Gypsy Wedding

The wedding dress designer sat down with me and made notes as I rattled off the changes I wanted to make.

'I'd like crystals scattered around the bodice and skirt. The train needs to be a lot longer. And it has to be very fitted on top . . .'

I had the perfect picture in my head. The designer had to take on two extra staff to get it ready in time, as all the silver thread embroidery was painstakingly sewn by hand. I didn't know how much the dress cost, but even Mam baulked at the price, though she wouldn't tell me how much it was. Instead she asked for me to pay something towards it, so I put in £600. It's the bride's family who pay for everything except for the best man's suit, the church and marriage licence. As soon as my sister and I were born, my dad would've saved something every day to put towards our weddings. But this dress was particularly extravagant so I was happy to chip in. Instead of a tiara, I commissioned a beautiful feather hair slide from a head-dress designer, with the strict instructions I didn't want anything crass.

I had a cake made by a cake decorator called Michelle in Wakefield. She often does Travellers' cakes and can make them for every occasion you can imagine. I knew I could never beat Maria's incredible wedding cake, a massive ten-tier cake with a real running waterfall underneath, so I just asked for a simple four tiers. Michelle did a double take. This was a very minim-alist order compared to most Gypsy cakes.

'You sure?' she said.

'Yep,' I nodded. 'I want it to look like a Chanel handbag with crystals all over it please.' She nodded, seeming to under-stand exactly what I meant.

Mam insisted I had a bride and groom on top, in keeping with tradition, so although I wanted just flowers I picked some icing figurines to sit on the side. Later I told George about the cake and he mentioned one of his aunties wanted to make one too. So I agreed, although it was unnecessary. I explained the flower theme was white Stargazer lilies but she ended up icing white trumpet lilies (death lilies to us) on the top. How ominous.

For the bouquets I chose Stargazer lilies and silver ribbon. I couldn't find a florist who understood the non-structured, hand-tied style I was after, so I made them myself.

Choosing the guests proved to be the hardest part. George's mother, Joan, wanted me to send out invites, but we don't do this for Gypsy weddings. As far as we're concerned, anyone and everyone can come. I have so many relations, and I didn't know where everyone was half the time, so it was impossible to track them down. The worst thing you could do was leave someone off a guest list, as that'd cause all kinds of ructions. Therefore the best thing was not to bother having invites at all.

'But think of your poor parents and the catering,' Joan said, after I explained.

'They are Gypsies,' I replied. 'They are used to it.'

Instead she asked if she could place an advert in *The World's Fair*, a newspaper just for show people.

'Yes, of course,' I said. 'As long as you mention my mam and dad.'

When I spotted the advert my heart sank. She'd worded it to say that all could attend the evening do, implying the service and the meal were invitation only. This resulted in large sections of her own family never showing up as they were expecting invites. Years later I met some of them and they knew nothing about our wedding at all.

Invites are so unnecessary. Word soon travels when someone gets married, gives birth or dies. I've never had a single invite to any wedding but have been to plenty. Of course that means there's no sit-down meal so we have a hot buffet, with lots of meat, potato and veg.

Despite the lack of invites there were plenty of other things to sort out. The next item on the list was the bridesmaids' outfits. I chose beautiful dresses made from white silk with delicate sleeves and full skirts. By this point Tom had become a dad three times over, with another girl, Maria-Cizzier, following Marnie, and a little boy called, you guessed it, Tom (though he was known as TJ, for Thomas-James). So I wanted to have my two nieces, Marnie and Maria-Cizzier, as bridesmaids and my nephew TJ as a pageboy.

George only had one female cousin. She was a teenager and a size twenty-two, bless her, so I knew if I put her alongside the wee ones she might feel a bit out of place. So instead he asked Howard's daughter, Tyla. Maria was chosen as my 'best woman'. At Gypsy weddings if you can have a best man you get a best woman too.

Two weeks before the wedding, my sister Maria became a mam for the first time when she gave birth to Violet-Theresa. As soon as she arrived we all went to see her and couldn't believe how sweet she was. With a layer of fine reddish hair, she took after my colouring, and it was love at first sight. As broody as I was, I've never been envious of my sister – although watching Violet-Theresa and her sister Maria-Suzannah (who arrived two years later) grow in to the most gorgeous little girls has been such an experience I often wish I had children like them myself. They grew in to such personalities and both shared my colouring so people often mistook them for my own.

The weekend before the wedding, I had my hen do. Again I chose the same place as we had our Maria's: the Batley Variety

Club. This place is often frequented by the Gypsy community and there's usually no trouble, so it's a good venue for a quiet drink. As usual I said I wasn't drinking, but on this night a few of my friends insisted.

'But I have no idea what to order,' I protested, looking at the optics behind the bar.

'Have a white wine spritzer: that's wine and lemonade,' said my cousin. 'You look like that type of girl.'

After three or four of those I was more than tipsy, dancing the night away and having loads of fun. Little did I know, a few months after marrying George, the supposed man of my dreams, that I'd look back at myself that evening, just a carefree girl sipping her spritzers and having a giggle, and realise that girl knew nothing about real life. She'd been so loved by her parents, so sheltered and basically so happy, she had no idea what real problems were.

On 5 March 2002, I woke up in the morning to get ready to marry George. Although I'd waited so long for God to provide me a Christian husband, I thought I knew what I was doing. This didn't feel as I'd imagined it, but then he seemed to be a decent man, who loved me and wanted to marry me. And after what I'd lived through with Moses, this seemed a sensible choice.

We hired a Beaufort, a classic convertible with a sweeping wheel arch, the same as Maria had, to take us to the church. Dad sat with me in the back, his eyes looking a little glazed.

We didn't say much; we just made polite chitchat about how the inside of the car smelled of leather and how we hoped the sun would come out.

I half-expected him to say the same line as he'd said to Maria: 'You can stop this now if you want.' Dad was always so keen to protect us. Even on Maria's wedding day, he wanted to let her know she didn't have to do it, despite all the guests waiting and the expense. But he didn't. Looking back I think I know why. If he had done, I'd have burst in to tears, turned the car back and tore off my dress.

As I walked in to the cathedral my dad held on to my hand tightly. Then someone waved and rushed over. I'd arrived fifteen minutes late expecting everything to be ready but the church canon hadn't arrived yet. So we had to stand in the doorway for a few minutes longer, with everyone waiting, the organ poised to start, just waiting, waiting . . .

Those five minutes in the church foyer felt like hours. No one uttered a word. Not a single word. I started to feel numb, any excitement waning. By then I just wanted it to be over.

Then a dress of white whooshed past us like a whirlwind: the canon had arrived, full of apologies.

'Just a minute,' he gasped, breathlessly, 'and we can get this show on the road.'

The first few notes of the honking organ told us it was time for my entrance and, slipping my arm through the crook of Dad's, he gave me the briefest wink, as we set off for the slow walk down the aisle.

My head started swimming as familiar faces of family and friends all caught my eye one by one. Finally I saw George at the end by the altar, looking hot and uncomfortable and out of place dressed in his smart suit. Though I had to admit he did look more grown up than ever.

I arrived next to him as he beamed like he'd won ten lotteries. 'I didn't think you'd turn up,' he whispered.

'Thanks,' I replied.

Not exactly the welcome I was expecting from the man I was about to marry but there you go.

I said the vows loudly and clearly, like I meant them. And I did. Every word. My voice came out all strange and robotic sounding as it echoed back off the concrete church pillars. I was happy to include the line 'to love, honour and obey'. This was going to be a traditional Christian marriage and yes, it might be unfashionable, but for me obeying my husband was part of that.

Then finally it was over, people were clapping, Mam was sobbing – more loudly than normal, it seemed – and I was smiling. I didn't know why but I suddenly felt tired. I wanted to sit down. It'd all been too much.

We took a car to the Midland Hotel up the road. Luckily no one had pointed out we were Travellers and perhaps because my dress was fairly understated it wasn't that obvious, so no one at the hotel made a fuss.

We made our way in to the reception room, where we could finally relax and let our hair down.

After taking our places, a few words were said. The Gypsy way is for the parents to stand up and say quickly 'Good luck and all the best', and sit back down again.

George's family had very different ideas. Both him and his best man spoke for about twenty minutes each and then they got out a whole pile of cards from people who couldn't make it. They proceeded to read out every single one of them in dull monotone voices. Up to that point the drinks were flowing and everyone was having a right good giggle. I just sat there thinking how the flow of my big day was being killed dead. But I was a Romany who'd married a showman. Like they had to respect our traditions, we had to respect theirs.

Of course, during the buffet George's mum Joan started to complain about the food, saying it wasn't up to scratch and the kitchen wasn't clean.

'All this money spent just on food,' she huffed over and over, even though she'd not put in a bean towards our big day.

During the buffet, drinks started to flow and it's seen as perfectly acceptable for the bride to get quite drunk. This is to prepare her for what comes later . . . the wedding night. This is a big event in any Gypsy woman's life as it would be the very first time she'd make love.

Up to that point, I'd still never discussed any of this with anyone, aside from the quick chat I'd had with Maria when she'd asked me if I wanted babies 'straight away'. I knew I didn't want this, because I didn't want folk 'finger counting':

this is when people gossip about how many months gone you are after the wedding. 'Well, if she had the baby seven months after the wedding . . .' folk would say, all counting on their fingers. It was a scandal if people thought you'd 'done the deed' before your wedding night.

All my cousins bought me drinks and because so many were men they soon made the singles I'd asked for in to doubles and then the doubles in to triples. Then my cousin Jimmy bought me a pint of beer. I laughed as I shook my head.

'A bride under the table is not a good look,' I grinned.

Not only do the bride and groom have a first dance, you have a last dance with members of your family. Life really does change when you get married. You're no longer able to hang around with your single girlfriends and your parents become more distant.

Just as I had lost Maria, she now felt a little like she was losing me. She knew I'd have to put George first now. I'd always be her big sister to look out for her, but my time wouldn't be so much my own.

I danced with Maria to Shania Twain's 'Man, I Feel Like a Woman', the same tune we danced to at her wedding. Then I danced with my dad to 'Wind Beneath My Wings', which had me blubbing on his new suit like a baby.

Then it was mine and George's turn. I should have seen another red flashing light when I realised we didn't actually have 'a song', as our relationship was so short and shallow.

After we realised we had to pick one for the first dance I simply said: 'OK let's go for whatever is number one on the day.'

It was 'Evergreen' by Will Young. Possibly the most depressing song ever.

Towards the end of the night George started nuzzling my ear. 'Shall we go to the honeymoon suite?' he whispered. I could tell he was itching to get me upstairs.

I brushed him off. In the pit of my stomach I actually felt rather nervous. 'We have to wait until all the guests leave or it's ignorant,' I said. At this point I also decided to stop drinking. I was very tipsy, and I didn't want my mam and dad to notice.

Later on an old friend, Harry, turned up. He was a bit tipsy himself, and without his wife.

'Can I ask your beautiful wife to dance with me?' he asked George.

George nodded as Harry whisked me off. 'This should have been me and you, Violet,' he said, very loudly and within earshot of the top table. I felt myself cringing, I didn't know if he was having a laugh or what.

My cousin Bernard showed up late too. I couldn't see him, but it was important to me he was there, so I rang his mobile to make sure he was coming.

As I danced around, my shoes started to kill me, so I pulled them off and held them in my hand. Then, wanting to feel free, I threw them high in to the air, too drunk to care where or on whom they landed. Next day I had to crawl around on my hands and knees for ages to find them.

A couple of hours later all the guests had left and it was finally time for us to retire to our room. I felt rigid with nerves as George waved goodbye to all the guests, while holding my hand firmly in the other. I couldn't even look Dad in the face or say goodbye. It made my guts churn to know he knew what was going to happen next. His little girl, oh, it didn't bear thinking about.

In our room, George flopped on the bed, a big smile on his face. 'Come here then,' he grinned, holding out wide-open arms.

But I sat down next to our big pile of presents. 'Let's open these first,' I said. 'Come on.'

As we sat encircled by torn wrapping it occurred to me just how much more generous my family were than his, even though they had more money. My uncle had given George £200 in notes just to buy pots and pans. My sister had saved for months to get me a limited edition vase. Another uncle had splashed out on two Crown Derby drummer boys at £100 a pop. Whereas his family got us a glass crystal ball that could have cost no more than £20, and a few cards.

I honestly don't remember a huge amount about what happened next. All I do remember is grabbing my discarded dress afterwards and clutching it to myself. I then walked to the bathroom, sat in the middle of the cold hard floor and sobbed quietly for ages.

I was married. To George. A showman I'd dated for five months, What had I done?

I ripped off a piece of toilet tissue, wiped my face and went back to bed to see my new husband sprawled across it, snoring loudly.

Chapter Twenty-Six

Marry in Haste . . .

My dear brother Tom had splashed out on a honeymoon for us, to Ayia Napa. Not exactly a normal honeymoon destination, but then that's typical of our Tom, and of course we were grateful.

Dad picked us up to drive us to the airport the day after the wedding. I felt so embarrassed seeing him. Dad knew what must have happened the night before and it killed me I wasn't his little girl any more, so I dived in the back, muttered a quick hello, unable to look him in the eye.

On holiday people seemed to notice our new wedding rings everywhere we went, and we were bought drinks by Gorja people and a couple of Gypsies alike. I felt happy to be swept along by the excitement, even though it was emanating more from other people than from us.

We did all the usual tourist things, playing the part of the newly married couple, visiting where the Apostle Paul was flogged, and wandering round the old town, peering at the architecture and mosaic work. Cyprus is divided in to two separate

Turkish- and Greek-controlled areas and there's a UN-controlled buffer zone between them that we went to visit one day.

We walked up to the top of a huge Woolworths to view the border, a no-man's land that separates the two parts of the country.

With my sunglasses on, the boiling sun beating down on us, I stopped and stared at this sight with my new husband. 'What a view,' said George, grinning, encircling my waist.

I nodded. But instead of appreciating the scenery, I just felt empty inside. It was no-man's land, a barren, empty space; somehow it resonated with me and I felt like I belonged there. I shook the thought from my head. I was probably just feeling a bit blue after all the excitement of the wedding.

We arrived home to find the wedding photos had been delivered. One caught my eye in particular. Dad and I were posing outside the church, I was wearing my veil and I hadn't noticed at the time, but Dad's face was filled with emotion. Biting his lip, his eyes were welling up. It was an expression I'd never seen before. I kept it separate from the others, as I thought it wasn't fair to show it to everyone in the album. Dad would be embarrassed.

And so we settled down to married life. Or that is what I thought the next line should be.

It's the man's job to provide the home and George had got us a Tabbert trailer, an old-style cheap one, costing around £1,000 when ordinarily most people spend around £4,000. Nothing worked in it, including the oven and the lights. Only the fridge flickered in to life now and then.

But I was a new wife, and this is what my husband had bought, so I was determined to make the most of it. Carefully I set about building up a home, the contents now being worth far more than the actual place. I polished and proudly set out my Crown Derby sets, my figurines and all my lovely wedding presents, and set about turning the insides in to a cosy palace. I'd bought a beautiful Hungarian goosedown bedspread, and as I threw it across our new bed, it really was the finishing touch. The trailer was parked in Mam and Dad's yard; however they respected we were married now and left us to get on with it. Tom wasn't quite so distant. Every time I started putting the dinner on he tended to walk past as if on cue.

'What you having?' he'd say, following his nose.

I wanted it to be a proper marriage though and it was only George I served for.

For both of us I think marriage was a huge adjustment. George had been used to going out most nights with the lads. At first he'd grab his coat after dinner and start to set off, leaving me in the trailer watching TV.

'Where you going?' I'd say.

'Out, see yous later,' he'd reply.

I would take one look at him and shake my head. He soon learned if he was going to set off out then I was going to disappear off with my friends too. I didn't fancy being sat in on my tod all night. And he didn't like that idea so stayed in too.

It wasn't just our social life we didn't agree on. I soon

learned that co-existing with someone as messy and lazy as George was a bitter pill to swallow. Living in a space around twenty feet by eight feet, you have to be tidy. I'd been brought up in a spotless house, so suddenly when someone was leaving bowls around and bits of food everywhere it was hard to deal with.

Then he bought a German Shepherd dog called Duchess, nicknamed Dutch, then later another one called Aphrodite, a wonderful idea in principle. Except he never cleaned up after them either, ever. Soon hairs and mess were everywhere. He just didn't care.

To begin with I just went round cleaning up after him, but even then he didn't respect my conventions. We'd never had any alcohol in our house, but he'd openly drink, leaving cans of lager around. People always drop in, no one phones or texts beforehand, so it's important for Gypsies to be clean and tidy. Plus I didn't want folk talking. If they saw open cans of lager strewn about whatever would they think!

Also George would leave bowls or cups outside and I'd then have to throw them away. Another of our customs is that something is dirty if it's been left outdoors.

I worked full time, but George's work was sporadic. He loved his PlayStation and sometimes I'd find him still sat on it when I got home.

Somehow though we managed to save the money for a bigger trailer, and we bought a static metal caravan. We got it from Auntie Sweetshop (Mary) and Uncle Jimmy, who had first lived in a yard in Bradford then moved in to a house, and used the trailer as a living room. They'd kept it immaculate and some of it still had the original plastic covers on it.

To me this was our first proper home and I couldn't wait to move in. I was sure once we'd left my parent's yard and got ourselves a decent place, things would improve. So we moved to Paley Road in Bradford, sharing a plot with other show people.

I knew before I arrived that it wasn't an area of beautiful green fields by any stretch of the imagination, as obviously I had previously visited George there. But living there and waking up to it on a day-to-day basis was a different challenge altogether.

The first thing you notice when you pull up is that you're basically living on a patch of dirt covered in enormous blocks, strange and foreign-looking to a Romany: these were showmen's wagons. With no windows, they weren't bright white but grey, streaky and dirty. People didn't scrub down their trailers like we did, maybe because they were so huge – it would've been hard to make a hosepipe reach. They looked so different to the pretty, shiny trailers with lots of windows that I was used to. On the showman sites there's no tarmac, no piece of ground that's yours, no fence around and no sheds, and on this particular site there was only one tap that belonged to five people. If someone put a washing machine on at the other end of the camp, it could take you four hours to fill a kettle. Electricity was the same: it was constantly tripping and if you had the telly on and someone else flicked a kettle on nearby the whole thing went off.

The view from our trailer was a mound of dirt that had some weeds going through it. On the other side was a spot I came to call 'the Showman's Graveyard', as it was the place where pieces of machinery, rides and old lorries were chucked before they made it to the dump.

'What do you think?' said George hopefully.

I managed a smile. 'We'll make it a home,' I said. The first thing I did was close the curtains to the view outside and I never opened them again.

Despite my reservations about the site I loved our trailer after I'd done up the inside. As you walked in there was a wardrobe and dressing table to your right, then a bed and a shower room to the left, and next to that was the table where I carefully set out my Crown Derby set, never used, but proudly left on display, just as my mam and grannies had done. All around the edges were more bunks, a couch and shelves. It was cosy, warm and inviting, just as I'd imagined a home of my own would be.

I picked an aubergine and biscuit colour scheme. Auntie Sweetshop had already put up royal blue-coloured curtains, which were lovely but didn't match. So I took them down and priced up some new curtains. Not able to bring myself to pay the £1,100 quoted, I decided to make my own. Having never done this before it was an effort and took forever, but I was determined and soon learned my way round a sewing machine.

OK, so the environment around my new trailer wasn't as I'd have liked but I couldn't wait to make new friends, get stuck in and really make this our home. We'd had a rocky first few months to our marriage and I thought a change of scene was all we needed. Although I was a Romany now living amongst showmen, I didn't see any reason why I wouldn't fit in. After all, I'd married one.

The first time I was called a pikey, a hot flush spread over my neck and up my face. This was quite simply the worst insult a Romany woman could hear from anyone, and showmen, of all people, knew this. It also wasn't just the word itself either, it was the way it was said.

'Oi, George. Tell your pikey wife to make us a cup o' tea,' laughed George's Uncle Paul, the man who ran the site, one day.

It was a joke, I told myself, a joke.

Even so, I didn't let him get away with it. 'Don't call me that, Paul,' I snapped.

He rolled his eyes and made an 'Ooooh!' face.

Ignoring it I made his cup of tea with extra sugar, just as I knew he liked.

Within a few months though I realised there are only so many times you can ask someone not to call you something. Even if the name has deeply offensive connotations, and even if that person knows it. Even the kids joined in sometimes.

One kid always turned up every time I made rice pudding. I handed him a steaming bowl once and he lapped it up like a cat. 'So nice!' he grinned, running off to play.

The following week, as I began to make another saucepan of it, I heard a patter of feet.

'Violet,' he cried. 'Can I have some more?'

'Sure,' I grinned. 'C'mon in.'

As he sat down to wait, a spoon clenched in his dirty hand, he said: 'No one can make a rice pudding quite like a pikey.'

I stopped stirring the pudding and turned slowly to face him. 'What did yous just call me?' I said.

George was sitting watching TV and overheard everything, but he didn't say a word. In fact he looked like he found it all rather amusing.

'A pikey,' said the kid loudly. 'Just saying, no one makes rice pudding like yous. How do you do it?'

'Oh,' I said, 'I put hedgehog milk in it, didn't you know?'

His face turned white. He wasn't so keen on my dessert after that.

All the residents of Paley Road went to the working men's club, including the women. They never asked me. But one evening, I decided to join them with George, invited or not. I just presumed that once I'd got to know them more they'd start to accept me.

As we arrived, I got chatting to a couple of people when George's Uncle Paul spotted us.

'Ah, it's George and his pikey wife,' he said.

I stopped draining my Coke, put the glass down and looked at him.

'You what?' I said. 'Can you stop calling me that? Please.'

'Ah, no offence, no offence is it.'

'Well, actually I do find it offensive.'

'Yeah, but it's the way we differentiate each other, innit,' he said.

'Well, maybe I should call you the Romany name for what we call showmen then,' I warned him.

Now, Romanies found out years back that showmen used a bucket to go to the toilet at night, and left it in their trailers. It made us all feel sick to the stomach and since then Romany people often called showmen 'shitinthebuckets'. Uncle Paul was well aware of this horrible tag and didn't like it as much as the next man.

'Aw, you're not like that,' he went on. 'You wouldn't dare. Pikey is different.'

'I am not a pikey, I am a Gypsy,' I said, through gritted teeth.

Paul started laughing. 'Pikey, Gypsy, it's all the same innit? C'mon, be nice, pikey.'

In the loudest voice I could manage I replied: 'All right, you shitinthebucket you, that's fine. Now I know your name and you know mine.'

With the much-hated nickname spoken aloud, all pairs of eyes turned on me. Paul's face was turning crimson. 'You whaaat?' he said.

'What's the matter, Paul? Sorry, shitinthebucket? Don't like your name? But that's just how we differentiate ourselves, innit? Only a name, no offence, none at all.'

Slamming his drink on the side, Paul stood up and walked away.

'Don't you ever call me a pikey in public again,' I shot after him.

George's face had turned a shade of white I'd never seen before. He was mortified.

'Violet,' he said. 'Think about what you're doing! What do you think you're doing?'

Tears sparked in my eyes. The last thing I wanted was to embarrass my husband, but where was he while I was being abused on a daily basis? I left the club and went back to the trailer, where I closed the curtains a little bit tighter to shut out the world.

Eight months after our wedding, we went on a day trip to Alton Towers. This is a popular destination for Gypsies and showmen alike. It's a place we're always allowed in and can let our hair down. As we arrived, I was holding George's hand when I felt a pair of eyes boring in to me. Call it a sixth sense, but my heart was in my mouth as I swung around. There, among the crowd, I picked out the familiar glossy black head of hair that belonged to Moses. For a split second our eyes caught and we held each other's gaze, long enough to make my heart thud in my rib cage and my cheeks flush. I just knew in that single transitory moment, with that one look, that my marriage to George had been a total mistake.

* * *

My marriage might not have got off to the best start, but my working life was going from strength to strength. In 2003, I started a job at a new venture called the Leeds Gypsy and Traveller Exchange (Leeds GATE for short). When I first began we worked in a horrible dingy little office with only one other person, but it soon grew to us having four full-time staff and many volunteers. Right from the start we all got on well together, having a right good laugh.

My role, just like Mam's, was to help Travellers find the right services they needed and to get an education. During my time here I also went on a few different courses to boost my CV and increase my knowledge. One chief executive kindly told me I could attend the courses but didn't have to be subject to the same tests as everyone else.

'You won't have to do the essay at the end like everyone else,' he beamed, as he explained the course to all the new students.

'Oh yes I will,' I said. Every pair of eyes in the room swivelled to look at me. 'What's the point of me doing a whole course and then not sitting the assessment like everyone else?'

His reaction to me joining the course couldn't have come at a worse time, as my confidence in my abilities was pretty low anyway.

Worrying myself sick about not getting my assessments right, I agonised over them, checking and double-checking my grammar until my head was in a spin. Luckily my tutor was very supportive, always pointing out my mistakes, and giving me praise when it was due. My own concerns at my lack of education were made worse when two girls on my course dismissed the assignments as walks in the park.

I was sent for the final exams at the Bradford Midland Hotel, the same place I'd held my reception.

As I sat chatting to the other students beforehand, some of them were intrigued about my life working with Travellers, not realising I was one myself.

'God, it must be a total nightmare sometimes,' one said.

'Of course!' I agreed. 'It's the professionals that get me. Some of them are absolute gits!'

During my stint in this job I was promoted three times. I started as a Connexions worker, then became a youth project coordinator and finally deputy director.

It was there I also made my first and only proper Gorja friend. Her name was Ellie.

Right from the start I liked her. She spoke so clearly with great empathy in her interview. She'd worked with homeless people in London and had a real understanding of the issues that Travellers faced. She wasn't afraid to tell it like it was.

Two months after starting the job, Ellie discovered she was expecting. Beside herself with distress she confided to me her mum and dad were going to kill her as they were strict Christians. She had no idea what to do and we talked intensely about it all. Although of course I didn't believe in the s-word outside of marriage myself, I've never judged other people and the way they lead their lives. I just loved Ellie for who she was and wanted to help. She went on to have her baby and marry her man, although they divorced later. But we stayed in touch.

I loved my job and enjoyed tackling prejudices head on. As I've mentioned, very often when a Gypsy person books a venue it can be cancelled at the last minute because of prejudices about Gypsies breaking things or being dirty. I took great pleasure in booking venues for conferences and the like under the name 'Leeds GATE', specifically leaving out the information that we were a Travellers' organisation, and then sending out a letter afterwards confirming the reservation with our proper name on it: the Leeds Gypsy and Travellers' Exchange.

One of the trustees of GATE was a lovely lady called Emma Judge. She worked for the Commission for Racial Equality, but once quizzed me about fortune-telling as she was fascinated by the subject.

'Are you able to read fortunes at all?' she asked. I just laughed. That stereotype is one people won't let go of.

Then one Saturday, I was in Argos picking up some bits and bobs when I spotted a woman arguing at the till, holding a copper kettle. She was saying it was broken and the man was telling her this couldn't be the case. Eventually the lady seemed to give up, grabbed the bag with her kettle and left the shop. As she walked out I realised it was Emma, though she didn't see me.

On the following Monday morning I thought I'd have a little joke with her.

'Hey Emma,' I said. 'Are you OK?'

'Yes, fine,' she said.

'It's just I had a right funny feeling about you on Saturday. A horrible sensation. You were angry, frustrated. It was something about electricity, water and a kettle. Copper I think it were . . .'

Emma's mouth fell open. 'Violet that's incredible . . . really freaky . . .' she began. Then she noticed my mouth crinkling in to a smile.

'It's amazing what fortunes can be told in Argos,' I laughed.

Chapter Twenty-Seven

The Real World

During part of my course I had to learn about child protection and we had talks by police and social services about child cruelty, how to spot it and how to report it.

I was horrified as we were shown pictures of injuries on children and told the lengths some parents would go to to hide them. Some of it was truly shocking.

It also highlighted to me just how blessed we'd been growing up with Mam and Dad travelling around, protected from the harsh cruelties of the outside world. OK, we were called gypos and followed round supermarkets and not let in to cinemas occasionally, but we'd also been protected from some of the extremes of society.

Here, in my early twenties, I found myself sat in a classroom, being taught not only a lesson in child protection but also something about the realities of the very cruel modern world of which I'd had little part. And at that moment I couldn't have been more grateful.

Over the next two years the Northern Network that I'd

started attracted hundreds of members, and before I knew it I was chairwoman. It became very successful and we were even awarded a government grant of £360,000 to help prevent homelessness amongst Gypsies. This money was well spent too: every eviction costs the government £5,000 and rehousing people is not cheap, so they definitely earned their money back.

The worst Gypsy sites are always found on local authority land. We heard of some terrible conditions that Travellers were living in, sometimes right under huge pylons or next to toxic land. We heard of one case when a group moved on to a site that had just been declared unfit for horses to live on.

It wasn't always easy being so young and dealing with such a huge organisation. The reaction from other Gypsies was also not always positive. At one meeting an old Gypsy lady came in, wanting to have her say about something.

As she waited, she looked over the minutes from the last meeting, pointing out loudly that they were wrong. I could see she'd made a mistake so gently I told her so, respectfully addressing her as 'aunt' as you always did with someone older.

Her sharp eyes looked at me. 'Shut up, little girl,' she said. 'The only reason you are here is because it looks good for the charity.'

I felt my temper snap, my hand shaking under the table as I clutched hold of the minutes, so I called for a few minutes' break, left the room and ran downstairs in to the street. Around the corner through gritted teeth I yelled: 'Fucking stupid old basket!' I never ever use bad language, so when Emma caught up with me, she asked if I was OK. I burst in to laughter. 'I feel better now,' I said.

Although I was working hard in my job, I took my role as wife very seriously too, looking after my man, however ungrateful he was. Once I had a day off, and with George out working on a fair for once, I thought I'd surprise him with a homemade lasagne. I carefully chose all the best ingredients and really went to town whipping up a bechamel sauce from scratch and layering it so it stood to attention when the pieces were cut and served.

George arrived home looking sweaty and tired. He'd spent the day helping his cousin Howard with rides. Proudly, I slipped on my oven gloves and pulled out my pièce de resistance. I knew he must be hungry.

Raising an eyebrow he peered in to my carefully prepared dish like he'd spotted an insect in his soup.

'Wha's that?' he said.

'Lasagne!' I beamed, triumphantly. 'From scratch.'

The sight of his wrinkled nose made my heart sink like a popped balloon.

'I don't like lasagne,' he said. 'I'll just have chips.'

I knew he loved spaghetti bolognese, and how this was different I'll never know. Saying nothing, I dumped it on the counter and pulled out the frying pan.

When we weren't bickering or rowing, evenings consisted of nights in front of DVDs. We had the biggest collection you'd ever seen. Sitting in silence, absorbed in a film, was preferable to niggling at each other. And we had one very big subject to avoid. Now a few months had passed, the baby 'issue' was starting to come up again.

Although of course I was desperate to be a mam one day, I found myself putting it off with George. It just didn't feel right. I wanted our marriage to be solid first.

His mam was also putting masses of pressure on me. Every so often, she'd give a little wink and say: 'Is there any news yet?' Sometimes she put it more plainly: 'I'm dying to be a grandmother, I think you need to get on with it.'

This was embarrassing and awkward. I knew Joan only had two boys so her family was very small compared to most Travellers, but bringing a child in to a marriage was a big commitment. My own mam was less pushy. By then she had six grandkids: Marnie, Maria-Cizzier, TJ and Bernadette-Dawn from Tom and Marie, and Violet-Theresa and Maria-Suzannah from my sister Maria and Fly. Looking back it's clear Mam had guessed my marriage to George was not love's young dream by any stretch. She knew I had to fix our relationship before I added kids to the mix.

Our first anniversary arrived and we had no money what-soever. My job supported us both, but only enough to pay the bills. I was pretty much the breadwinner. I decided we should still celebrate our anniversary anyway. George didn't seem bothered but I insisted we did something – our marriage hadn't got off to a good start, but I wanted at least to make the effort.

I borrowed a *Reader's Digest Atlas of Britain* and, looking down the coastline of Yorkshire, I picked out Hornsea, a little seaside town.

George rolled his eyes as I showed him the atlas.

'Looks like it's in the middle of nowhere,' he grumbled.

'That's the exact point,' I said.

There's nothing that cheers a Romany up more than going somewhere new and seeing a bit of open space when things get tough. So I booked the cheapest B&B I could find and we set off for two nights. The most memorable part was walking around an ex-army barracks that had been turned in to a bird sanctuary. But we did so in complete silence. I was with my husband, yet it seemed like he had nothing left to say to me.

Back home in the trailer at Paley Road, however much I tried I still didn't seem to fit in. No one asked me to go for a drink or over to theirs for dinner. I was so used to the Romany way of people turning up for cups of tea or just popping in for dinner. No one ever minded – everyone's trailer was an open house all year round. Loneliness was a very new feeling for me. The only people who made any effort were Thomas and Elizabeth Peel and the Wilkinson family. The Wilkinsons had three beautiful little girls called Dempsey, Darcy and Regan. I fell in love with pretty little Regan, she was all smiles, teeth and blonde hair.

After work, I'd get home and would soon hear a soft knock on the door. It was always Regan, wanting to come in for dinner or to snuggle up next to me and watch TV. She'd even want to accompany me to the supermarket to get the week's shop. I never minded, she made me giggle again and just accepted me for who I was. I loved those kids so much. Although my brother and sister had children of their own, I didn't see much of them.

In fact, very slowly and almost imperceptibly, I realised I didn't see much of anyone these days. George didn't encourage me to go out and the twenty questions I'd receive if I did try and organise anything made it not seem worth it. Seeing those kids was like a breath of fresh air.

Years later the tragic news came through that Regan was found dead at nineteen in her trailer. A faulty boiler had caused carbon monoxide poisoning. Such a terrible tragedy, but Gypsies and Travellers were often vulnerable to such things. Sometimes health and safety was poor on sites.

Although our home was finally fixed and looking lovely, the atmosphere inside was deteriorating. Our small rows about cleaning up and tidying subsided as I decided it was less hassle to just tidy up after him. But communicating with George on a day-to-day basis was getting harder.

'What do you want for dinner?' I asked every evening after work.

'Not bothered,' he'd reply, his eyes fixed on the PlayStation.

Sometimes starting any sort of conversation with my husband was like getting blood out of a stone.

My two years at Paley Road were miserable to say the least. It was a tight-knit community of showmen, and I soon realised they were not the most welcoming towards outsiders. Some made sure I always felt like one.

George's work was always sporadic, but it grew even worse after we married. The frustrating thing was that he was extraordinarily clever with his hands. Once he set his mind to it he could create anything. For example, one time he made an incredible catering unit from scratch, buying parts from scrap, designing it himself and putting it all together. It was a hot-dog stand, and if it were possible to call a fairground caterer's stand 'beautiful' it was a good description for this one. The shiny straight edges and curved sides drew attention from other showmen who copied his design.

He sold the stand for £18,000. Excited about the money, I congratulated him. Three years had flown by since our wedding and I thought perhaps he was going to turn a corner work-wise.

I was wrong. Shortly afterwards he paid £1,000 for a position on one of the shows but spent just six months working there. As with most things, he got bored easily and gave up.

He also wanted me to work with him. I was incensed at this idea. I was already working six days a week at this point and I had done for years, and if he expected me to get up at 3 a.m. on a Sunday morning to go and stand behind a hot-dog stall with him he had another thing coming.

So he did it by himself, grew increasingly disenchanted and gave it up. I didn't even pass comment, I realised by now this was going to be the way of my husband.

In the summers of 2004 and 2005, we ended up going back to Hornsea, the place we'd spent our anniversary, to work at a small fair. I'd managed to help George get a doughnut stall there while he sorted out what he was going to do next.

To escape to Hornsea was just heaven. Sitting on the grass under the trees with laughing kids around me while I handed out doughnuts . . . it felt like a holiday. Just to be away from Paley Road and with happy people again was such a treat.

But in 2005, another tragedy struck our family, and it was caused once again by a terrible disease that we now felt too familiar with. The year before, Babby John, my Aunt Margaret's surrogate boy, had been taken ill with cancer aged just eleven. He was such a lovely little boy, and devoted to his mam. Initially doctors dismissed his complaints as growing pains, but Aunt Margaret put her foot down, insisting on a second opinion, another common theme in our family.

Eventually they found that tumours riddled his body. It was devastating. Babby John never complained, despite the awful treatment he had to endure. Once again we all gathered together and prayed like mad. I absolutely believed God would help Babby John through. It seemed impossible to me that God would put a little boy like that through such horrors and that He would not let him survive.

But in July, he was admitted to a children's hospice, Martin House in Boston Spa, West Yorkshire, to be given palliative care.

I visited a few times. It was a place full of suffering, with parents sat around bedsides, in tears, praying and hoping – the hope so alive you could almost reach out and touch it. In the face of such adversity, the nurses were cheerful every single day, the wards rang out with laughter and the staff's positivity shone through as they organised endless games, songs and activities. We were all inspired.

Aunt Margaret insisted on staying with Babby John, even though she wasn't in the best of health herself, God love her. She suffered from another illness that ran in our family: diabetes. Staying in the hospital meant she stopped following a strict diet and lived off sandwiches, pizzas or whatever she could quickly grab in between seeing to Babby John. Soon she fell ill, without realising it, and suffered a terrible stroke.

She ended up in hospital herself, lying there like a vegetable with only a machine keeping her alive for a time. She wasn't there to be with Babby John when he passed away on 9 August 2005.

At this point I questioned my faith in God. I couldn't believe that He could put an innocent like Babby John through all that pain, giving him the false hope of treatment and even taking his mum away – then finally allowing him to die. I felt like raging with anger, it was so deeply unfair. Why should I believe in such a God who could allow such cruelty to happen?

It was Mam who called me to tell me the news that John had died. I just couldn't stop crying as I put down the phone. I grabbed a few belongings to go and drive over to Mam and Dad's but when I went out to my car I realised it had been blocked in by another vehicle. My face blotchy and red with crying, mascara running down my cheeks, I felt a right state and was embarrassed to ask the men whose car it was.

I rang George. 'Babby John's dead,' I sobbed. 'I need to get home but can't get out, can you find out whose car it is and ask them to move it please?'

George let out a long sigh, but agreed to do it.

Finally the cars moved one by one as I waited in the trailer, and eventually the path was free so I was able to get in my car. Even driving seemed like a struggle, as I just felt so beside myself with emotion. As I pulled away, a man flagged me down.

I wound down the window. 'Next time, you get out of your trailer and ask us youself to move ya car,' he snapped. 'You little pikeys think you're too good to speak to the likes of us.'

I couldn't believe he was so angry. Having a go at me for such a little thing. All this on top of Babby John was too much. I just snapped.

'You what?' I cried. 'I am just about to go home to see my eleven-year-old cousin who has died! Next time I'll just call the fire brigade . . . As for *you*, you can drop dead, you ignorant, racist bastard!'

Chapter Twenty-Eight

Till Death Do Us Part

Babby John's funeral was enormous. Around 400 attended the church, where we heard moving readings and poems from his family, his dad/brother John driven to despair with his grief.

Auntie Margaret came to attend too, pushed in a wheelchair by my mam. We all turned as she was wheeled in to the church and just one look at her face told us that she was here physically but not mentally. She'd gone, her whole personality and mind stripped bare by the cruel stroke. And for that we thanked God, as she'd have jumped in to the grave to be with her Babby if she'd understood he'd gone. She couldn't have lived without him.

Two weeks later we were back at the church, burying Aunt Margaret's coffin on top of Babby John's.

Mam helped me through my period of questioning the Lord. She told me Margaret was with her Babby again. And that was exactly what she would've wanted. In some strange way it made sense of it all.

Soon afterwards, I insisted to George enough was enough.

I'd hated Paley Road from the start and however much I'd put a brave face on, I needed to leave. I wanted somewhere I could call home.

As I had a steady job I decided to do what Mam had done and get a mortgage, move from the trailer and buy a house in Castleford. The idea was to feel a bit more settled and obviously buying a house was a way to 'get on'. And let's face it, my husband couldn't afford it, so I'd have to do it myself.

Meanwhile George had had another brainwave for a way to earn money. He made the announcement he wanted to be a machine man (owner of a large fairground ride) and he'd make it work this time. He and his cousin Howard decided to pool some money and buy a ride outright to earn a steady flow of cash. They went off to get it and three whole days later turned up with a contraption apparently known as a 'Grasscutter'.

Staring at what look like a heap of junk outside our trailer I wasn't sure whether to laugh or cry.

'And you expect to do what with this?' I said.

George laughed. 'You'll see,' he said. 'A few lights, a bit of paint and some music, this will be a right money spinner.'

Although I knew nothing of fairground rides, aside from which ones made me throw up, before meeting George, I took my husband's choice of profession to heart and tried to support him as much as possible. I bought an inflatable slide, and every weekend at local fairs I would take it out. Unlike the Grasscutter ride, which still hadn't been finished, the slide made a good few hundred pounds here and there. I loved sitting in the sun, chatting to kids, too.

Weeks after the purchase of the Grasscutter ride, during which time it had been sat outside gathering dust, George decided perhaps he couldn't do anything with it after all. He heaved it back in to the lorry and told me he'd sold it for £20. I was completely staggered at his total lack of sense. I worked out he'd spent £30 on diesel just to drop it off with the buyer, if one existed at all.

Around this time I was lucky enough to get a tax rebate as I'd been taxed at the basic rate for three years in my previous job. When the £3,000 cheque landed I couldn't have been happier, and as I was used to having to pay for everything, I thought it'd be nice to give myself a treat.

I'd always wanted a real Rolex, so one Saturday I took myself off to look at a few. Having completely fallen in love with a Rolex Midi watch, I tried it on and smiled as it sparkled and shone at me. All Gypsies love jewellery and sparkly things. We wear less gold now, as it's seen as tacky since people started copying us, but wearing a nice watch or having a nice ring on you proves you're a worker, someone who takes care of themselves.

Then I thought of my husband, and how we needed to move on in life. I knew I couldn't rely on his wage so it'd have to come from me. How could I justify spending this much on a watch when we needed so much?

Carefully unlatching it, I handed it back to the jeweller, who'd been keeping a watchful eye on me.

'I'll have a think about it,' I said, sadly.

Later that night I asked George: 'What could you do with £3,000 that would really help set you up once and for all?'

He thought for a minute and decided on another catering unit. 'If I build one like last time we could really go places,' he said.

Of course I'm not stupid and knew there was a risk involved but when I thought of the gorgeous unit he'd built before, I knew he was more than capable.

Six months later bits of an unbuilt catering unit were lying outside our trailer, getting soaked in the rain. Once again all his enthusiasm had dried up, fizzled out. He'd just got bored.

Let down once more by my husband, I turned my attentions to a new house. I'd fallen in love with a rundown early nineteenth-century two-bedroom cottage. I'd seen a picture in an estate agent window, and it had a garden on three sides so I could fit a trailer in there too. Perfect.

When I went to visit it, I completely fell in love with the place. What did it for me was a gorgeous cream enamel stove in the kitchen. It was built by a company in Yorkshire that only existed for a few years, so was a real one-off. I imagined myself with a pinny on, knocking up all kinds of treats in that kitchen. Ooh, I couldn't wait. Plus the original fireplace was also incredible, with beautiful tiles around the edges.

We went on a group viewing, and all the other prospective

purchasers seemed to be as keen as me. There were a fair few trailers next door with a Traveller family living there, so I loudly pointed this out to some of my competitors for the house.

'Oh, you want to watch them lot next door,' I said. 'I've heard they cause a right racket, always playing music and the like. You can see the awful caravans from the windows too, terrible, isn't it?'

A few of them looked visibly worried, straining out of the window to spot smoke curling from a trailer chimney. 'Such an eyesore,' one lady muttered.

My plan worked and within a month or so the house was mine. I could've jumped for joy.

We got a date for moving in, but tons of work needed doing on it. George of course stepped in to say he'd help. The worst thing was I knew he was capable of fixing everything. It was just a case of whether he could be bothered or not.

Despite her tiny stature, my Granny Winnie not only had an iron personality but also appeared to have iron insides as well. Aged just ten years old she had suffered a terrible accident while riding her bike, and her handlebars went in to her stomach, coming out the other side of her back. She was rushed to hospital and not expected to survive. As if this ordeal wasn't bad enough, this accident took place during the war, and one night while she was still recovering in hospital an air raid took place. All the nurses wheeled the children in the beds to the cellar for safety, and they were left there all night as the bombs raged above. Terrified and alone, poor Granny Winnie developed a lifelong fear of hospitals and nurses.

This came out years later during her final illness. Again, it was cancer. My dignified and very private granny, who always worried so much about what other people thought, swore and cursed at the nurses as they tended to her. Convinced they were trying to trick her in to being thrown in the cellar she would shout with terror at them when the delirium from her morphine kicked in.

One of my aunties dared to tell Granny Winnie in a lucid moment what she'd been doing and she was mortified. 'I never said that to any nurse,' she hissed, shaking her head. 'I'd never do such a thing.'

So after that we stopped telling her and just tried to keep her calm as the nurses tried to attend to her needs.

When she was dying in hospital we were desperate to bring her home. Romany people don't ever leave their relatives alone if they are ill and in any case it was clear Granny Winnie didn't want to stay in hospital.

It's not just immediate family who care, everyone gets involved. Soon around twenty people – my aunts, cousins, Mam and Dad and various other relations – were milling around her bed and waiting in corridors for visits. But hospital rules stated only two people were allowed per visit.

Ever resourceful, we soon got around this little hindrance. We all got chatting to other patients and when the nurse came in to disperse our group we'd scatter to different patients' bedsides and pretend to be their visitors instead.

Once I rushed over to one old man and quickly looked at his name on the wall. 'Er, hello Mister . . .' I said, frantically looking for his surname as a suspicious-looking nurse walked past. 'Lovely to see you!'

This way, we did genuinely get to know some of the other patients. Many of them were elderly and didn't get visits from their own families for weeks on end. Even after Granny Winnie had left hospital my grandad kept in touch with many of them by letter. They became friends.

One visit didn't end so peacefully. A nurse asked us to move in to the corridor, which we did, but then someone else asked us to move off the premises altogether.

'But we can't leave Granny,' I explained calmly. 'We stay with our folk when they're sick.'

I was then told to leave or face having the police called, so not wanting to create an even bigger fuss we did immediately. Outside, however, a police car was already waiting.

I felt incensed we'd been treated in such a manner. It's part of our culture to be close to very sick or dying relatives and this was our granny, the figurehead of our family. So later on, as the chairperson of my Northern Network of Travelling People, I rang the hospital, not telling them I was also a relative, to complain there'd been a racist incident.

'We're not racist,' said the hospital lady. 'We're in Bradford.' I never could work that one out!

Finally, Granny was allowed out of the hospital on the day

of the funeral of another member of the Varey family. One of her nephews had committed suicide. He was only in his thirties but sadly it was not uncommon.

Granny came out and while back in the trailer with my grandad she passed away peacefully on 3 August 2007. We knew she just wanted to come home.

Around this time my working life took another turn. I left my job to start as a Gypsy and Traveller Inclusion Officer for Doncaster CVS. Finally the Labour party had woken up to the fact that the Gypsy people had not been properly recognised as their own ethnic group and had started employing people to bridge the gap. My colleague Zoe left, so the role of assistant community development worker became available.

Suddenly everyone I knew seemed to want the job. I was wanted to sit on the interview panel, but I explained to my boss I couldn't as I knew all the applicants. One of them was a good friend's sister, another was married to my dad's cousin, another was my sister-in-law's sister . . . It went on and on. It was decided that because I knew all of them I couldn't be prejudiced towards any of them.

The weeks leading up to the interview became a bit of an assault course. Wherever I went people winked and nudged me. 'You'll give that job to our kid, won't you?' So and So's mam would say. Or someone else would grin, and say they couldn't wait to be my colleague. I kept saying it wasn't my decision but no one seemed to want to hear that.

The first interview was with the sister of my friend. Chrissy was a lovely girl, a real livewire, but she was very nervous on the day. I think in order to compensate for this she went completely the other way and pretended to be anything but bothered about the job.

She turned up wearing a pair of jeans, a shirt and a Swarovski crystal headband. She looked like a cross between a tomboy and a Spice Girl. As she sat on the chair in front of us she pulled out her mobile phone, twizzling it in her hand, holding it to her ear and pressing the buttons. I felt like reaching across the table and telling her to stop. But I knew for her it was like a security blanket.

Next up was my sister-in-law's sister. She seemed very calm, collected and super-confident. When we went through the scoring I had to explain why mine was so high for her answers. Then I realised I was the only one who'd actually understood her accent well enough to hear what she'd been saying.

Then came my dad's cousin's wife, Paula. Now everyone I'd met always told me what a lovely woman Paula was. I'd met her many times but never really had a proper conversation. She turned up at the interview, looking a little nervous. She'd reached the age of forty and never had a proper job before. But on paper she looked great. She'd not only held responsible positions in the church, looking after their accounts, but she also answered all the questions in a confident, straightforward way, telling us how she'd deal with situations on a practical level, giving us real-life examples of being a mum to her many kids.

She might never have sat in an office before but we all

agreed she should have the job. When our boss rang her on the Friday afternoon to let her know she was very excited. 'When can you start?' she asked her.

'Well, it's a bit late coming in now as I have to get the tea on,' she said. 'So Monday do?'

Although I knew she was the best candidate my heart sank a little when I heard Paula had got the job. All I knew of her was she was very hardworking and very in to church. I imagined working with her would be a proper bore, as all we'd have in common would be work and God. But she proved to be nothing of the sort.

On her first day we had a multi-agency meeting. I'd completely forgotten to warn her about the jargon used in these sorts of groups. I'd become so used to the strange terminology and acronyms I'd forgotten how confusing it could be for someone who had never set foot in that sort of corporate environment before.

As we sat down, I met Paula's eyes and saw them fill with panic as the meeting kicked off. I wanted to reach over the table and tell her it'd be OK, but realised this would be out of place and rather patronising.

During the break, she looked horrified. 'I have to quit, Violet. I can't understand a single word they're sayin'.'

I reassured her as best I could and after a while she relaxed. Soon Paula was part of the furniture and proved to be a great worker.

Always outspoken, Paula could be relied on to call a spade

a spade. Once we were in a meeting when one of the top honchos, Julia, came in late. At one point, Paula chipped in, meeting a frosty look from Julia. 'And who are you?' she said, looking down her glasses. Someone introduced Paula and Julia softened a little, saying she'd not been introduced before. Then Paula piped up: 'Well, you weren't introduced because you showed yerself up late.' The whole room fell silent as Julia cleared her throat and changed the subject.

Some of the bosses were lovely but sometimes we couldn't help but wind them up. Sometimes me and Paula would rib each other just for the heck of it. 'Oi, pikey,' she'd say. 'Pass me the stapler.'

'You ronker, I'm pikey nothing.'

Karen, our manager, was horrified. 'Stop, sshhhhh!' she'd cry. 'You can't say that, others might hear and think that language is OK!'

Once we had to move office three or four times in a year. 'Yeah, keep moving us gypos on, why don't you?' I laughed when someone told me the decision.

We did genuinely struggle sometimes to understand things that we weren't used to in our culture. Like we were told to wear 'smart casual' clothes to work. I kept turning up in jeans until someone pulled me aside to explain that smart casual was anything but jeans and Bermuda shorts. But many of my jeans are smart, I reckon, so I got away with it. Once I was invited to an event with the dress code 'black tie casual'. What was *that* all about?!

It was brilliant working with all the different cultures. Again I couldn't socialise much with my colleagues, but I really hit it off with Nazia, a Muslim girl. Like me she didn't drink, have casual relationships or go out much. We understood each other and she acknowledged how 'un-white British' I am.

Both of us were expected to marry early. Once, for a laugh, I wound her up about it when she turned twenty-two.

'Oooh Nazia, you're twenty-two now, you'd best be off finding yourself a man quickly now, eh?'

'Shut up,' she laughed.

Another time I was chatting to someone in the kitchen, making a cup of tea when I realised there wasn't any milk. I said to Paula in half Romanese 'Let's steal some from downstairs', when Nazia walked in. 'What you talking about stealing for?' she said. She'd recognised the Sanskrit word for 'stealing'.

Chapter Twenty-Nine

The Darkest Hours

Despite all our difficulties, or perhaps because of them, George was putting increasing pressure on me to have a baby. As much as I yearned for one, I was also determined to put the cracks in our marriage right first. I suppose buying a house was another distraction, another project to sort out since I couldn't seem to sort out George's behaviour. Deep down I knew I didn't want kids with this man, someone who couldn't or wouldn't provide. Growing up with my hard-working dad as my hero, someone who believed in an honest day's work every day, it was hard to accept being with a man who seemed to have the complete opposite stance.

So first of all I used the excuse of hating Paley Road as to why I didn't want children. Then I said I hated the house being in disrepair. George's mother Joan was furious with me. She told me outright that it was my duty to stand by my marriage vows and my husband. She said people would talk if we didn't start producing children.

What made matters worse was the constant rowing

between me and George. I'd learned to accept I had to clean up after him, but paying for everything while he was so frivolous with money was harder to stomach. Plus he was unhappy about me having any social life at all and would moan constantly even if I wanted to see Mam and Dad or Maria. I just started to stay in more. When his friends came round, I found he'd always have an excuse to send me out to fetch something from the shop or make cups of tea for everyone, like he never wanted me to join in. I started to feel isolated, lonely and depressed. My husband didn't feel like my friend.

I didn't have to look far to see where a lot of George's habits came from. He had a cold, distant relationship with his parents and money wasn't their strong point either. His own parents lived a hand-to-mouth existence in a rented council house. They barely had enough money to pay the bills but then every so often would splash out enormous sums on holidays abroad with their friends. A classic case of being seen to keep up with the Joneses. It wasn't an attitude I could understand.

I always stuck up for my husband, though, if I felt he'd been treated badly. Once I came home from work to find George looking a bit upset about something. 'Listen to this,' he said.

It was his mum, ranting and raving on his answerphone message. Except it wasn't directed *at* him, just *about* him. She was talking about her son when her phone had accidentally called him. Spitting feathers she was, shouting about always bailing George out, how we owed her money – which I knew nothing about – and how ungrateful and awful we were.

After listening to this bile, I calmly called this woman up. 'I got your message, Joan,' I said. 'And imagine speaking about your own son like that. You need to learn to be a mother before you can ask to be a grandmother. Don't you ever darken my door again.'

I felt sick on behalf of George. No wonder he was troubled, with parents like that. My heart went out to him. To hear him being ripped in to like that made my blood boil.

But despite my sympathy for him, our marriage continued to flounder. Eventually, after one row too many, I felt so worn down and unhappy that I packed up a bag and went to stay with Mam and Dad. They didn't say a word when they saw my car pull up. Mam just stuck the kettle on and gave me a hug. Afterwards they told me how they always knew I was suffering with him, but didn't dare say anything.

During this time, George begged me to come back to him, promising me he'd improve his behaviour and take over the redecoration of our house. I'd got a 110 per cent mortgage so all the building work, new kitchen and bathroom, was being paid for by me. But I felt that if he did all the redecoration and some of the building work, that would be fair. So I agreed to give him a chance.

George insisted I let him get on with it if he was going to do it. I knew he was capable of building incredible creations, like the stall, so I took a leap of faith after explaining in detail what I wanted to get the job finished.

One day I turned up to see how he was getting on. My heart nearly stopped still when I saw bits of broken tiles from the fireplace on the floor.

'Wha— . . . what have you done?' I gasped, looking at George's dust-covered face.

'You told me to take the fireplace out,' he said.

'No!' I cried. 'I said take out the old parts and get it working again, not smash up all the gorgeous tiles! You *knew* I loved them!'

He'd not only smashed the tiles, he'd replaced the iron grille with a horrible, cheap, two-bar electric fire from Argos.

Looking back at this time it was the perfect opportunity for me to just walk away. I wasn't happy, George had proved himself to be controlling, erratic, lazy and more than unpleasant at times. I felt so unloved. I'd moved out so I knew I could just stay away. But my Christian beliefs and traditional values proved this to be impossible to carry out. I just knew people would raise eyebrows and say or at least think: 'I told you so.' My pride was going to keep me in this marriage, if nothing else. Within weeks I moved back.

It was like jumping from the frying pan in to the fire. Or hell on earth. Now we were in a settled house, our rows intensified when we were together, and we had dreadful arguments about anything and everything.

I don't think it suited either of us to live in four walls. I had reasoned with myself that a permanent base might help, but the reality was that the claustrophobia of the marriage matched the claustrophobia of living in bricks and mortar.

During one barney George accused me of tricking him in to marriage. 'You told me you were pregnant,' he said. 'You told me I was the father of your baby so I had to marry ya.' The first time he said it I just laughed – I *was* pure, I had expected the Romany rules, waited until marriage, as was this old supposed second, third, fifth, tenth time he brought back. Maybe I had done up during a row I started to think

'You couldn't wait and got yourself pregnant to spite me,' he'd scream.

Shouting and screaming at me, saying things I didn't understand, I simply couldn't keep up with his mind games. I was questioning my own sanity by the end of it.

By now I had some money behind me so decided to buy a plot of land to go and live on while we finished doing up the house. Before I knew it though, George was also inviting his mam and dad to stay with us. Family still meant everything to me, and even if they were my in-laws and I didn't especially like them, it was my duty to make the best of it.

We moved on to the plot of land, a lovely small green field, and I felt much happier living a more outdoorsy life, free again after the claustrophobia of staying in our building site of a house. But adjusting to his parents living so close by was a little harder to deal with.

His mother would rant and rave every day, rowing and picking fights about almost anything. One day I plucked up the courage to ask George to tell her to pipe down. She really did shatter the peace of living in such a lovely place.

By the age of twenty-nine, I started to seriously question myself. I'd always said I wanted kids before I was th[...] here I was, working very hard but still putting off [...]imes by of children. I'd watched Maria become a m[...]n were my life now as Ely-Tom arrived in 2007. Th[...] them as I could, and I loved spending as much [...]eeded a babysitter. I adored letting them sleep over if M[...] them. I suppose it wo[...]e been natural for me to feel envious of Maria and h[...] life, but I didn't. I was happy she was happy. My nieces and nephews were adorable and spending time with them simply made me feel: 'I want my own kids to be like these.' They were such fun, with strong personalities. One day I put a little pair of overalls on Ely-Tom just after he'd learned to talk and he came toddling over to me, all cute and adorable, demanding a cup of tea. In a flash I felt my heart melt. I knew I really wanted one of my own.

With each baby, I'd always coo over their clothes, oohing and aahing over some pretty designer dress or a pair of adorable booties. Maria would put them aside for me. 'I'll save that then for when you have yours,' she'd say, adding it to a growing pile, then squashing it in to a drawer. Looking at the pile of clothes, I would say a little prayer, hoping she was right.

One night I gazed at George while he slept, my mind racing

with thoughts and worries about my future. I knew I didn't want kids with this man, but then I also knew I'd rather have children than none at all. I made a decision. I would make it work whatever.

Within two months of having that midnight chat with myself, in March 2009, I found out I was expecting.

George was delighted when I told him the news. I didn't go to the doctor's as someone had told me they give you an internal examination. I couldn't bear the idea. I'd never had so much as a smear test. The thought of a stranger, even a doctor, poking around made me feel sick.

But one night at home, a few weeks later, I started feeling really ill. My stomach was killing me, and I knew, I just knew, that I was losing this baby. I didn't call anyone, I didn't ring an ambulance, I just lay on my bed, praying, moaning softly and crying in to my pillow.

'What's happening?' George said.

'I'm losing it,' I sobbed. 'There's nothing I can do.'

George sat in shock on the bed as I closed my eyes, feeling so helpless.

The following day, I took some time off work and just sat in the trailer staring at the closed curtains. Everything seemed so bleak. I felt so alone. George didn't seem to know what to say or do, so he flicked on the PlayStation to kill some soldiers or whatever they were.

I didn't call Mam and Dad or even Maria. I just couldn't bring myself to tell anyone. Plus the shame of talking about my body like that wouldn't be right. I just had to try and put it behind me.

At least I now knew what I wanted more than anything. A baby of my own.

Four months later, in July, I was at my desk at work, when a terrible and familiar pain shot through my stomach. Rushing to the loo, and seeing what I saw, I knew I must have been expecting without realising it and was now losing it again.

History repeated itself. I left work, went home, closed the trailer door and laid myself on the bed, feeling like all my dreams were literally draining out of me.

George gave me a cuddle and we both cried. Then he wiped his tears, leaving me in bed alone, my mind in turmoil. I didn't go to the doctor's afterwards either. I just couldn't bear the idea of being prodded and poked, especially now. Although George seemed to have cried all his tears completely, he knew I was still upset, but also desperate not to let anyone know.

'Just don't tell anyone,' I said to George. 'Not even my mam or dad, and especially not yours.'

He nodded. 'OK, doll,' he said. 'Whatever you say.'

I hated the looks of sympathy or gossiping around me, much like my Granny Winnie had done. He promised not to breathe a word, especially to his mother who I didn't get on with at the best of times.

The next few days passed in a blur. I avoided everyone and just stayed inside, praying, hoping I'd somehow manage to move through this bleakest of times. It seemed so unfair to lose two so close together. I didn't know where to start with the grief.

My relationship with George still wasn't the best, so I thought I'd focus my energy on that. If I was going to have a child with this man, I wanted to bring out the best in him. I gave him some of my savings, around £7,000, to buy another catering unit. He promised me he'd make it work this time, as he wanted to sell it and buy a ride to set us up for life. His cousin Howard had five or six rides at this time and really was doing very well for himself and his family. I wondered if George might simply be a late starter.

'This machine will make us, doll,' he said.

I knew I'd heard it all before, but now I was planning on having a baby with this man, I thought he deserved another chance.

After taking the money, George disappeared again. This time he returned at 2 a.m. I got out of bed to make the men cups of tea after they had heaved the machine back to the site. As I opened the door, even in the poor light, I felt my heart sink.

'Please tell me that piece of scrap metal isn't the ride,' I said.

George rolled his eyes. 'Honestly, you have no idea,' he said. 'This is going to be amazing. I'll build it up, all it needs is chrome and you know it's the lights and music that make a ride. So have a bit of faith and give me some time.'

Howard nodded. 'It will be a good 'un once it's finished,' he agreed.

Later on, George admitted he needed another £3,000 to do

it up. But I'd never seen him so full of enthusiasm and posi-tivity. I really thought that this time, knowing he was hopefully going to have to support a family sometime soon, the change had come.

The aim was to get it all painted and finished for a particu-larly busy fair at Thurnscoe in Barnsley. We knew the ride could hold fifty people so quite easily we'd make £80 a spin. It would be a good wage and one that would last.

Every day I'd get back from work to see how much progress George was making. He started off well, buying all the paint and chrome and explaining how good it would look when it was finished. Then after a few weeks, I noticed he seemed to be doing less and less. One evening I got in and he was playing on the PlayStation.

'What you done today then, George?' I asked. He took me outside and pointed out a section of the ride he'd painted.

'But you did that yesterday,' I said, my temper rising. I swallowed it down and walked back in to the trailer to get the dinner on. I didn't understand this almost stubborn laziness.

His mother came over the following day and started rowing with George about something or nothing. As they went at it hammer and tongs, I turned up from work without either of them noticing. Closing the door of the trailer, I could still hear them, ranting and raving at each other, more like cat and dog than mother and son.

Listening to my husband trying to avoid answering some

question about a loan of money I knew nothing about, his next words cut like a knife.

'Do you know what pressure we're under here?' he yelled. 'Violet's just lost a baby . . .!'

This statement obviously had the desired effect as his mother immediately dropped whatever argument she'd had – which sounded perfectly valid from where I was sitting – and began filling up with tears and murmurings of sympathy.

I couldn't believe he'd betrayed me like that or used the worst thing that had ever happened to me to wheedle his way out of a row.

Marching up to the pair of them, I brushed past Joan and sat down.

'I am so sorry,' she sobbed, like a baby. 'Losing my grand-child, oh, it's just devastating.'

I waited for her to finish. Then with a cool stare, I said very calmly, 'I am sorry, I've cried all the tears I can about this and have to put it behind me.'

Afterwards I gave George a rollicking. 'You *promised* to keep schtum!' I cried. 'Just don't tell anyone else then.'

Chapter Thirty

Parting Gift

Two days before Thurnscoe, George's much-heralded ride was still waiting for coats of paint and proper chrome fittings. His cousin Howard had kept a space for his wayward cousin and couldn't believe George had missed this opportunity.

'I jus' don't understand it, mate,' he said, shaking his head. 'You'd've had it made, y'know.'

Looking sorry for himself as usual, George just shrugged like a little boy.

We attended the fair anyway, and I was chatting with Howard's sister, Chelsea, when I looked across and saw George talking to Howard intently.

I wondered what he was saying, as Howard had been royally pissed off that his cousin had wasted space and therefore money. But as he spoke, Howard's expression changed from one of severity to open-mouthed surprise, shock and sympathy. Then, searching the crowd, his eyes landed on me before he quickly looked away.

I just knew, I just did, that my weasel of a husband had

once again used me losing a baby as a way of worming his way out of his own laziness.

The only reason he'd not finished the machine was he couldn't be bothered. The amount of time he'd spent consoling me hadn't lasted longer than an hour at most.

My conversation with Howard's sister faded to silence, and I stood there biting my lip with rage. All trust and respect for my husband fizzled completely in those seconds. I just couldn't believe my life had come to this. This wasn't what my dream wedding was supposed to lead to. This wasn't what I grew up believing marriage would be about. Unless, I thought grimly, you marry the frog who never turns in to a prince.

Tasting the salt on my tongue and feeling the cool sea breeze in my hair certainly seemed to blow away the cobwebs and helped to soothe the pain and frustrations of the past couple of months. For my thirtieth birthday, George treated me to a trip to Scarborough for the weekend. Once again, our marriage had been sorely tested and once again I'd turned to prayers mixed with sheer stamina to keep it going.

While we were there my phone started ringing and looking at the number I didn't recognise it. To be fair I didn't have many numbers on my phone these days. George insisted I only needed close family. Even on Facebook he'd made me place a profile pic of myself in my wedding dress, and he would inter-rogate me about any men I was friends with on there.

Answering the phone, I heard Sunshine's voice. 'Wow, how did you get my number?' I asked her. She explained she'd had to ask a few people who'd looked me up and then asked another friend till finally she'd found it.

'You need to come home, Violet,' she said, breathlessly.

'You what? We're only away for a night and it's my birthday. What you on about?'

'You need to come home. Really. Your place has been done over . . .'

I listened, holding my forehead as she started telling me how someone had broken in to my trailer, still in the safety (or so I thought) of my yard.

'Everything's everywhere, V,' said Sunshine. 'Just get yourself home.'

'Have you called the police?' I asked, my voice shaking.

'Yeah,' she replied. 'But they ain't come yet.'

In tears, I jumped back in the car and ordered George to drive. 'Don't worry, I'm sure it can't be that bad,' he kept saying, like a broken record. I couldn't believe how calmly he was taking it. He looked so collected behind the wheel, despite the panic-stricken tears sliding down my cheeks.

Mam and Dad met me at the trailer, wanting to shield me from the worst of it, but I brushed past them all, insisting I see it.

'Mam, how bad is it?' I said, the look on her face telling me everything I needed to know.

'Bab, not good,' she said. 'They've said we're not to go near it.'

346

I grabbed my mobile and called the police again. They told me it had been logged as a caravan burglary. 'It's not just a caravan,' I said. 'It's a Gypsy trailer. It's my actual home.'

While the house was being rented out, I continued paying the contents insurance for it. Yet stupidly, my home, my trailer with everything I owned in it, was completely uninsured. Desperate to see the damage for myself, I opened the gate of the yard and walked in.

The scene of destruction took my breath away.

The most expensive window, known as the chocolate box window, had been smashed, and the insides looked like such a mess it was almost impossible to see what was actually there.

The first thing I noticed that had disappeared was the silver salver Granny Winnie had given me. My jewellery box had also gone, along with the charm bracelet I'd been given as a baby and the charms that had been bought for me every single year on my birthday by my grandparents and aunties. Granny Suzanna's pictures were gone, plus some white porcelain wedge shoes I'd bought to remind me of Auntie Winnie. The Crown Derby drummer boys that Uncle Jimmy had bought for my wedding were gone, as was the limited-edition vase my sister had given me. Then there was the tea service Mam and Dad had given me for my twenty-first birthday and my Jimmy Choo shoes that I'd treated myself to after saving up for years. All gone. My clothes, of which of course I had many, were ripped up and strewn about. I felt violated, frightened and humiliated, all rolled in to one. Looking around, I simply didn't know where to start.

'Mam, why would anyone do this?' I whispered.

Picking through the stuff, I wanted to be sick. What the hell had I done to deserve this?

Dad cornered George as soon as we arrived. I could hear him outside.

'So, how's this happened do you think, George? Eh, son? Why do you think they picked on Violet's trailer? They've given her stuff a right going over, y'know. How much of your stuff's actually missing?'

George was hunched, hands in his pockets, kicking at the gravel in the yard. 'I dunno,' he kept saying. 'How would I know? Don't ask me. No idea.'

Dad wasn't letting up. I could hear him switching to a low murmur, a warning sound if ever I heard one.

After a few more minutes of to-ing and fro-ing George's voice grew louder, harder.

'You don't know what we've been through, Tom!' he shouted indignantly. 'Your Violet has lost two babbies in the last few months. She's been devastated, we both have.'

It felt like a vice had gripped my throat as Mam looked at me, also overhearing the words, her eyes full of nothing but love and sympathy. 'Oh, my Violet,' she whispered. 'We never knew.'

Tears stung my face as I turned to her. ''E shouldn't be telling my dad such things,' I whispered. This was personal, private. I didn't want my dad to have to know this about his daughter; it was embarrassing, something we never spoke about. Yet again George had let me down in the worst possible way.

I picked over what was left of my possessions, counting all the things that had been stolen. Then I noticed George's watch on the sideboard, untouched. I'd bought him it three years ago from Harrods for his birthday. Picking through the debris I also found his much-loved hollow gold football necklace. This was personal. Whoever had done this had clearly had it in for me and not him.

We called the police again and three hours later they'd still not shown up so Dad and I went down there ourselves. Finally an officer came to see the trailer, and surveying the situation he looked visibly shocked. 'Well, this is no ordinary burglary,' he said. 'It seems to be a vendetta against you. Too much destruction for just a smash and grab.'

He confirmed what I'd suspected already, but I couldn't think who would do such a thing to me.

The officer pulled out a notebook and pen, licked his finger and turned a page.

'Right,' he said. 'Can you please tell me the approximate value of the items in your caravan?'

'Trailer. Our home,' I corrected him. 'Right, well, the antique Crown Derby set was worth around £2,000, my sister's vase was a Waterford limited edition so that was £500, the pearl necklace was £1,500, my gold bracelet was around £500 . . .'

The more I spoke the more the policeman's face changed. 'Right,' he started to say, his scribbles slowing down, his eyebrow raised.

'And what insurance exactly did you have for this?' he said, a wry smile flitting over his face.

My eyes welled up with tears again. 'Nothing!' I cried. 'I'd had the house insured for three years but stupidly not my trailer!'

After I told him this, his voice suddenly changed to one of complete sympathy. 'Oh, I am so sorry,' he said.

Then the penny dropped. This copper had thought I was doing an insurance scam! Unbelievable. I went white with annoyance, and if I hadn't known some coppers are all right after having worked with them, I would've lashed out. But it wasn't worth it. The best I could hope for would be he'd catch whoever had done it, although I wasn't going to hold my breath.

Sifting through the remains of my belongings was the hardest afternoon I'd ever spent. I'd lost so much of my history. Things were missing with such high sentimental value they could never be replaced. I wept when I thought about the bracelet my mam and dad had got made for me, with my name across, which was a copy of my Aunt Kay's, who I loved and admired so much.

As we cleared up I found a few items untouched, like the diamond ring I'd bought from my Tesco's wage, my set of Wedgwood, still on its stand – probably too heavy to lift – and a few favourite items of clothing such as my mink coat and a Chanel handbag. Mam told me how my niece, little Maria-Suzannah, had spotted a belt I'd always worn strewn half out of the door when they'd arrived.

'What's Violet's belt doing?' she'd asked, all confused.

For the bairns to have seen the destruction upset me even more. After the big tidy-up I felt shattered, physically and mentally. My entire being felt stripped away to the core. It felt like there was nothing left of me.

Later that night I climbed in to bed at Mam and Dad's house, with George lying beside me snoring like a foghorn. He'd not shown a jot of sympathy today. He'd been more annoyed that my dad had had a go at him. Once again, for the third time in six months, he'd let me down in the most horrible way. I might have been married but I had never felt so alone.

Two months later in October, I was driving back from work when I spotted a fair on at Brotherton. George was away selling chestnuts at Hull fair, although Maria had been there and later said she never saw him, but I knew some of his mates would be there so thought I'd be sociable and pop in to say hello.

After finding a group of them we stood around chatting happily for a while. As much as I didn't want to admit it, it felt good to be away from George, not having to explain why I was laughing or with who. Some of his friends also noticed this difference when I wasn't with him.

'You're a right laugh, Violet,' said one. 'I always thought

you were a dolly bird. But when George's not around you get right out of your box.'

I laughed. 'Well, he gets a bit jealous sometimes.'

'I never thought you were just a dolly bird,' chipped in another. 'Once I saw you sitting outside a stall on a fair when it were freezing cold, while all the men were huddled around a fire. I knew then you were like one of us.'

I smiled again. It felt good to start to be accepted at last. They were right as well: without George around me I did feel more at ease.

After drinking a cup of hot chocolate, I said goodbye, hopped back in the car and set off home. When I arrived, George was fuming.

'Where've you been, then?' he snapped.

'Just popped in to Brotherton to have a chat,' I said. I was opening a cupboard to look what we had in for tea when he slammed it shut, almost catching my hand.

'You what?' he yelled. 'So what were you doing there then, eh? Looking for someone to chat up? Someone to sleep with?'

I stared at him, his eyes wild with jealousy and anger. Emotions I'd seen cross over his face so many times before.

'Oh shut up,' I said. 'I am not having a row about such a ridiculous, pointless thing.'

His face tight with fury, George picked up my set of Wedgwood, including the stand, and lifted it up high. His eyes bright with rage, he stared at me.

'Go on then,' I said, calmly. 'Do it. Destroy one of the last things I still own in one piece. Go on! Seriously, break it. Go on, George! It's the end anyway.'

His mouth fell open, his arms shaking under the weight of the stand.

'Go on!' I said, screaming now. 'What you waiting for? Drop it and smash it to smithereens; that would be brilliant. It's the perfect ending.'

Staring at me strangely, he was momentarily lost for words, then he slowly put it back on the sideboard.

'What do you mean it's the end?' he asked, quietly.

I stared at my husband. However seriously I'd taken those vows, however much I believed in marriage, I knew I just couldn't take any more.

I'd been stripped of everything. My belongings, most of my friends, my family, even the person I was I didn't know any more. Violet Cannon. I needed to find her again. But first I had to get this excuse of a man out of my life.

'It's over, George. We're done. I am done. I really mean it.'

He slumped on to the couch, his head in his hands. 'You don't mean it,' he said.

'I do,' I replied firmly. As my words hung in the air of our trailer, we both knew I did.

He started sobbing in a way I'd never seen anyone do before. Tears dripping on the trailer carpet, his fingers swiping his eyelids as new tears formed.

But as I watched him a piece of my heart sealed shut for good. I'd been through too much with him to have any pity

353

left. He left me nothing but numb and cold now: all his anger, jealousy and lack of consideration over the years had chipped away any love I'd had left for him and left nothing but dust.

'I told you so many times you have to change your ways or there'll be nothing left,' I said, sadly. 'So many times.'

He cried and cried, all evening and in to the night. Even after I'd pulled on my nightclothes and got in to bed he was still crying.

There was nothing to say, so I fell silent, thinking surely he'd stop. Please stop. By 3 a.m., he was still snivelling, sobbing in to a soggy pillow next to me. After a full four hours of this, I was exhausted and lost my temper.

'Will you just shut up now, George?' I cried at him. 'Just shut it. Now. Please.'

Shocked at the harsh words, he rolled further away from me, curled himself in to a foetal position and rocked back and forth.

I didn't feel a shred of sympathy.

The next morning, I simply got up and like a robot on autopilot, I started gathering as many things as I could – clothes, make up, money . . . George watched me, laying in bed, his tears starting to well again. Ignoring him, I rapidly moved around, then started loading the car.

'You're not really going, are you?' he said. I didn't even reply.

I managed to squash as many items in to the car as I could, including a big milk urn with 'Tom and Violet' written on the front, a present my mam and dad had been given at their wedding and that had been passed on to me.

Right now, I felt so lucky to have them. I was going home.

Grabbing the car keys, I took one brief look around the trailer, scouring it for anything I'd forgotten. My heart lurched a little as I saw my gorgeous Hungarian goosedown bedspread, which I'd so proudly placed on our marital bed when I'd set up this home eight years ago. Back then I'd never imagined it'd come to this. That bride, full of hopes, dreams and romantic ideals, seemed to exist aeons ago now. I felt very sorry for her and what she'd had to live through.

Chapter Thirty-One

Game Over

As my car pulled up outside Mam and Dad's they both came out to meet me. I'd already called Mam the day before, and all she said was: 'Come home.' Wordlessly, Marnie and Maria-Cizzier, now teenagers, arrived, to clean out and wipe down the empty trailer in Mam's yard while someone else made me a cup of sweet coffee. My marriage was over but thankfully my family was here as always.

As I unpacked my suitcase, I realised I'd left Andrew Alan and many photo albums behind. Of course my beloved doll had come everywhere with me and had even survived the break-in. It only seemed right he'd be by my side today too.

Taking a deep breath, I plucked up the courage to text George to ask him for them. I soon got a reply: 'You want your doll and your pictures then you come and meet me at the park and I'll give them to you.'

I simply pressed delete. He hadn't changed and he didn't care. He knew how much that doll meant to me, but as usual it was all about him.

Later that day news got out he'd also started spreading rumours about me. Already he was telling people I'd left him for another man. Breaking up a marriage was a huge stigma for any Romany woman, and to be having an affair on top of this would have been unforgivable. Even my dad would have seen fit to punish me if this had been the case. Dragging my name through the mud was the only thing George could do. For my dad and brother Tom it was hard to watch. As men it was their job to protect the family name and George was sorely trying their patience.

A few months later he asked me again to meet him so he could return some of my stuff. Still keen to have Andrew Alan back as well as some other bits, I reluctantly agreed, telling him there'd better be no funny business. He sounded calmer, kinder – all he appeared to want to do was help.

At this point I did question whether I'd ever have him back – I admit it did cross my mind. Ultimately I wanted him to see the error of his ways, to beg for forgiveness, to be truly sorry. The reality was I knew it was unlikely to happen but I suppose there was part of me living in hope.

When I watched him climb out of the car in the car park we'd arranged to meet in, any semblance of hope was dashed. He wasn't carrying Andrew Alan, he was dragging my wedding dress along the ground and brandishing an album of pictures. The look on his face told me this was no friendly encounter.

'What you giving me these fer?' I asked.

He started giving me lip and I just shook my head. 'Forget

it, George!' I pulled the dress off him and squashed it in to the boot of the car. Tears smarting in my eyes, I dumped the album on the passenger seat and put my car in to reverse. If he thought handing over my stuff like this would make anything better he was sorely mistaken.

A few weeks later, I jumped in the car and returned to my former marital home to try and rescue Andrew Alan myself.

George's face turned to grey thunder as he opened the door. 'So you think you can just waltz back and pick up what you want?' he sneered, giving me a shove so I stumbled back on the bunk. I jumped out of his way and got back in the car as quickly as possible.

As I slammed the car door, he kicked it hard, denting the side. My heart thudding like a drum, I slammed my foot to the floor, tearing off at speed.

Drying my eyes hurriedly as I pulled up at Mam and Dad's, I knew I couldn't tell them what George had just done. Tom and Dad were already barely able to contain themselves, desperate to mete out justice Gypsy-style, in a field with fists.

But just the look on my face told Dad all he needed to know. And when he spotted the side of the car he knew instantly who was to blame. Marching round to George's he went to give him a piece of his mind.

George wasn't having any of it though. He grabbed his mobile and rang up Tom, then Ely, and as Dad tried to calm him down, they began arguing. Tom only lived seven miles away, so he jumped in the car and drove straight round there with his wife Marie.

By now George's brother, Bob, had also arrived and all five of them started rowing. George turned to Marie and said something very disrespectful. The touchpaper was lit. Tom thumped George and Bob grabbed an iron bar, to join in. Dad stepped in to save Tom and within a few minutes it was a complete punch-up.

A passerby spotted the field full of shouts, fists and kicks, and soon the police arrived to find my brother-in-law Bob chasing my sister-in-law Marie down the road with an iron bar.

Feeling terribly guilty about the trouble Dad and Tom had run in to, I contacted the police myself later but they were not interested in hearing who was innocent or how it was started. The police just arrested all of them and all were charged with affray. I wanted to explain they'd been defending me but it fell on deaf ears. I could see in their faces they saw it as nothing but a nasty gypo fight, a bunch of hoodlums fighting like the animals they were in a field. Nothing to do with honour, respect or love.

Obviously I stayed away from George from this point onwards, to let the dust settle. To step away from your marriage as a Romany was still almost unheard of, but after what he'd done to my dad and brother I just never wanted to see him again.

I was struggling with my own emotions enough without

having to deal with his. Coming back to my community as a woman who'd broken off her marriage wasn't going to be easy. Very few women leave their marriages. It's just not what happens.

Here I was finding myself back with my parents again, battered and bruised emotionally, trying to pick up the pieces. Dad bought me a trailer and a car, something that I felt terrible about. He also insisted on paying for my food as well when we went shopping. I'd have a separate trolley, containing my expensive bits of chocolate and Ben & Jerry's Cookie Dough ice cream and things like that, but when we arrived at the till Dad insisted it went on his bill.

'But you've already paid for me, Dad,' I said. 'You paid for bringing me up, you don't have to do this now.'

'You're my little girl, put it on the belt,' he growled back.

I carried on getting up in the morning, plastering a big smile on my face. I went out as much as possible, joining in all the church activities, many of which I'd missed over the years as George didn't like me going to them. I started reading the Bible all the time again, something George would openly complain about, and listening to my church music.

Slowly, day by day, the sad, unhappy wife was turning back in to single, confident Violet, who spoke her own mind and knew who she was. It was a struggle finding her, though.

There were some uncomfortable moments with family members who, not knowing the ins and outs of our unhappy marriage, couldn't understand why I'd left him. One of my dad's cousins came over and had a chat with me about it.

'Ooh, I can see in your eyes you want to get back with him,' she said. 'Don't worry, I'm sure you will.'

'But I don't, Aunt!' I began to protest. I could see she couldn't understand a word. In her mind she simply couldn't fathom why I'd voluntarily put myself in this situation. Single and childless in my thirties.

Once I was dropping off Maria's kids at nursery when I bumped in to Ely's cousin. 'I've heard you've left George,' she said, shaking her head like someone had died. 'That's such a shame, I am so very sad for you.'

'Oh don't be sad,' I breezed. 'I'm not.'

Her mouth opened and closed like a goldfish. She was genuinely baffled. Again, in her eyes any situation was probably better than the one I was in now.

At night when the trailer door was shut and I was on my own, I could never drop off to sleep easily. I was so relieved George wasn't in my life any more, but sometimes, despite the brave face, the enormity of my situation was overwhelming. I was thirty now, a decade older than most brides, and most of the men from my community would be married. I had no idea what would become of me. I so desperately wanted children too, and couldn't imagine my life without them. Would having kids now be nothing but a pipe dream too?

Of course it also killed me knowing how much money my parents had spent on the big day. It must have cost tens of thousands of pounds, all for nothing: a weeping daughter in a trailer eight years later.

At first Mam and Dad took a step back, saying nothing, simply repeating: 'We're just pleased to have you home.' And they were. During my marriage they'd not seen me very much, as we never came to visit as a couple. And when we did, George did nothing but badmouth me to my parents. Later on I found out that when I left the room he'd say things like: 'You know, Violet's been drinking again. I've been finding bottles of wine everywhere.' Mam used to laugh, she knew I didn't touch drink. Quietly, painfully, they all thought George was off his rocker. Watching me go back with him to Paley Road was horrible for them.

When things had settled down a bit, months had passed and it was obvious to Mam and Dad that I wasn't going back, Mam sat down with me one afternoon.

'We knew he was never right for you, my love,' she said, quietly. 'I think after what you went through with Moses and the whole Annie business you had a nervous breakdown. You lost the plot and married the next man to come along, which unfortunately was George. But we had to let you make your own mistakes. If we'd interfered and stopped you marrying him, it wouldn't have been right either . . .'

Tears pricked my eyes, as Mam reached for my hand. My family meant everything to me, and during the past eight years only now I realised just how alone I'd been.

'But you'll get through this, my Violet,' she nodded.

I started to turn to God for help, praying I'd somehow make sense of everything that had happened. Then one night I had a dream about a piece of brown thread. A horrible dirty-brown colour it was, and it was right in my face. So I turned and walked backwards away from it and as I did, a beautiful tapestry emerged in front of my face. I knew then it was God's way of showing me that even when you're mired in some terrible situation, if you can look at the bigger picture, you will see it can still make something beautiful.

Finding myself single again I tried to embrace my freedom. As a child I'd always wanted to do a skydive, but Mam and Dad always said no. Then when I got married I'd said to George, 'Right, I'm old enough to do a skydive and live the dream now', but he also wasn't impressed with the idea. So now I was a woman alone I booked a skydive to raise money for Martin House Hospice, the place in which Babby John had been so lovingly cared for before he died. The smiles on those nurses' faces looking after such sick and desperate kids had never left me.

I signed up for the day, got a bit of sponsorship and my family took me up there in the car. As the airstrip I was flying from came in to view, Dad pulled over. 'Violet, are you sure you want to do this?' he said. 'You can always just jump over the fence and run back if you change your mind. We can just tell everyone you've done it and that'll be that. You can still get your sponsor money.'

I laughed. 'Nooo Dad, that's not the point. The point is actually doing it and I *want* to do it.'

'Well, as long as you're sure . . .'

During the practice run, my bravado fell a bit flat when our group was shown the harness holding us to the tandem diver. The clips my dad used for keeping stuff attached to the trailer were bigger than the ones they showed us. Next they talked us through the parachutes. There were three cords, each one following on if the other failed. The last chute to go off – if all else failed – was set off by a tiny microchip computer. I started laughing at this point. I couldn't believe my life was in the hands of a computer. I'd never found a reliable computer: my laptop had a mind of its own and my iPod had frozen umpteen times. But then I thought how it was really God's hands that I was in and decided not to worry.

We all went off up in the plane, the same one used in the *Bridget Jones* film for the bit where she landed in the pigsty, something I hoped wouldn't happen to me. As I poked my head out to jump I yelled the biggest 'Whooooooooaaaaaaaaaaah!' of my life.

Suddenly, I experienced the most incredible sense of freedom. Falling the first five thousand feet, feeling the rush of the air around me as we hurtled towards the green fields and trees below, was so overwhelming I'd completely forgotten all about the parachute opening until we were jolted from our thoughts and shooting skyward again.

Drifting down to earth was as heavenly. For the first time in years I felt truly free, as free as I did when I was a kid running through fields, with corn whipping my ankles. All the upset, anger, everything I'd endured over the past few years . . .

it all just flew away behind me and I experienced a sense of complete tranquility.

We landed softly without incident – although I did break a nail, which as a war wound disappointed me somewhat. I'd imagined maybe a sprained ankle, so I could tell people what I'd been up to when they enquired after it. Not only did I raise some money, but I raised my spirits. I knew how to live again.

I also found solace and help in the unlikeliest of places. I decided that after payday every month I'd treat myself to a facial to cheer myself up. Maria suggested I used a beauticians in place called Wetheralls, which surprised me as I always thought they looked quite stuck up in there. Certainly not a place Gypsy women were welcome.

But as soon as I walked in to the room a therapist called Theresa put me completely at ease. I told her straight away I was a Gypsy, as if it turned out she was racist I didn't want to deal with her. Her response was just to laugh and say she'd met Maria too and was she one as well?

To begin with I was cautious, but we soon got chatting every month and there were times I ended up pouring out my troubles to her. She was so lovely. Unwittingly for both of us Theresa became my therapist, and I went away with softer clearer skin and a lighter heart each time.

Chapter Thirty-Two

Return of the Princess

I left George in 2009 and within three months served the divorce papers. I tried to divorce on the grounds of his unreasonable behaviour, but he'd never concede to any of the points, surprise, surprise. The echo of his words 'I will never let you go. You will never be free', rang in my head every time my letters were returned or not signed. I tried being nice to him, asking him over and over to please just sign them, but this was the one last hold he had on me.

I had to serve the papers three times in the end, but then a change in law meant he didn't have to sign. Two years after our marriage ended it finally arrived. I tore it open, read the words 'Decree Absolut', and sat on my bed and cried. It really was over now.

I couldn't wait to get rid of George's surname. I sent off for it to be changed by Deed Poll and, always looking for ways to get my money's worth, I decided to add a name or two of my own. I wanted to add a middle name of Tallulah Belle or

Betty Boop, but Mum vetoed both. So I am now proudly known as Violet Margaret Princess Cannon.

I felt so happy, so good, I knew what I wanted to do next. In February 2011, I decided to organise the biggest divorce party I could. Inviting everyone I knew, I booked a night in OK Karaoke in Leeds. The night had to kick off with a rendition of Dolly's 'D.I.V.O.R.C.E', of course!

I set about organising my dress. I'd put my old wedding dress in to a shop in Leeds to be resold. I'd only get £200 for it so when I saw it still hadn't been sold I picked it back up.

Sitting in my trailer, the dress hanging off the wardrobe, I gazed at it for a while, deciding what to do. I wanted to customise it for the night out. Deciding I wanted it bright pink, I bought some dye. In the end it took four boxes of Poppy Red Dylon, and still it only turned a pale pink, there was so much material.

After changing the colour, I set about the design. I decided all the embroidered silver flowers had to come off. Grabbing a pair of small scissors I set about unstitching the lot.

The phone rang as I set to. 'What you up to?' asked Ellie.

'Just unstitching the flowers on my wedding dress for the divorce party,' I replied.

She started laughing. 'Oh V, I love you. You're mad, you know,' she said.

For the next few evenings, I slaved away cutting, stitching and redoing my dress. I opted to shorten and remove the train, and reattach it to the back with a button. I wanted to look like a bride, but I didn't have to look pretty this time.

Next I decided to go back to the woman who'd designed the wedding cake to ask her to do my divorce cake. Over the years I'd used her for every big birthday, including George's. She smiled when she saw me. 'What's it this time? Another birthday? Or something even more special?' she winked.

'A divorce cake please,' I said. 'For a divorce party.'

She looked a bit puzzled and admitted she'd never had a request like this before. Especially from a Gypsy. But I knew exactly what I wanted. A pink cake with a bride wearing boxing gloves, standing over her groom with a foot on his chest.

'But I want the groom's eyes to be open,' I laughed. 'I don't want him to look dead.' I also asked for the same quilted design as my wedding cake.

'Would you like any writing on it?' she asked, scribbling.

'Yes,' I grinned. 'My Big Fat Gypsy Divorce.'

Mam thought I was mad doing this, but also thought it was rather funny. My dad didn't say anything. They were both just pleased I was finally free of my ex-husband. A couple of family members were less impressed that I was happy to tell the world I was divorced.

'Don't you think you should just leave it?' said one aunt. 'Let it go quietly, unnoticed by folk?'

Another cousin also shook her head when I explained what I was doing. 'Can't you just let it drop, Violet?' she said. 'Let it be.'

I invited a big group of cousins and friends. On the night,

I pulled on my wedding dress and set out, head held high, determined to have a good night. And what a night! No one could believe how amazing the dress looked. We got stares and whoops everywhere.

One group of Irish lads were stood outside the club. 'You getting married?' asked one.

'Nope, divorced,' I grinned. 'This is my wedding dress, chopped up.'

His mouth fell open. 'Here, lads,' he shouted, calling friends over. 'Look at this lady, she isn't getting married, you know. She's celebrating her divorce!'

Quickly a group of lads gathered round, smiling and laughing, giving my dress the once over.

'You know what we'd call you back home?' said one.

I felt my hackles rising, colour creeping up my neck. 'What?' I said.

'An effing legend!' they cried, giving me a high five.

After singing our hearts out to Dolly we headed down to Revolution for a boogie. The skies opened and splats of rain started to hit the pavements, the drops slowly turning bigger and bigger until a mini monsoon was washing the streets of Leeds.

Ellie stuck out her arm and hailed a cab, but the driver took one look at us and shook his head. 'I'm not taking a bunch of Traveller girls, rain or no rain,' he snapped.

'Right,' I said, whipping off my train. 'You lot, get under this then!'

Eight of us all huddled under my wedding train as we marched down the street, laughing. It was such a brilliant use of it.

Being a divorced woman in the Romany Gypsy world was isolating. I could pretend otherwise but this was the reality. All of my friends were married, busy wives and mothers. I still saw Maria and Tom of course, but they were also parents themselves.

Joining Facebook was an amazing thing for me, as it gave me back my voice. Going online and logging on was like meeting all my friends at Appleby again, chatting away about whatever was going on, having a laugh. It didn't matter if you were married, single or divorced, it was just about reigniting the friendships I'd missed out on.

Then someone mentioned Desiree, the poor girl who'd married Barry, the non-Christian, and she'd soon realised he wasn't who she thought he was. A devout believer herself, their marriage hit the rocks and reluctantly Desiree left her husband, with her daughter, who was aged two by then. Seven years later she was alone, and a single mum. A double whammy for any Romany girl. A few people suggested I meet up with her, but I was reluctant. Just because we were both divorced didn't mean we'd get on, I thought. But when we finally did have a chat on the phone and arrange to meet up, I knew I'd found a friend for life.

We'd both been hurt, we'd both made painful mistakes, but

we could also both laugh at the silliest things, and support each other. Sometimes she'd simply ask me what was wrong and all I'd have to say was 'You know', and she got it. Completely. In the way only another divorced Romany woman could do.

Today I live in a trailer, on my parent's plot of land, a small-holding near a lovely village green in Yorkshire. It's the pinnacle of fifty years' hard work and finally my dad's found a happy medium. He lives in four walls, in a small chalet they have built on the site, but it's surrounded on all sides by green fields with a view of the horizon stunning enough to melt anyone's heart when the sun sets.

The plot includes a small stable and the fields contain around thirty horses, including Gypsy Cobs, the same breed Grandad Tom once had, and Shetland ponies. Mam and Dad still go to fairs but don't get away as much these days. Having horses to work with is something Dad says keeps his Romany roots going. But neither Tom, Maria nor I have any intention of forgetting them. Recently, when Maria was eight months' expectant, her husband Ely drove them by horse and cart to Appleby. It took nearly ten days as opposed to the two and a half hours in a car, but they wanted to experience what their ancestors had done for years.

Now I'm thirty-two, and still working for Travelling people. Like Mam, I am and always will be an advocate for our people and way of life. I don't have kids of my own but am a proud auntie to Tom's and Maria's. Things might have ended with George for good, but thankfully that terrible, dark period is in the past. I am still a romantic at heart. I still believe my prince will come, and one day I will have the children I long for. For Romany people are not beaten very easily and never give up the fight. We're a race who've survived despite the odds for years and I am so proud to have their blood coursing through my veins. There's no one else I'd rather be.